*The Campus History Series*

# Presbyterian College

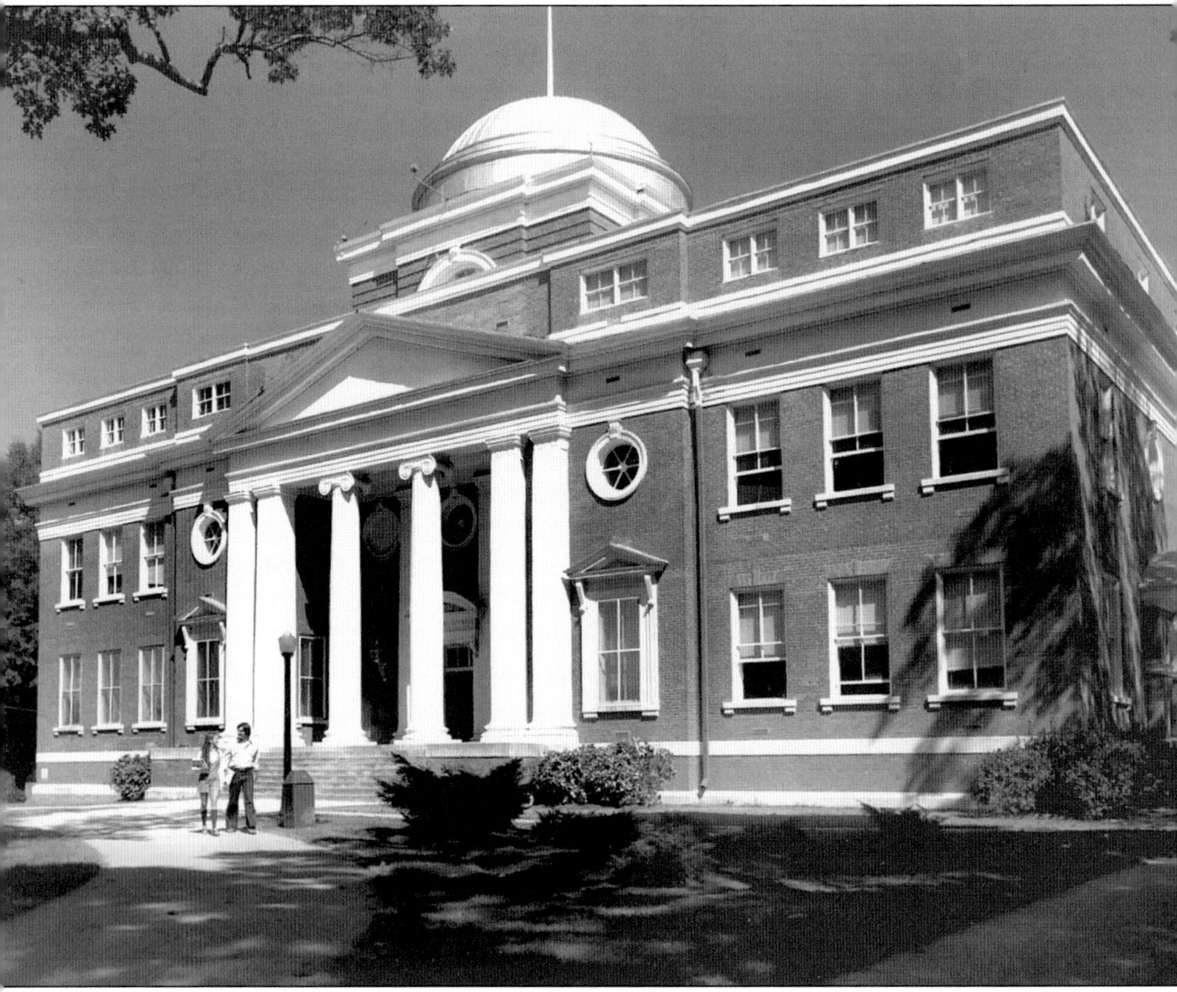

**Neville Hall.** This landmark building, constructed in 1907, stands at the center of the PC campus and serves as a symbol of the college. It exhibits the collegiate Georgian architecture which typifies PC. (Courtesy of Presbyterian College Archives.)

*The Campus History Series*

# PRESBYTERIAN COLLEGE

NANCY GRIFFITH

ARCADIA PUBLISHING

ISBN 978-0-7385-1409-3

Published by Arcadia Publishing
Charleston, South Carolina

Printed in the United States of America

Library of Congress Catalog Card Number: 2001095832

For all general information contact Arcadia Publishing at:
Telephone 843-853-2070
Fax 843-853-0044
E-Mail sales@arcadiapublishing.com
For customer service and orders:
Toll-Free 1-888-313-2665

Visit us on the Internet at www.arcadiapublishing.com

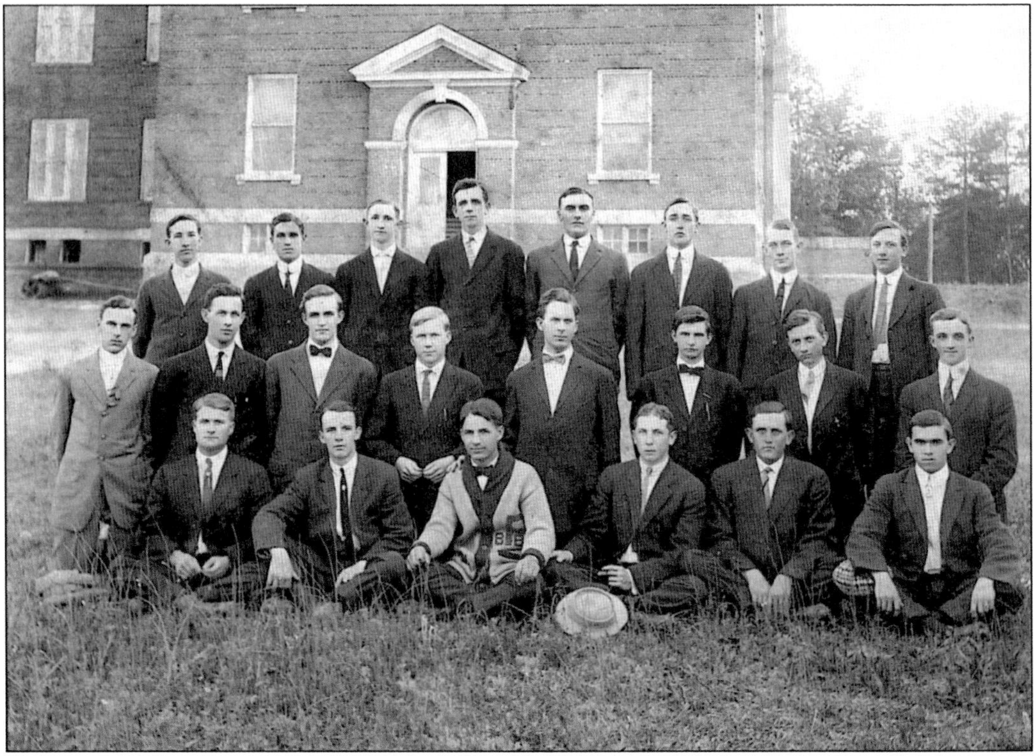

**Sophomore Class, 1912–1913.** From right to left are the following: (front row) Hicklin, Ballenger, Jacobs, Perrin, Anderson, and McLin; (middle row) Carrigan, Miller, Davis, Adams, Winters, Neely, A. Kennedy, and Anderson; (back row) Fickett, Whats, Johnson, McCutcheon, Gresham, Nickles, Gorham, and G. Kennedy. (Courtesy of Presbyterian College Archives.)

# Contents

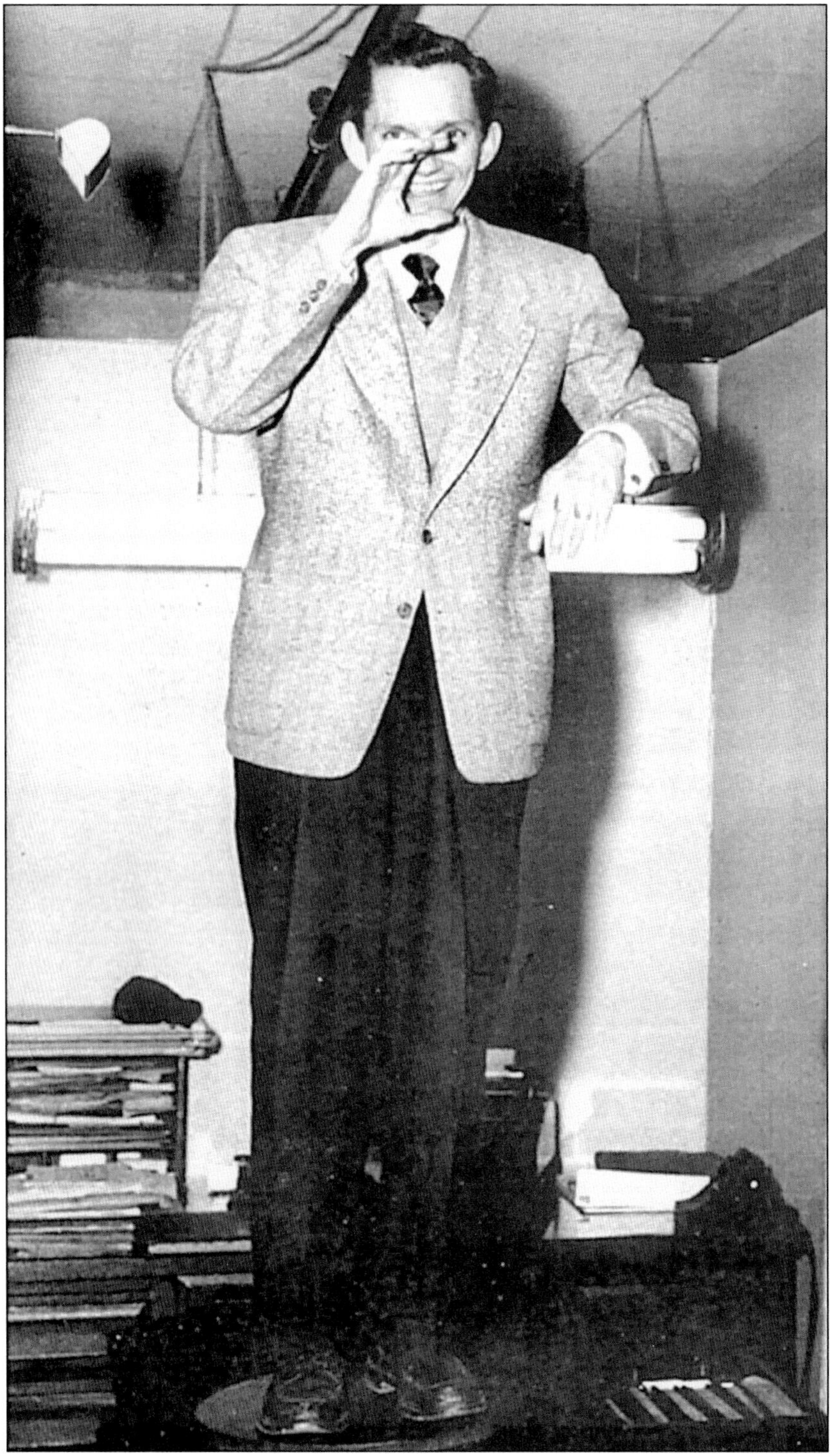

**"HAMMET THE HUCKSTER," 1955.** This book is dedicated in memory of Ben Hay Hammet, Presbyterian College's leading advertiser and chief publicist, who did so much to preserve the history of Presbyterian College. (Courtesy of 1955 *PaC SaC*.)

# INTRODUCTION

When Rev. William Plumer Jacobs arrived in Clinton in 1864, the forlorn village boasted approximately a dozen dilapidated storefronts, and only a half-dozen houses along the whole length of Broadway (now Broad Street). Public schools were non-existent. By 1872, this energetic minister of the First Presbyterian Church had founded Thornwell Orphanage, and had been instrumental in the formation of the Clinton High School Association. It was this association, under Jacobs's leadership, that transformed itself in 1880 into the Clinton College Association, with the purpose of establishing a college in Clinton. By 1881, the co-educational college had been chartered, its primary purpose to send out graduates, "whose lives shall be epistles to Christ's honor and glory."

In 1883 this "vigorous tree of knowledge" graduated its first class. Given its later history as a men's college, it is interesting to note that this first graduating class contained three women, including Reverend Jacobs's daughter Florence. By 1886 the college's first building, Recitation Hall, graced South Broad Street. College life during this period was quite different from that of today. Social life centered on the various literary societies, with their schedule of performances and debates. There was no dating during the week, but parties were held in private homes on weekend nights. Long walks, buggy rides, and picnics at Musgrove Mill were other pastimes. The town had no paved streets, and few streetlights; studying was done by the light of oil or gas lamps. During the 1890s, the first sport, baseball, was introduced, and the first social fraternity, Pi Kappa Alpha, was established.

The early 1900s was a time of uncertainty for the college. Synod considered relocating it to another town, and several submitted proposals. Despite attractive offers from Chester and Bennettsville, Clinton's proposal won out, and the college remained where it was. Building began on what is now the West Plaza. This period also saw the short-lived but inspirational presidency of William G. Neville, and the disruptions of World War I. The 1920s was an optimistic time. While there were only three cars on campus, and no radios, students managed to make their own fun. One graduate remembers catching one of Johnny Young's mules and leaving it in the bathroom in the "B" section of Smyth. Meanwhile, a weekly batch of home brew was left to ferment under the "A" section. The freshman "rat run," a feature of orientation, provided entertainment not only for students, but for townspeople as well.

The Depression befell the country in 1929, and while it brought hard times for all, it also brought out the make-do, can-do PC spirit. Professors, always underpaid and sometimes not paid at all, turned down more lucrative offers and remained at PC. Among the more memorable figures of this period were the well-dressed B.H. Boyd, the stately Dudley Jones, "Demon Dan" Brimm with his chew of tobacco, and A.E. Spencer, who reputedly washed dishes in his raincoat.

The 1940s brought war, but the period also brought a football victory against Clemson. According to Mike Turner, the 1940s was also the period of an unforgettable prank. According to Turner, a wonderful feat was pulled off by the freshman "hoodlums." They removed the doors of Neville Hall to ensconce John Gannt's Model A in the rotunda. And who can forget the campus dog "Psycho?" According to Shields Croker, "Psycho" audited several of his education psychology classes, and "participated in the work of the class about as much as a few of the students at the time did."

The years since World War II have been years of constant growth in all areas of the college. Record student enrollment in the 1950s resulted in the enlargement of the campus and the construction of numerous buildings. The 1960s brought full co-education and integration. The unrest of the 1960s and 1970s touched the campus, but one of its most lasting legacies was a positive one, the establishment of Student Volunteer Services. Continuing progress has been made during the 1980s and 1990s, with the college steadily advancing in the college rankings. But the essential character of Presbyterian College has remained—a friendly campus, where everyone wears a smile, and where students are encouraged not only to excel academically, but to engage in service to their community and the world.

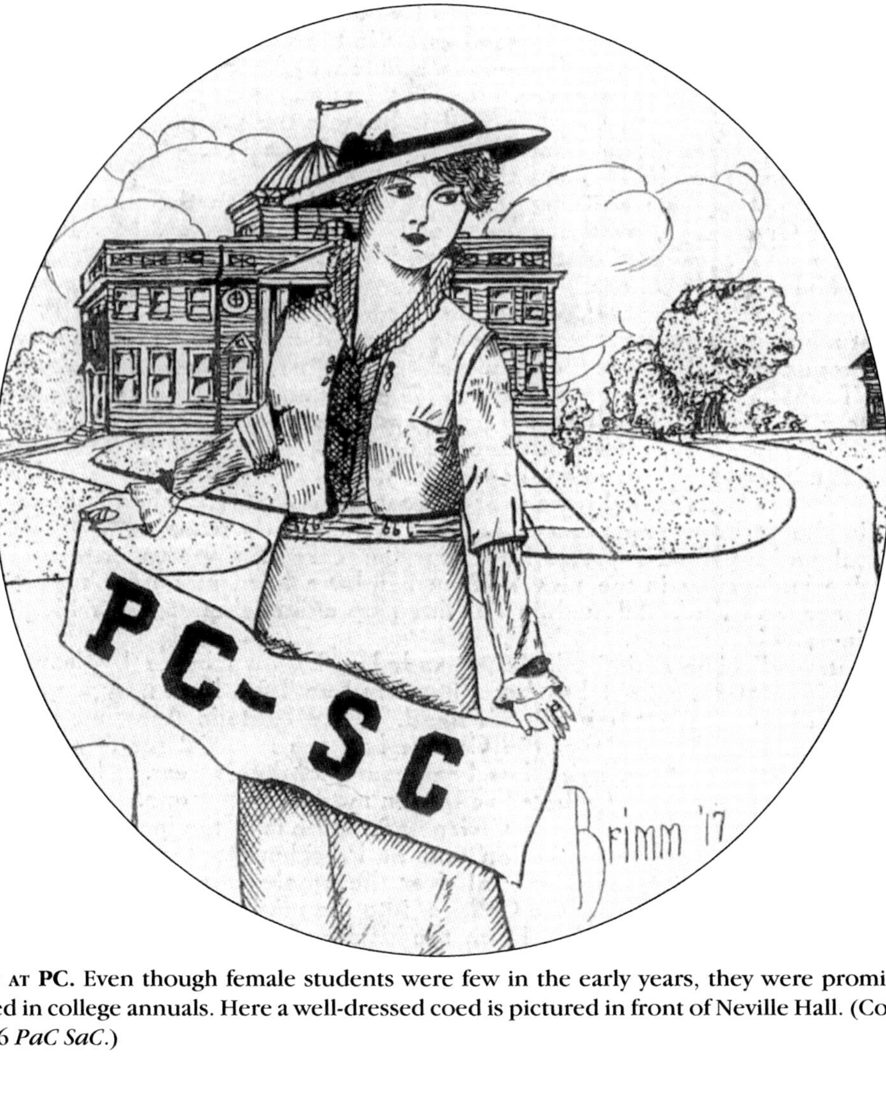


**Women at PC.** Even though female students were few in the early years, they were prominently featured in college annuals. Here a well-dressed coed is pictured in front of Neville Hall. (Courtesy of 1916 *PaC SaC*.)

# *One*

# History

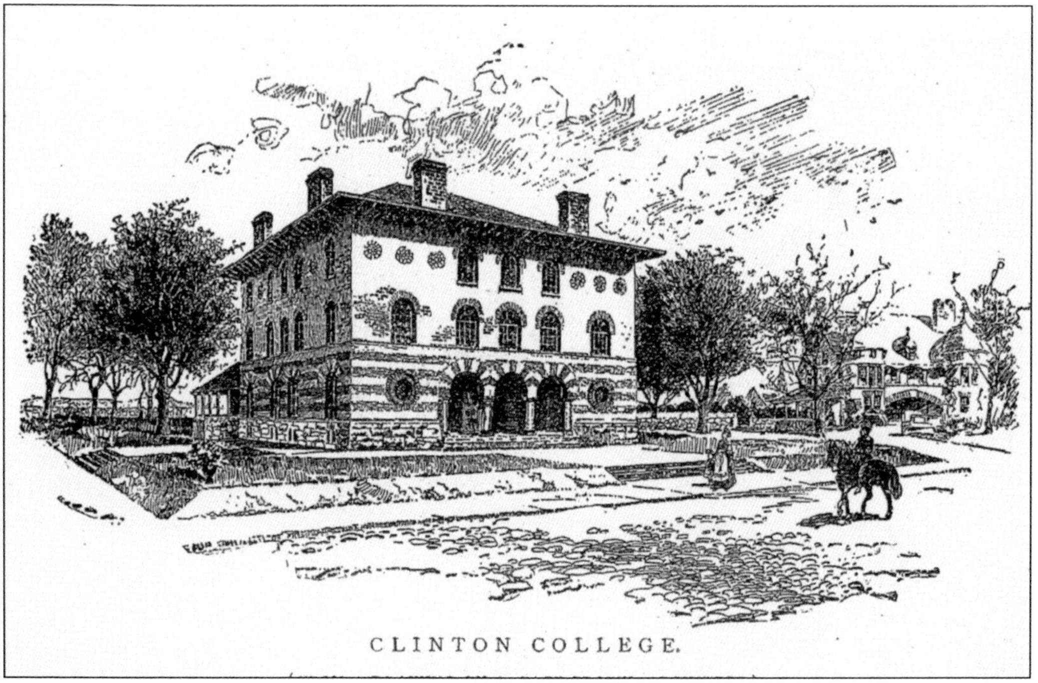


**Original College Building.** This is an architect's rendering of Recitation Hall, the original college building, which opened in 1886. The stately brick and stone building was designed by A. Page Brown of New York. (Courtesy of 1887 College Catalogue.)

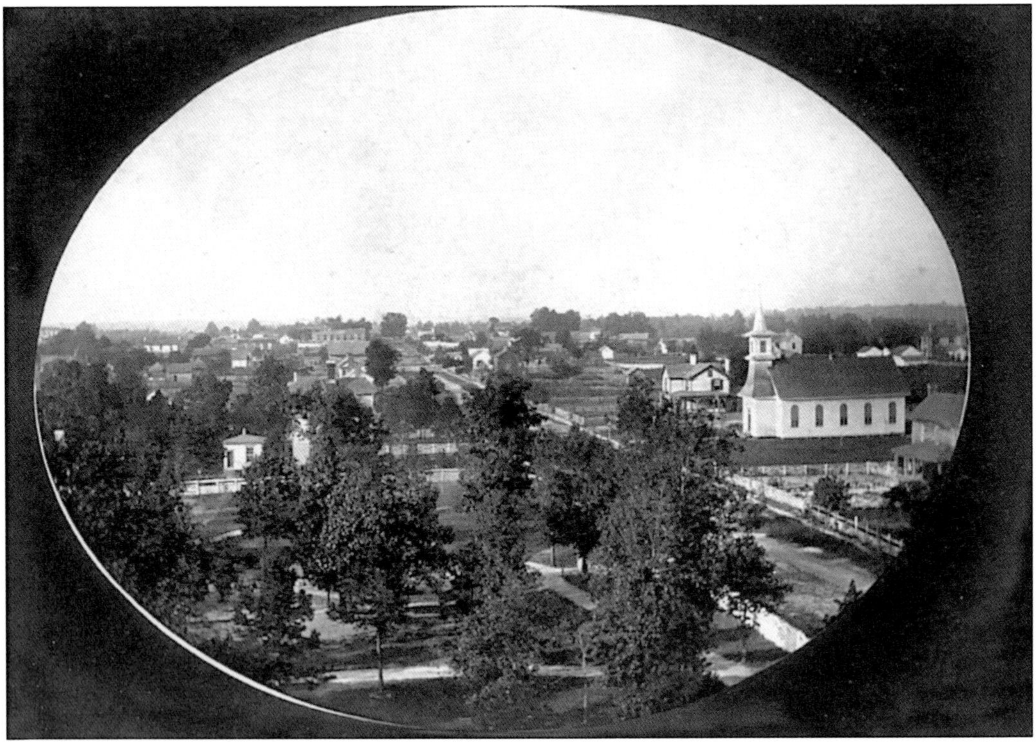

**EARLY VIEW OF CLINTON.** This view of Clinton was taken from the steeple of the Thornwell Seminary. At the time of Dr. Jacobs's arrival, Clinton was a struggling crossroads town known for its barrooms. He was the town's first resident pastor. (Courtesy of Presbyterian College Archives.)

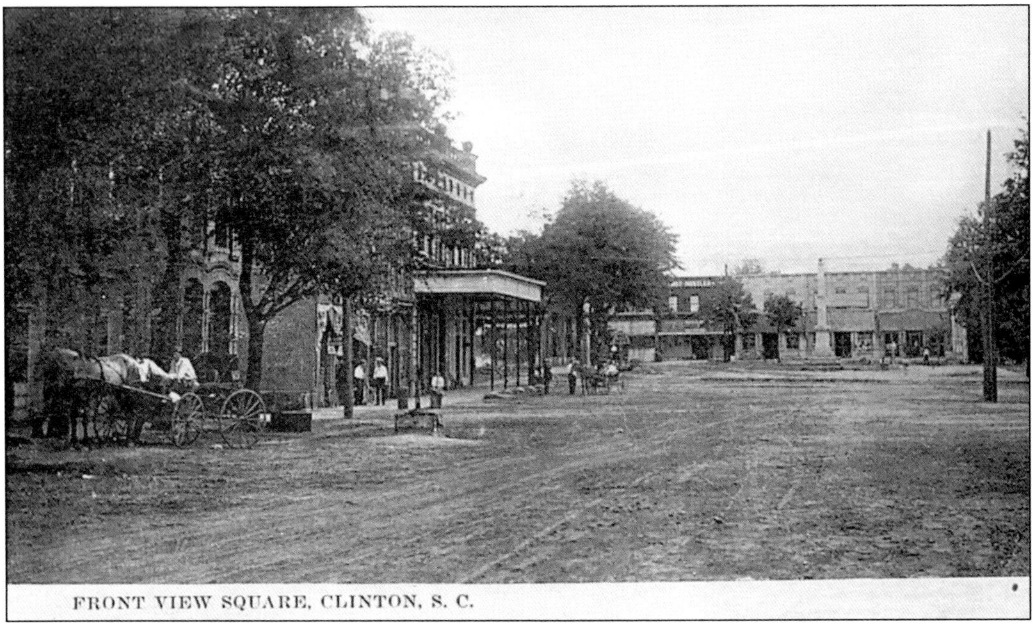


**CLINTON.** This photograph, looking east down Main Street, captures the front view of the square. The Confederate monument, erected in 1911, is at the far end of the street. (Courtesy of Presbyterian College Archives.)

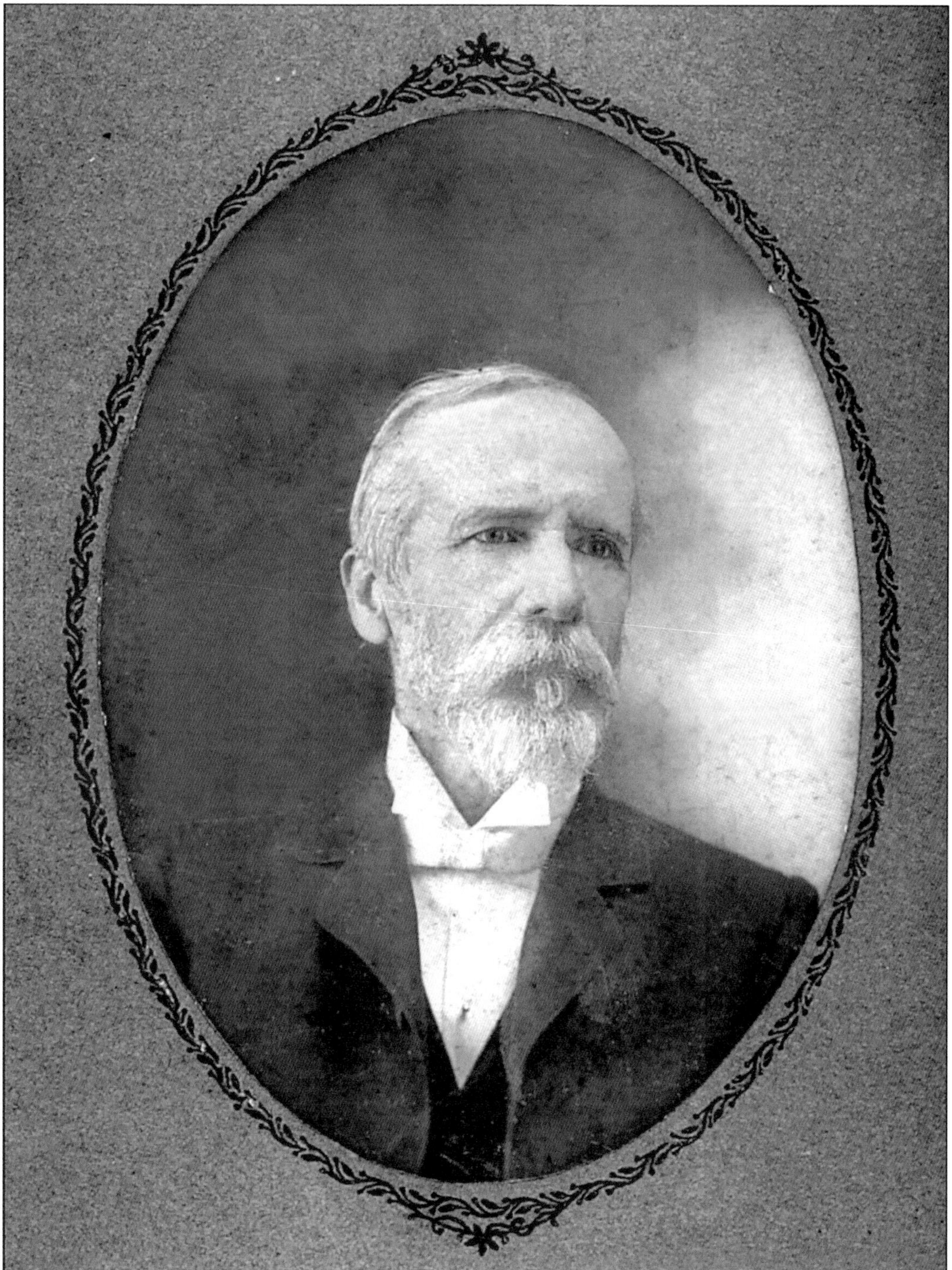

**WILLIAM PLUMER JACOBS.** Born in 1842 in Yorkville, South Carolina, William Plumer Jacobs was a graduate of the College of Charleston and Columbia Theological Seminary. He came to Clinton as pastor of the First Presbyterian Church in 1864, and was instrumental in founding both Thornwell Orphanage and Presbyterian College. He died in 1917 after serving the town and its various institutions for more than 50 years. (Courtesy of Presbyterian College Archives.)

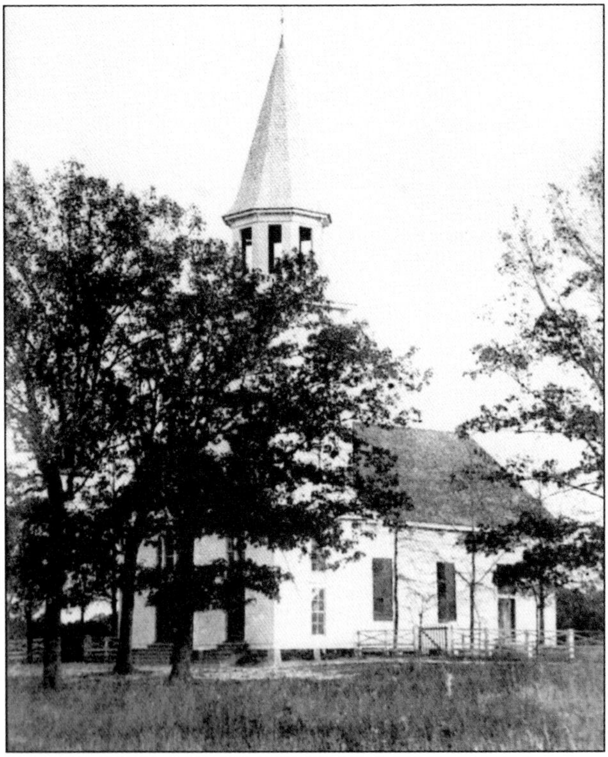

**Original Building of the First Presbyterian Church, Clinton.** The college has always been closely associated with the First Presbyterian Church in Clinton, which first held services in 1855. The college's founder, William Plumer Jacobs, was the minister of this church for 47 years. (Courtesy of Presbyterian College Archives.)

**Clinton High School Building.** This frame building on Academy Street housed Clinton High School classes prior to the organization of Clinton College in 1880. This photo was taken during a later era, after a porch had been added. (Courtesy of Presbyterian College Archives.)

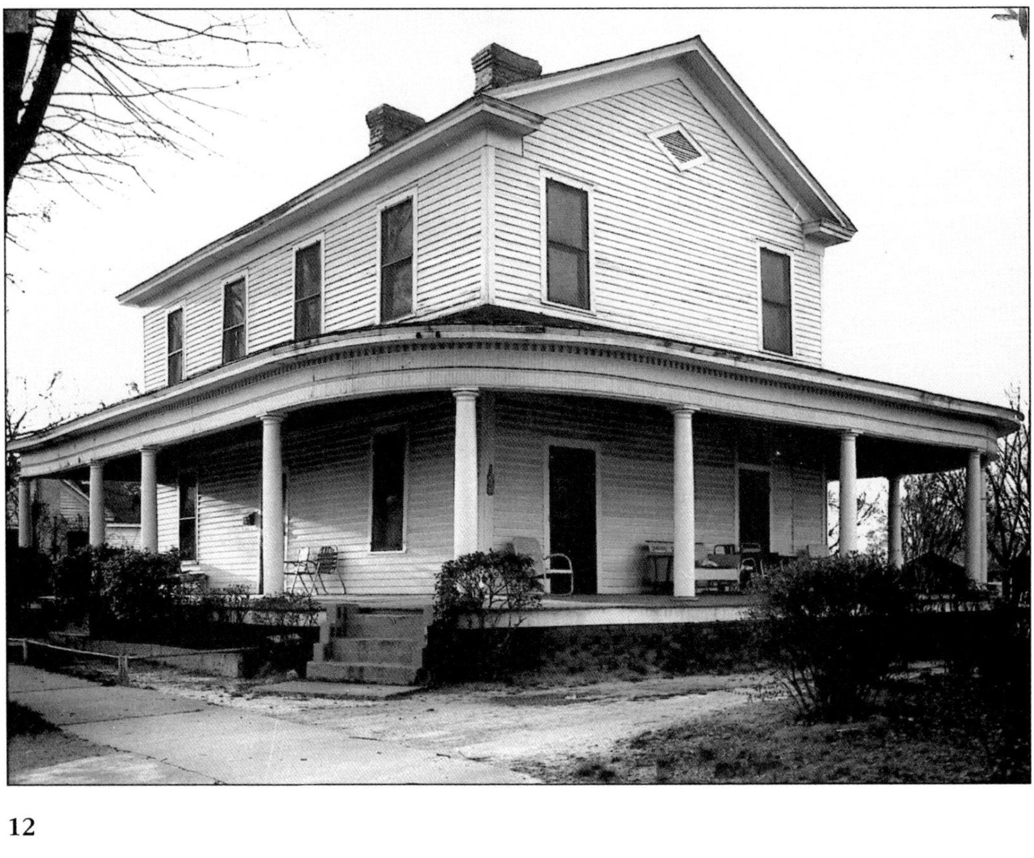

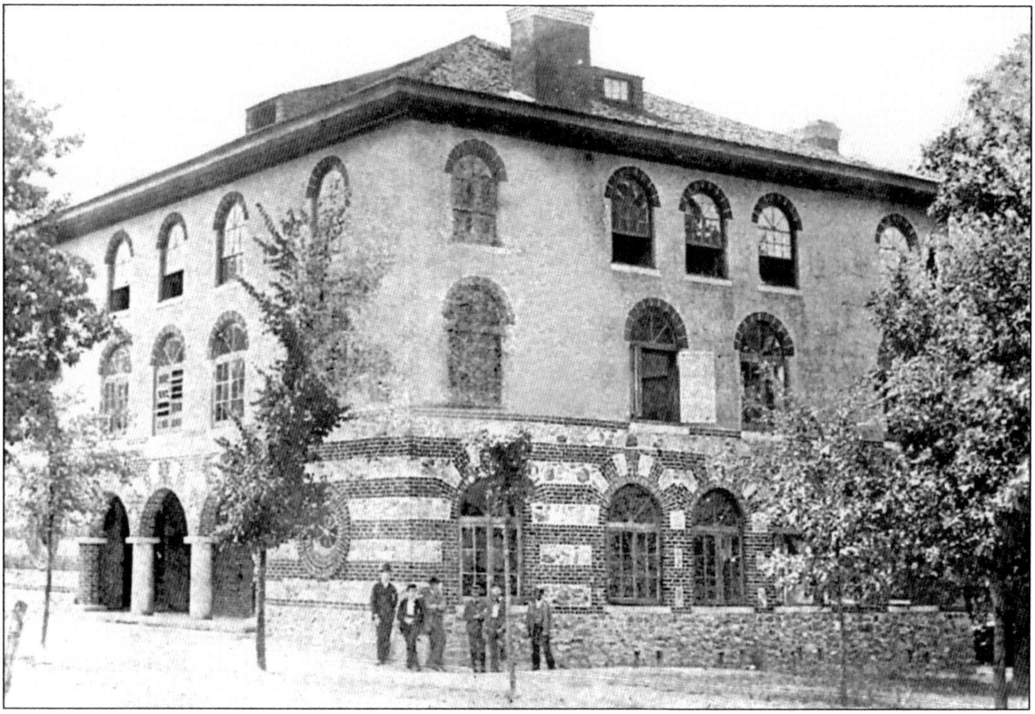

**Recitation Hall.** Recitation Hall was the first building on the campus, and was located on four acres on Broad Street, on the present-day Thornwell campus. The building was the realization of Dr. Jacobs's dream for a "nice college building . . . which will be an ornament to our town." (Courtesy of Presbyterian College Archives.)

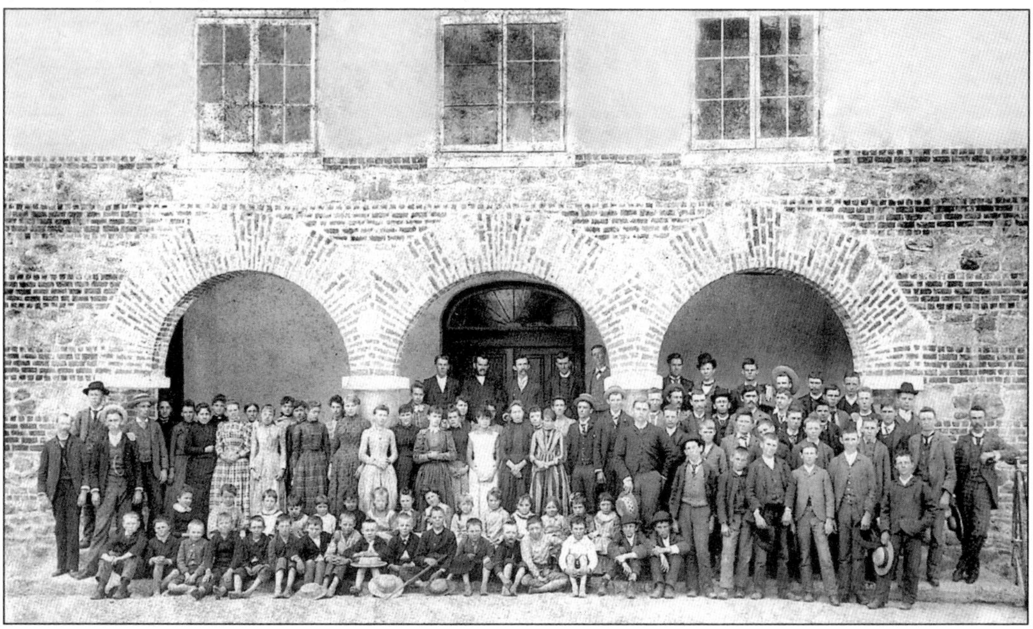

**Early Student Body.** In the early years, the college also offered preparatory classes. Here, the student body of the fledgling college, including the preparatory classes, assembles in front of Recitation Hall. (Courtesy of Presbyterian College Archives.)

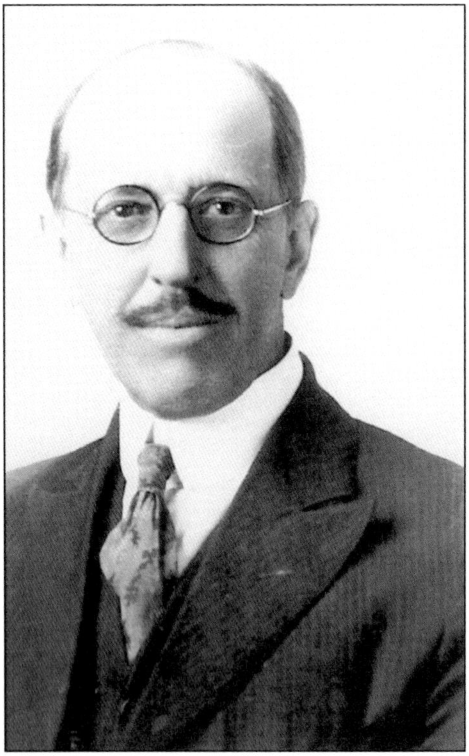

**Almon E. Spencer.** A.E. Spencer served at various times as professor, bursar, president (1897–1904), and acting president of the college. He was ultimately to serve the college for 54 years, from 1891 to 1945. During his presidency, development was begun on the present campus. (Courtesy of Presbyterian College Public Relations Office.)

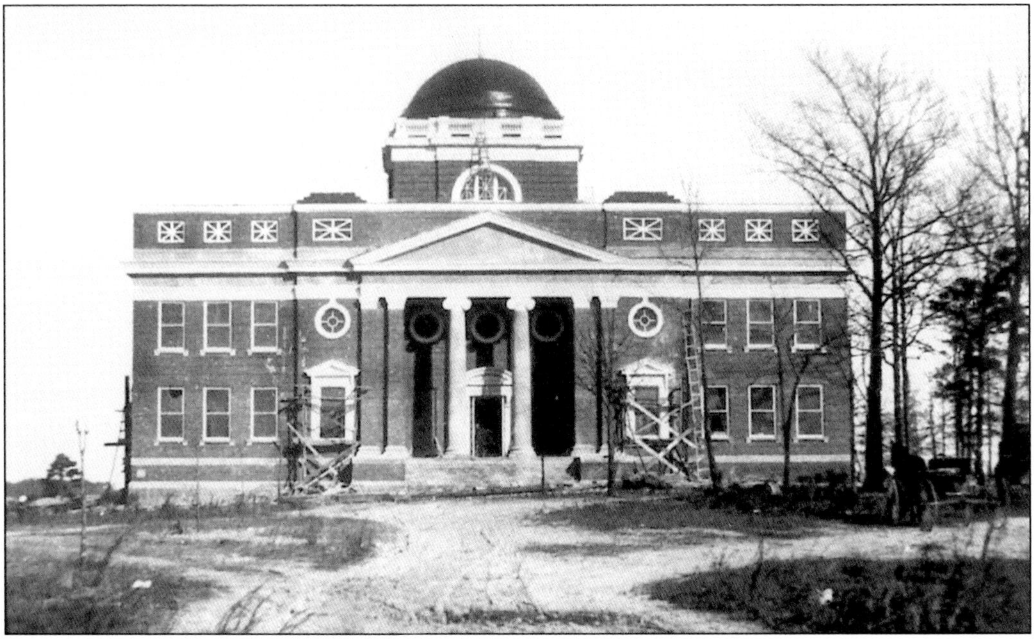

**Neville Hall Under Construction, 1907.** This campus landmark, pictured above, was originally called the Administration Building. When it was built it was the centerpiece of college life; the building housed administrative offices, classrooms, a large auditorium, and fraternity rooms. Its name was later changed to honor former president William G. Neville. (Courtesy of Presbyterian College Archives.)

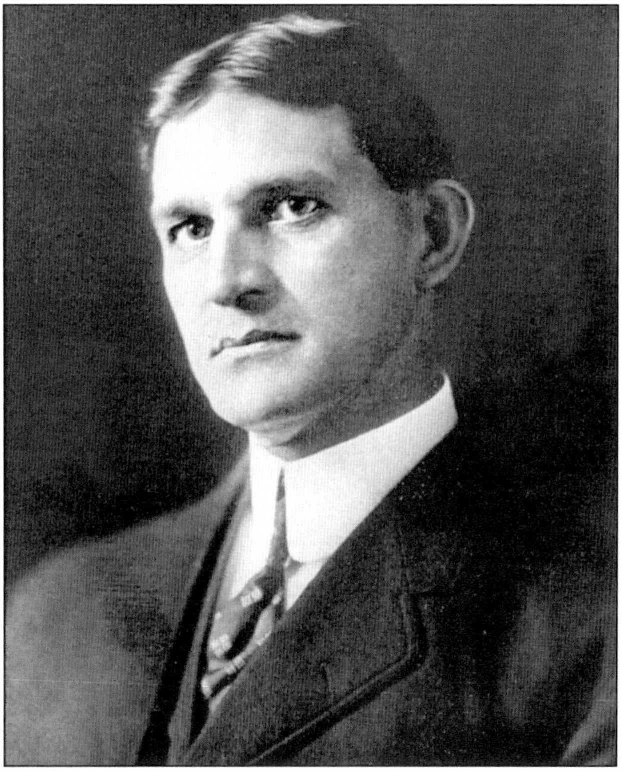

**DAVISON MCDOWELL DOUGLAS.** Douglas served the college from 1911 until he accepted the presidency of the University of South Carolina in 1926. During his tenure the size of both the student body and the faculty tripled, four major buildings were constructed, and the total assets of the college increased from $150,000 to over $1 million. (Courtesy of 1914 *PaC SaC*.)

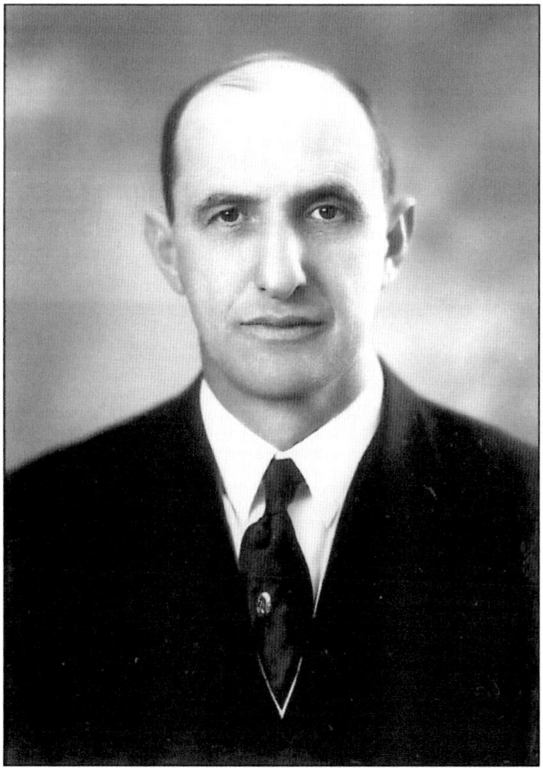

**PRES. JOHN MCSWEEN.** Rev. John McSween served as president from 1928 to 1935, and helped guide the college through the troubled years of the Depression. During his tenure the college expanded its relationship with the Presbyterian Church, and its reputation grew. (Courtesy of Presbyterian College Archives.)

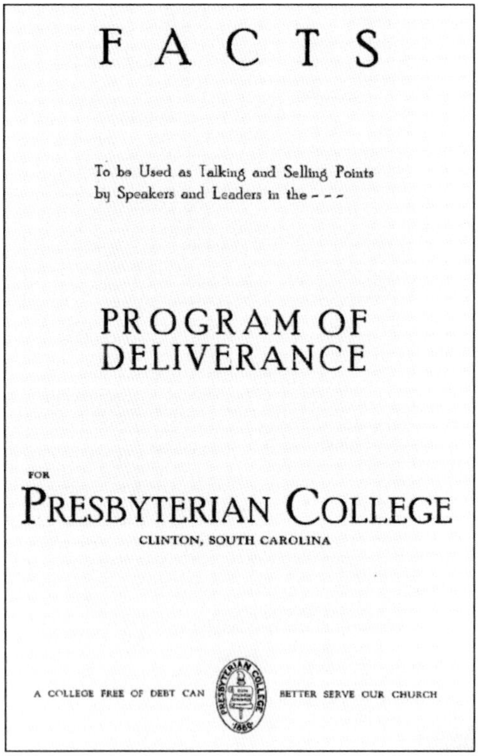
FACTS

To be Used as Talking and Selling Points by Speakers and Leaders in the - - -

PROGRAM OF DELIVERANCE

FOR

PRESBYTERIAN COLLEGE

CLINTON, SOUTH CAROLINA

A COLLEGE FREE OF DEBT CAN BETTER SERVE OUR CHURCH

**PROGRAM OF DELIVERANCE.** This ill-fated fund-raising campaign was launched by President McSween just weeks before the collapse of the stock market. The $350,000 campaign netted only $148,000 for the college coffers. (Courtesy of Presbyterian College Archives.)

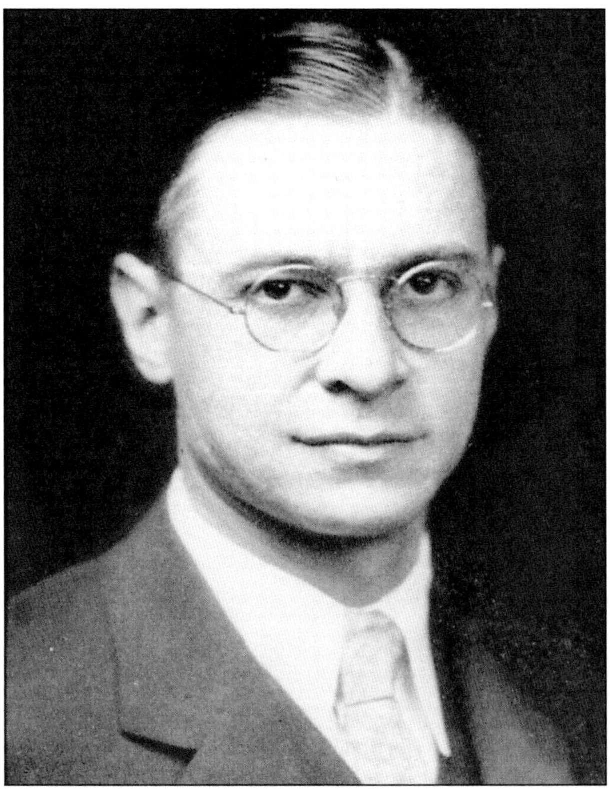

**DR. MARSHALL W. BROWN.** Marshall Brown arrived at PC as a history professor in 1925. He was later to serve as academic dean (1928–1945) and president (1945–1963). During his presidency college assets and church support increased dramatically. The campus was enlarged by 100 acres, and three new buildings were added, with three additional structures in the planning stages. (Courtesy of Presbyterian College Archives.)

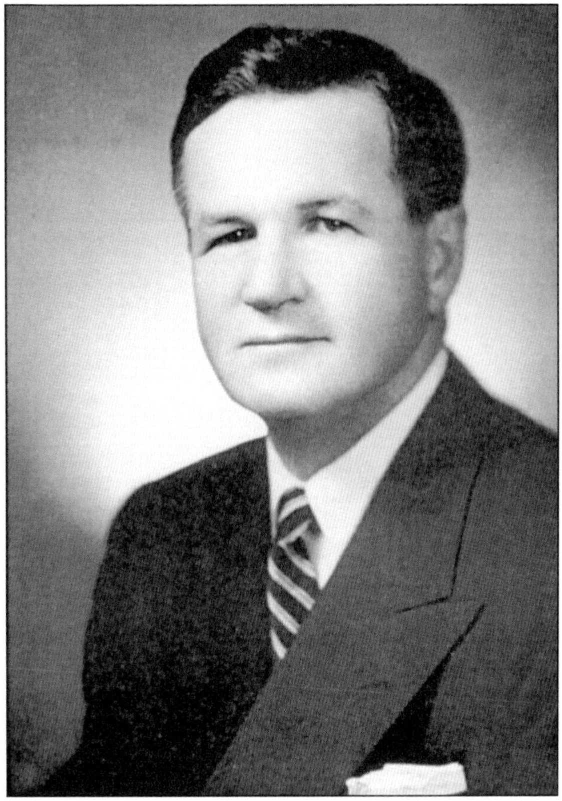

**William Plumer Jacobs.** Jacobs, grandson of the college's founder, served as president from 1935 to 1945, a period that included the upheavals of World War II. While president, he continued his regular business activities, handling fund-raising and public relations for the college while Dean Marshall Brown supervised the daily operation of the campus. (Courtesy of Presbyterian College Archives.)

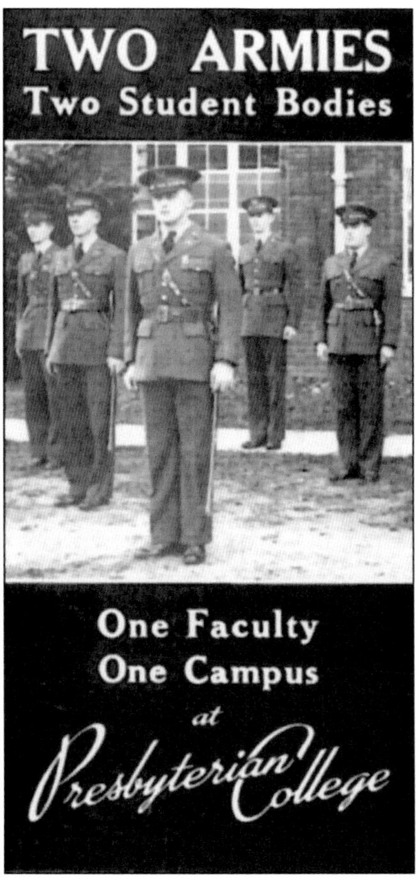


**Wartime Training.** During World War II, PC trained both its own ROTC troops and the 39th College Training Detachment of the U.S. Army Air Force. (Courtesy of Presbyterian College Archives.)

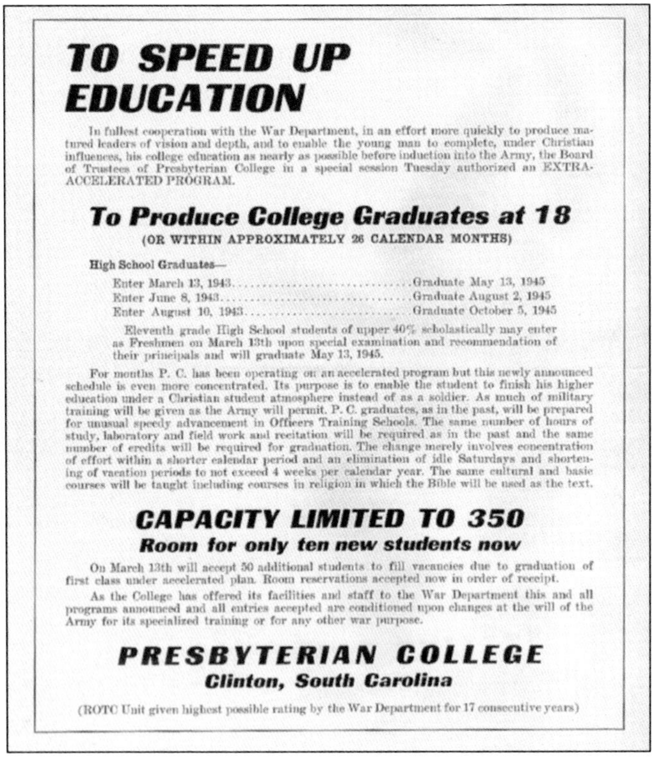

**TO SPEED UP EDUCATION**

In fullest cooperation with the War Department, in an effort more quickly to produce matured leaders of vision and depth, and to enable the young man to complete, under Christian influences, his college education as nearly as possible before induction into the Army, the Board of Trustees of Presbyterian College in a special session Tuesday authorized an EXTRA-ACCELERATED PROGRAM.

**To Produce College Graduates at 18**

(OR WITHIN APPROXIMATELY 26 CALENDAR MONTHS)

**High School Graduates—**

Enter March 13, 1943 .......... Graduate May 13, 1945
Enter June 8, 1943 .......... Graduate August 2, 1945
Enter August 10, 1943 .......... Graduate October 5, 1945

Eleventh grade High School students of upper 40% scholastically may enter as Freshmen on March 13th upon special examination and recommendation of their principals and will graduate May 13, 1945.

For months P. C. has been operating on an accelerated program but this newly announced schedule is even more concentrated. Its purpose is to enable the student to finish his higher education under a Christian student atmosphere instead of as a soldier. As much of military training will be given as the Army will permit. P. C. graduates, as in the past, will be prepared for unusual speedy advancement in Officers Training Schools. The same number of hours of study, laboratory and field work and recitation will be required as in the past and the same number of credits will be required for graduation. The change merely involves concentration of effort within a shorter calendar period and an elimination of idle Saturdays and shortening of vacation periods to not exceed 4 weeks per calendar year. The same cultural and basic courses will be taught including courses in religion in which the Bible will be used as the text.

**CAPACITY LIMITED TO 350**

**Room for only ten new students now**

On March 13th will accept 50 additional students to fill vacancies due to graduation of first class under accelerated plan. Room reservations accepted now in order of receipt.

As the College has offered its facilities and staff to the War Department this and all programs announced and all entries accepted are conditioned upon changes at the will of the Army for its specialized training or for any other war purpose.

**PRESBYTERIAN COLLEGE**

**Clinton, South Carolina**

(ROTC Unit given highest possible rating by the War Department for 17 consecutive years)

ACCELERATED PROGRAM. During the war the college also provided an accelerated program that produced graduates with army commissions in just 28 months. (Courtesy of Presbyterian College Archives.)

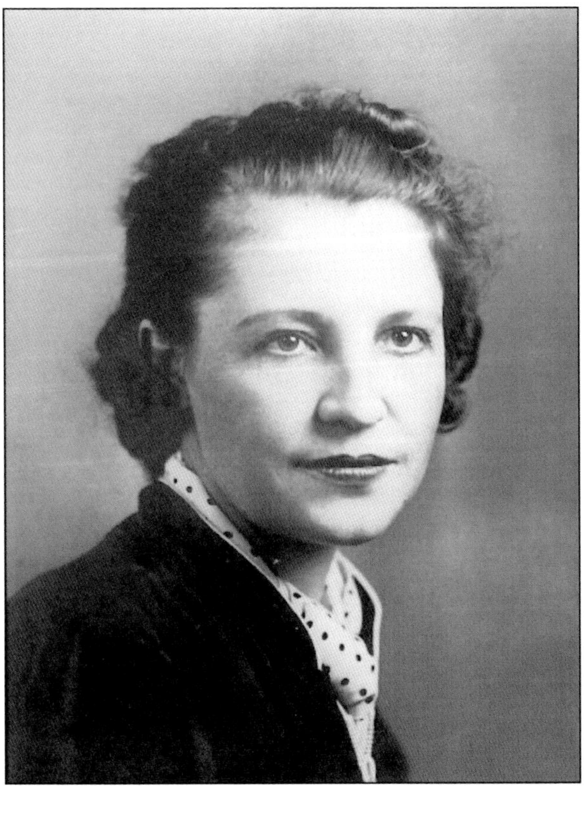

MRS. BEE. Marshall Brown's wife, Lillian Gross Brown, arrived at PC and took on the job of registrar in 1928. Her "Bee Mail" letters went out to all PC servicemen during the war. She died in July 2001 at the age of 103. (Courtesy of Presbyterian College Archives.)

**In Memoriam.** Approximately 1,500 PC students and alumni served in the armed services during World War II, and 65 lost their lives. (Courtesy of Presbyterian College Archives.)

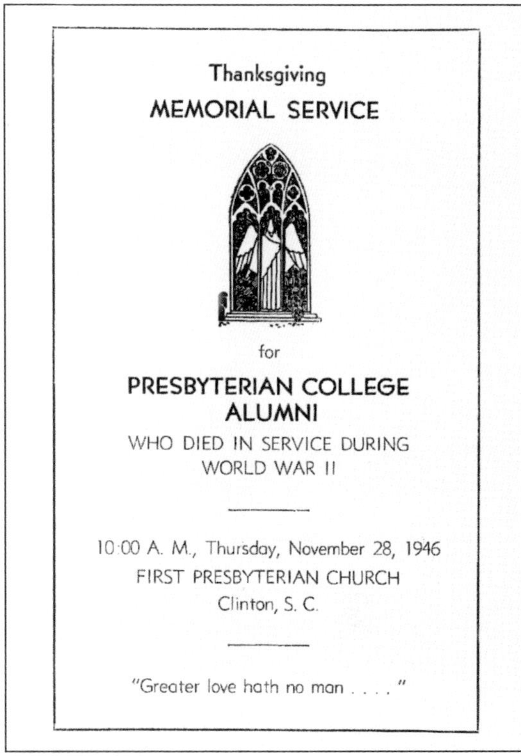

Thanksgiving

MEMORIAL SERVICE

for

PRESBYTERIAN COLLEGE ALUMNI

WHO DIED IN SERVICE DURING WORLD WAR II

10:00 A. M., Thursday, November 28, 1946

FIRST PRESBYTERIAN CHURCH

Clinton, S. C.

"Greater love hath no man . . . ."

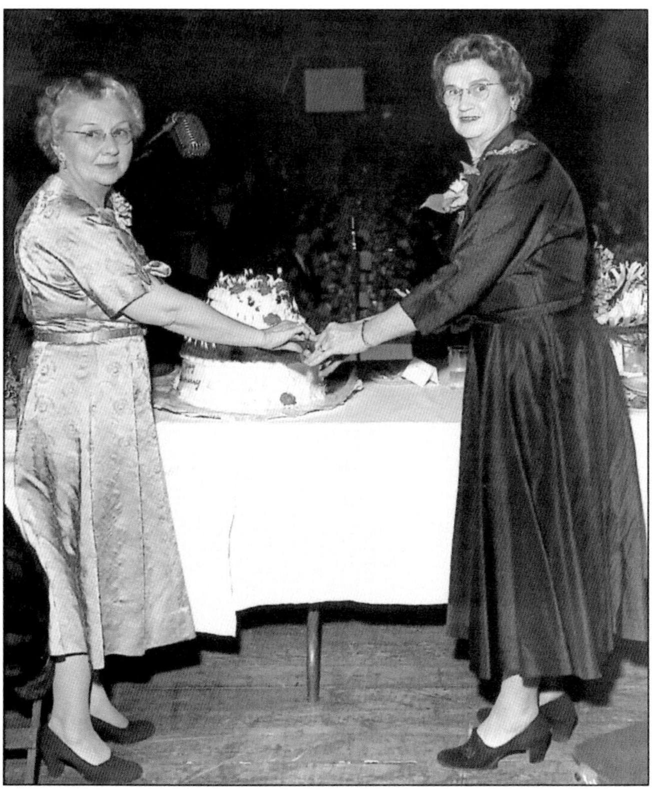

**Diamond Jubilee.** The college celebrated its 75th anniversary in 1955. Here an anniversary cake is cut at the Atlanta Jubilee Dinner, which was part of the celebration. (Courtesy of Presbyterian College Archives.)

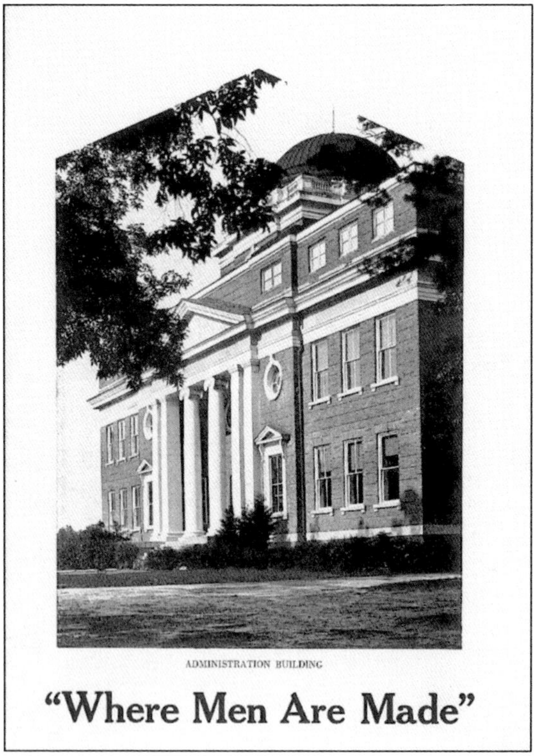


**"Where Men are Made."** This early PC motto definitely became a thing of the past when the college became fully co-educational in 1965. (Courtesy of Presbyterian College Archives.)

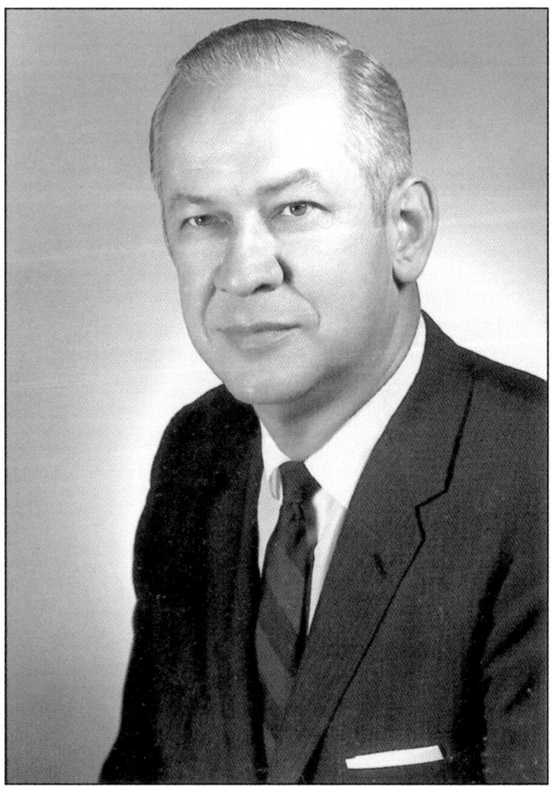

**Marc Weersing.** Weersing, a former trustee, served as president from 1963 to 1979. During his tenure, full co-education was achieved, and African-American students were admitted to the college for the first time. The college's assets grew dramatically, and the number of students and faculty increased. (Courtesy of Presbyterian College Archives.)

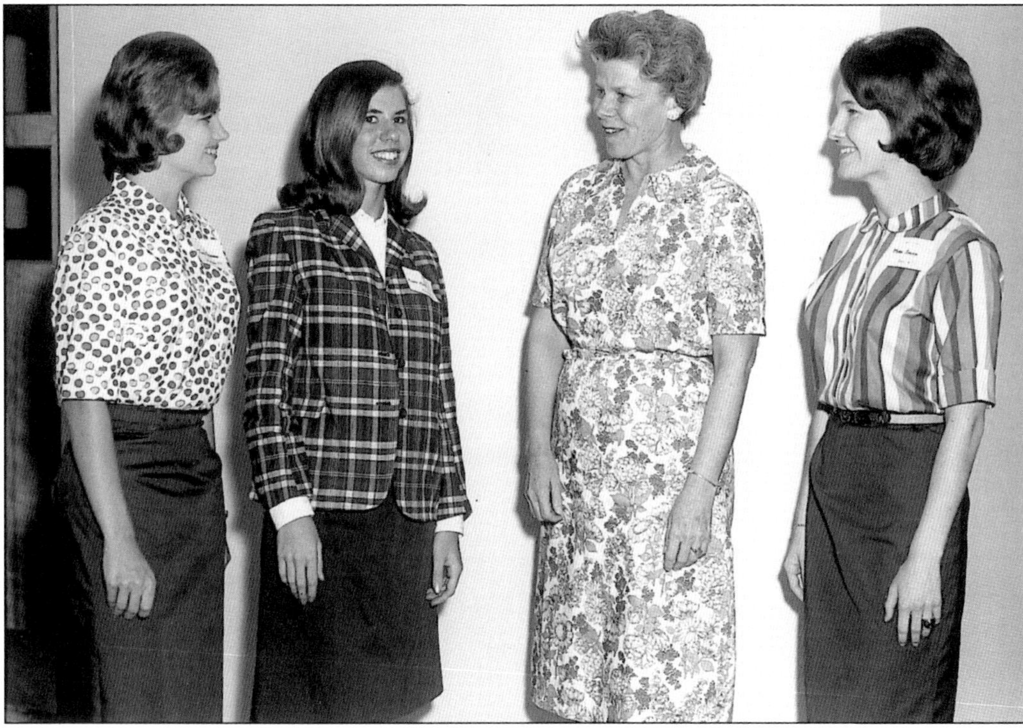

**FULL CO-EDUCATION, 1965.** Dean of Women Marion Hill welcomes coeds Faye Kirkman, Elaine Mason, and Myra Smith to campus in 1965. While local women had been allowed to attend classes at the college throughout much of its history, PC did not become fully co–educational until 1965. (Courtesy of Presbyterian College Archives.)

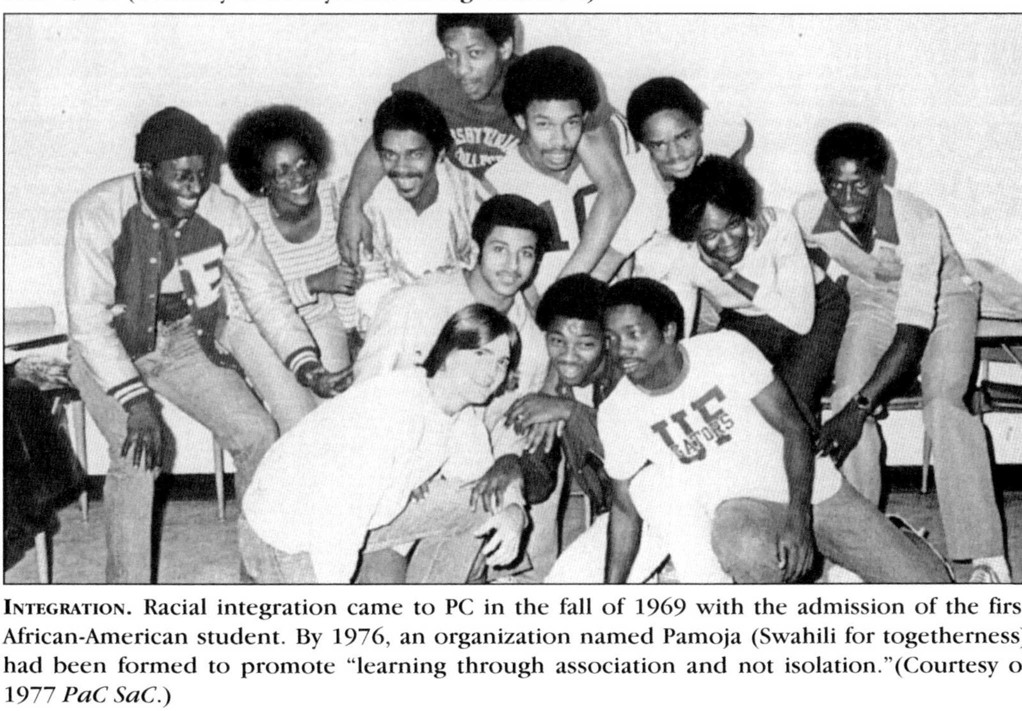

**INTEGRATION.** Racial integration came to PC in the fall of 1969 with the admission of the first African-American student. By 1976, an organization named Pamoja (Swahili for togetherness) had been formed to promote "learning through association and not isolation."(Courtesy of 1977 *PaC SaC*.)

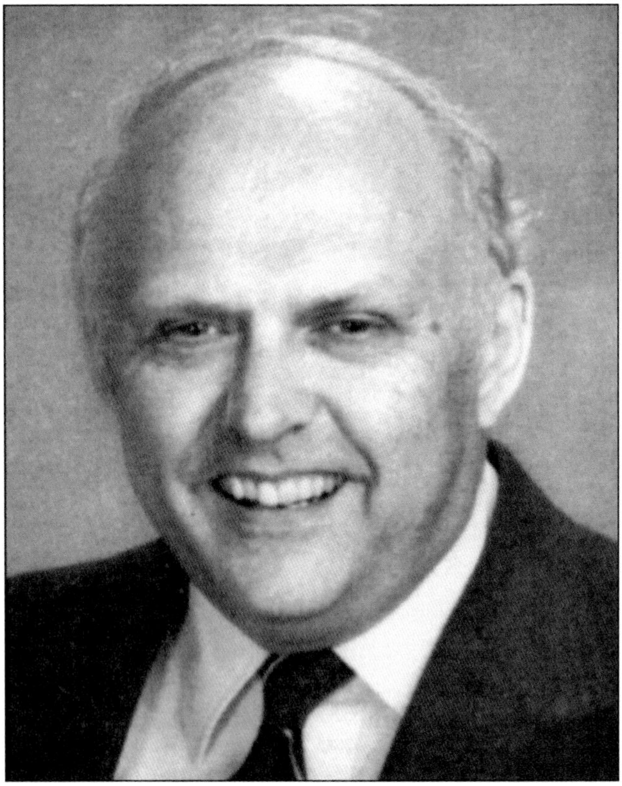

**Kenneth Bradley Orr.** Dr. Orr served as PC's president from 1979 to 1997. During his tenure, such campus landmarks as Edmunds Hall, the Harper Center, and the Harrington-Peachtree Academic Center were built, and the college completed a $38.5 million fund-raising campaign. The college's enrollment, endowment, and ranking increased steadily over this 18-year span. (Courtesy of 1987 *PaC SaC*.)

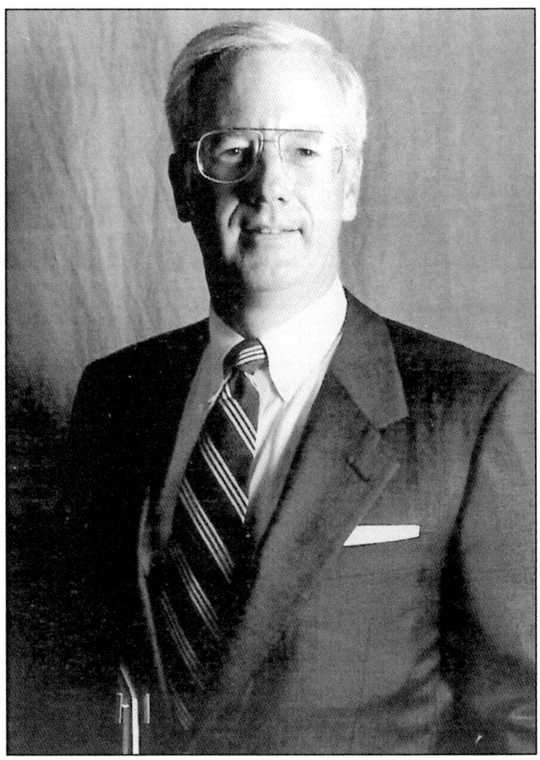

**John V. Griffith.** PC's current president is John Griffith, who took office on January 1, 1998. Armed with a rich history and a new long-range plan, the college is well equipped to enter the 21st century. (Courtesy of Presbyterian College Public Relations Office.)

*Two*

# The Campus

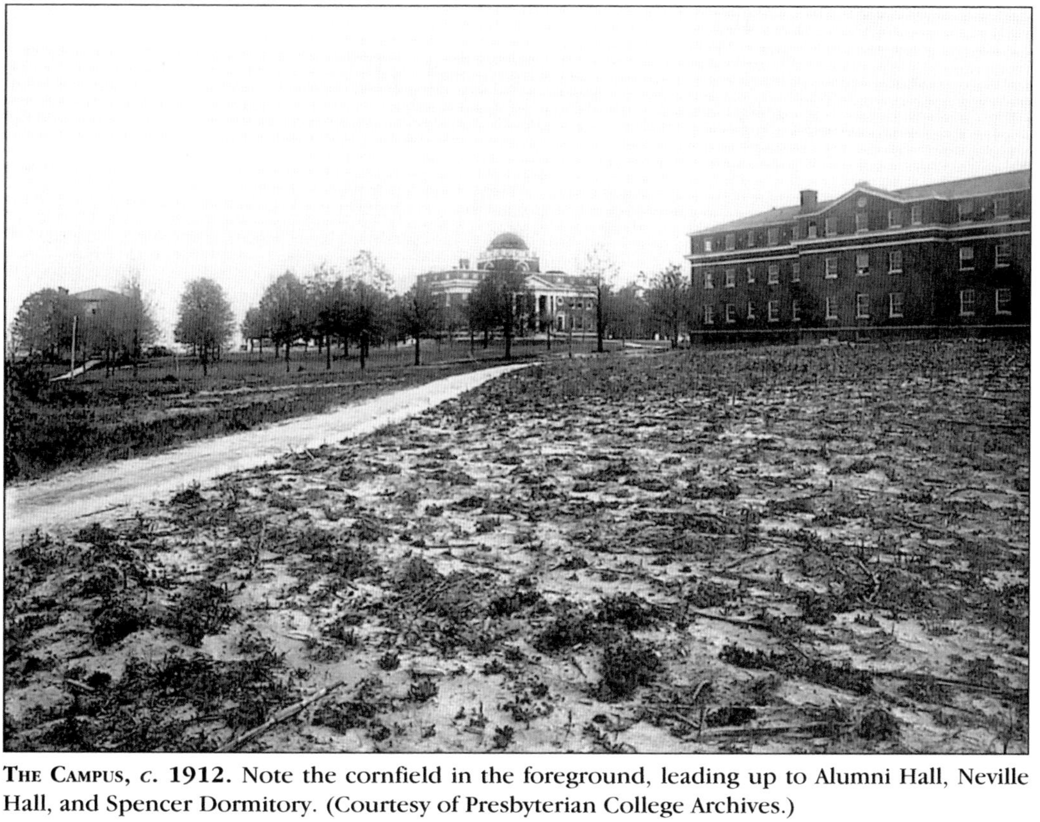

**The Campus, *c.* 1912.** Note the cornfield in the foreground, leading up to Alumni Hall, Neville Hall, and Spencer Dormitory. (Courtesy of Presbyterian College Archives.)

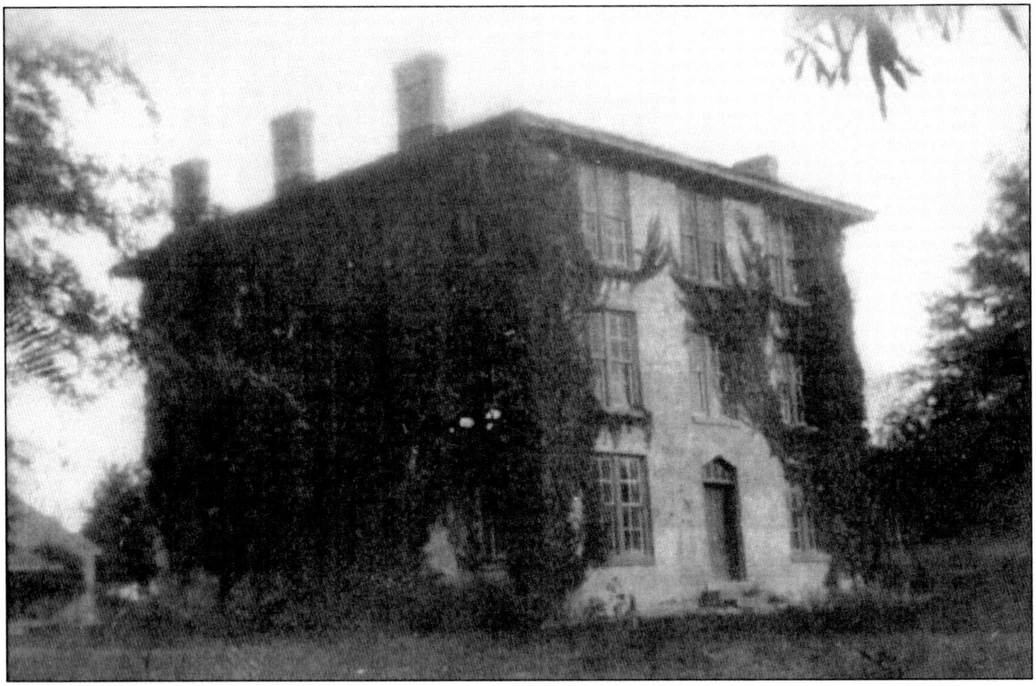

**ALUMNI HALL.** Alumni Hall dormitory, the first building to be erected on the present campus, was built in 1891. The three-story building contained 6 rooms on a floor, and housed 36 students. The rooms were described as "large, well lighted, and heated by steam." In 1942 it was renovated to serve as Doyle Infirmary. (Courtesy of Presbyterian College Archives.)

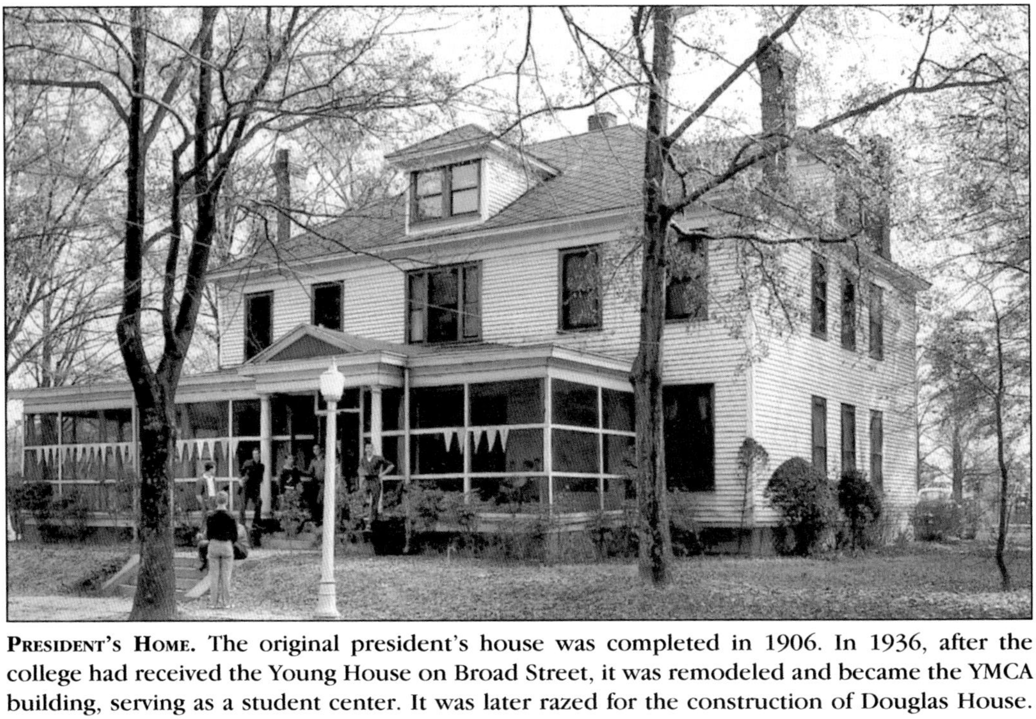

**PRESIDENT'S HOME.** The original president's house was completed in 1906. In 1936, after the college had received the Young House on Broad Street, it was remodeled and became the YMCA building, serving as a student center. It was later razed for the construction of Douglas House. (Courtesy of Presbyterian College Archives.)

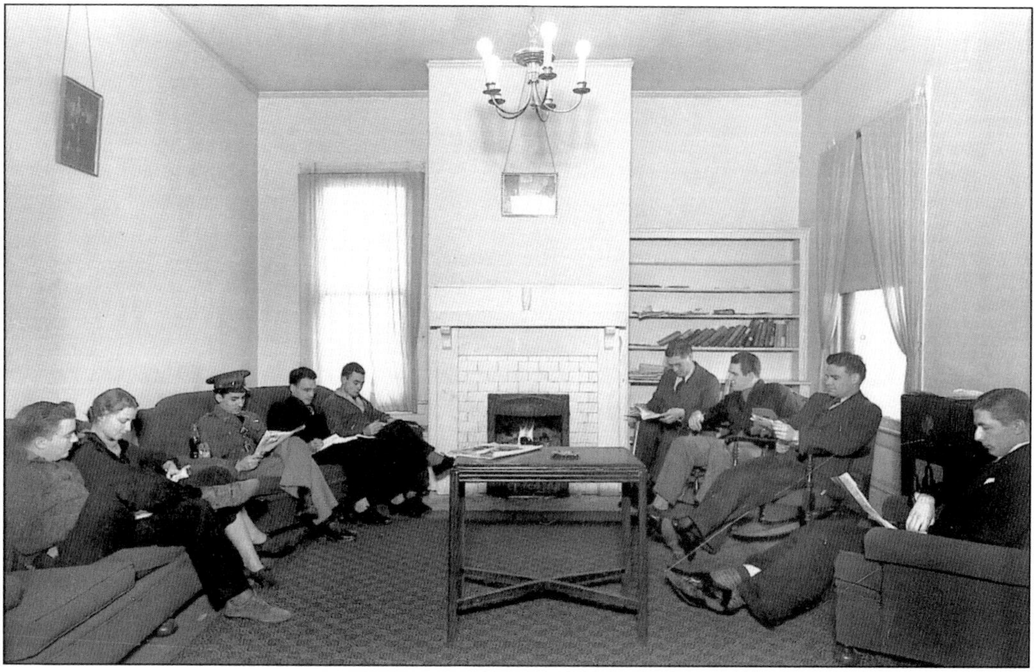

**Student Center.** This photo shows the lounge in the YMCA building around 1938. (Courtesy of Presbyterian College Archives.)

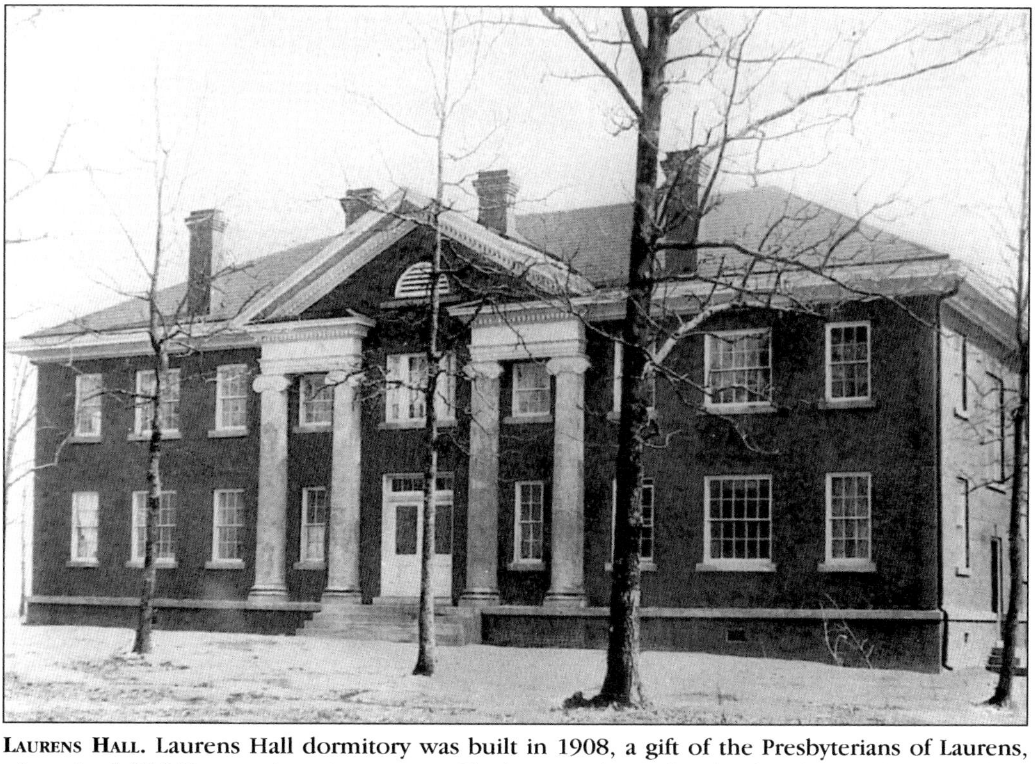

**Laurens Hall.** Laurens Hall dormitory was built in 1908, a gift of the Presbyterians of Laurens, who raised $7,000 to underwrite its cost. Charles C. Wilson of Columbia designed the building. (Courtesy of Presbyterian College Archives.)

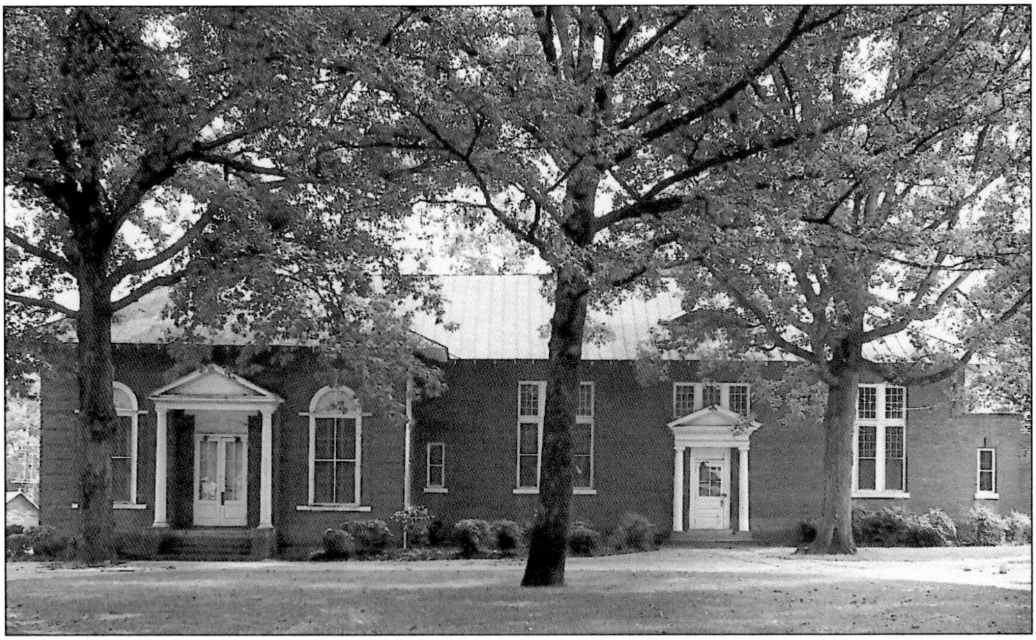

**Judd Refectory.** Judd Refectory, the dining hall for PC students, was the result of a gift from Mrs. E.A. Judd of Spartanburg. It was originally built in 1908 to seat 300 people, and was enlarged in 1923. Following the admission of women in 1965, it was renovated to house women's physical education activities. It burned in 1973, the result of arson, the first major fire in PC's history. (Courtesy of Presbyterian College Archives.)

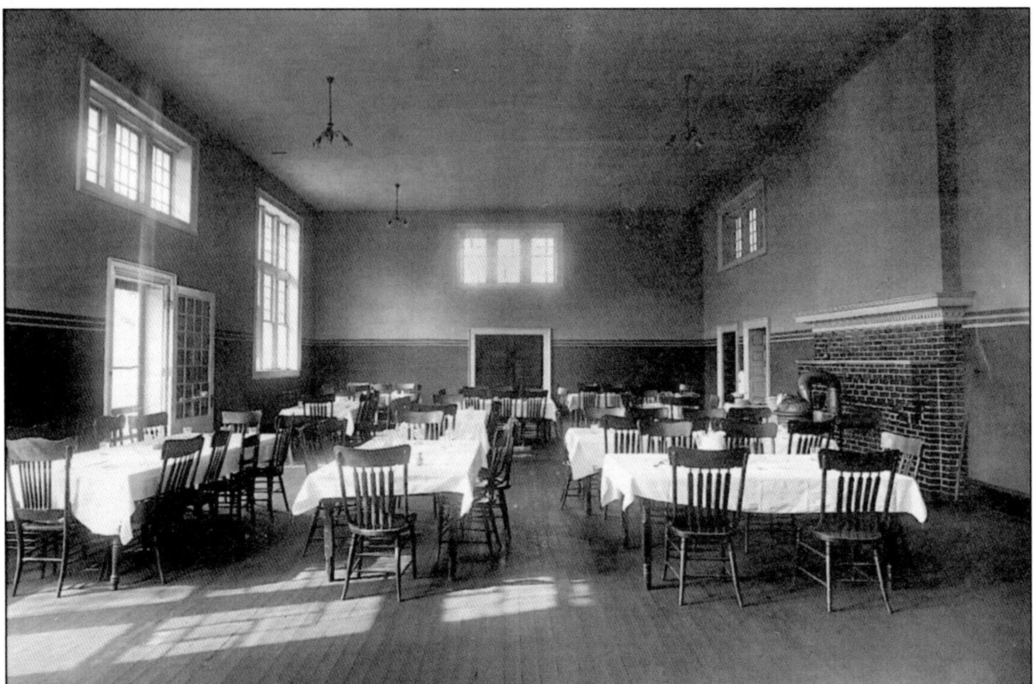

**Interior, Judd Dining Hall.** Under the supervision of Matron Myrtle Hunter, tables were traditionally set with tablecloths and cloth napkins. (Courtesy of Presbyterian College Archives.)

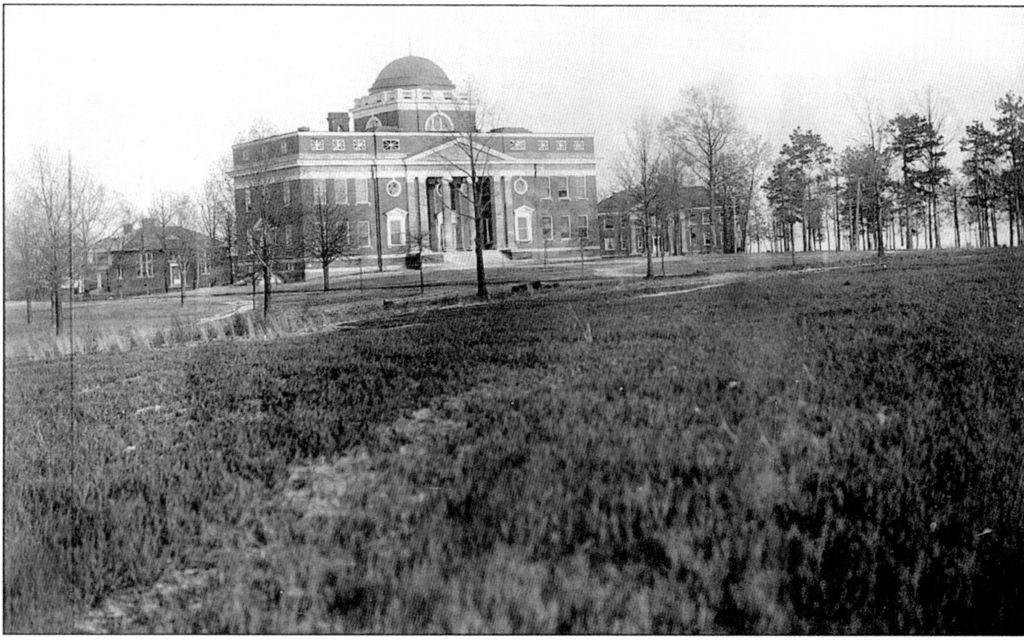

**Neville Hall, Judd Hall (left), and Laurens Hall (right).** This view of the rather barren 30-acre campus was taken around 1910. (Courtesy of Presbyterian College Archives.)

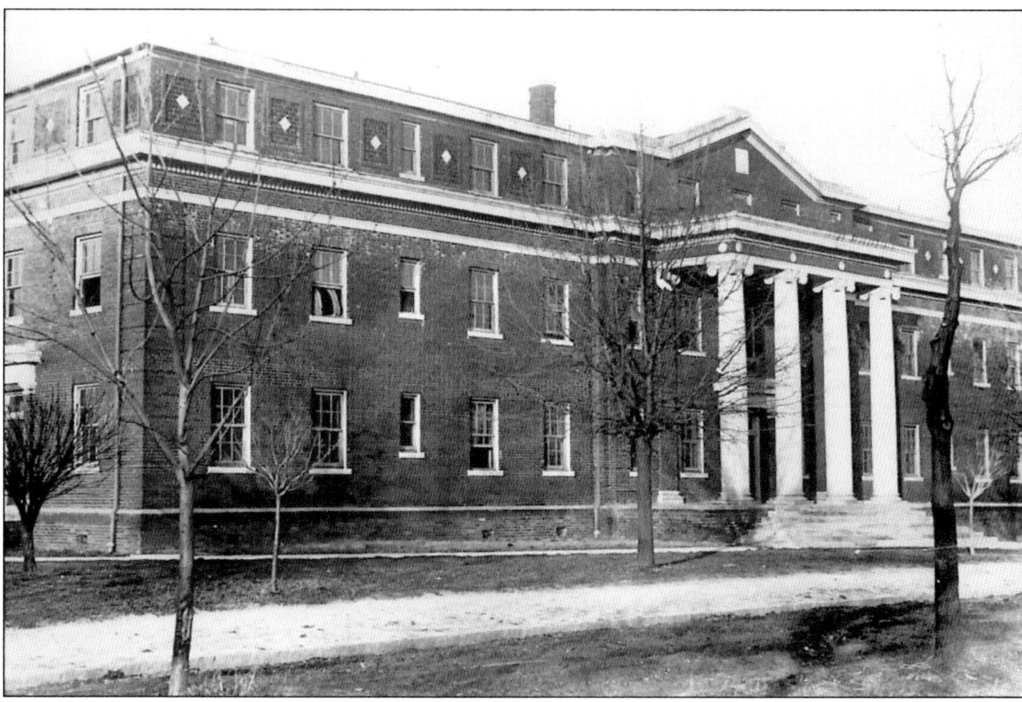

**Spencer Hall.** Built as a dormitory in 1912, Spencer Hall was named after former president Almon E. Spencer. It housed 90 students, and rooms were arranged in suites. It was later razed and replaced by the Harrington-Peachtree Academic Center. (Courtesy of Presbyterian College Archives.)

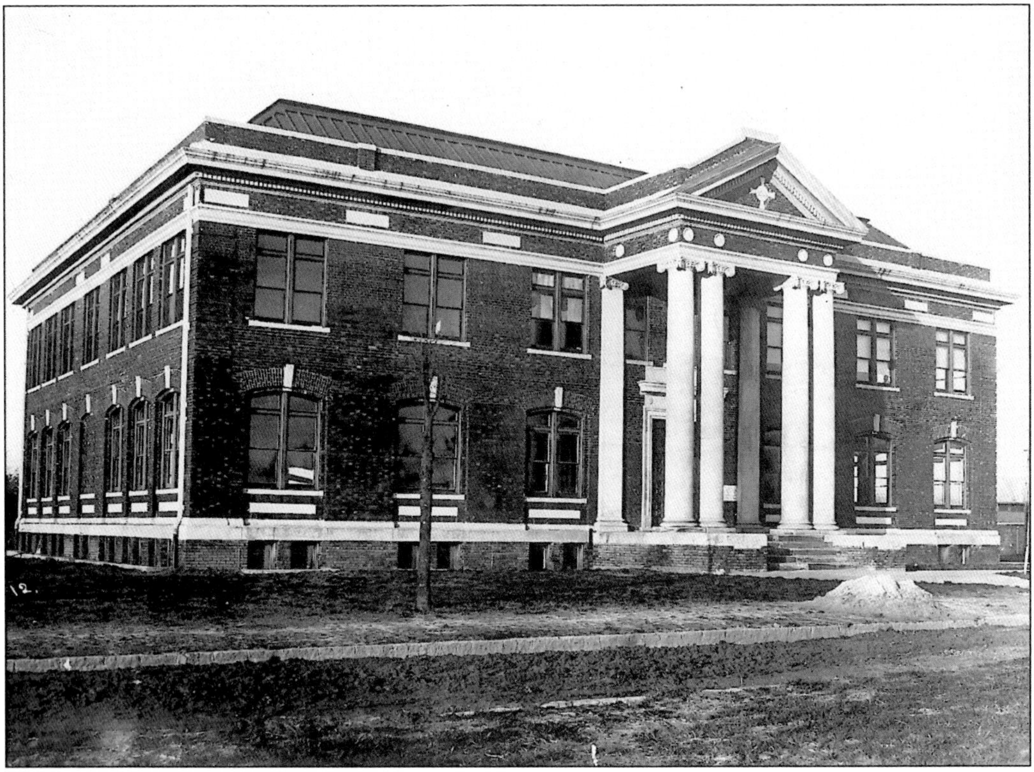

**Jacobs Hall.** Jacobs Hall, named after college founder William P. Jacobs, was built in 1915 as a combination library and science facility. It also contained a gymnasium. It underwent extensive renovation in 1987. (Courtesy of Presbyterian College Archives.)

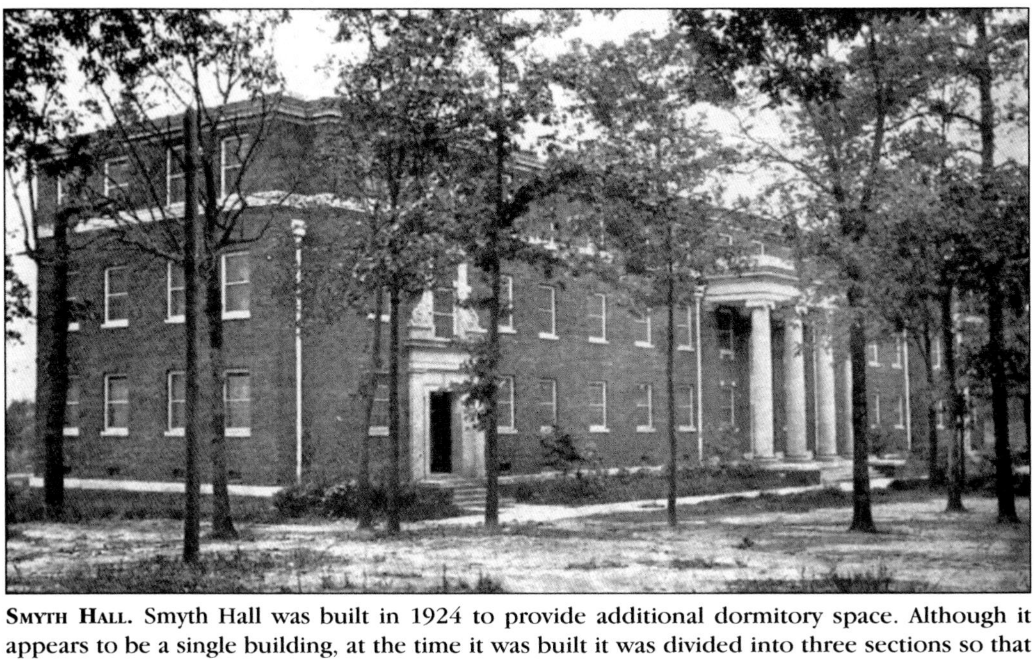

**Smyth Hall.** Smyth Hall was built in 1924 to provide additional dormitory space. Although it appears to be a single building, at the time it was built it was divided into three sections so that students could be housed in smaller groups. (Courtesy of Presbyterian College Archives.)

**THE CAMPUS BELL.** The campus bell dates back to the first academy building in 1880; during the first 65 years of the college's history, it rang to announce class changes and football victories. (Courtesy of 1982 *PaC SaC*.)

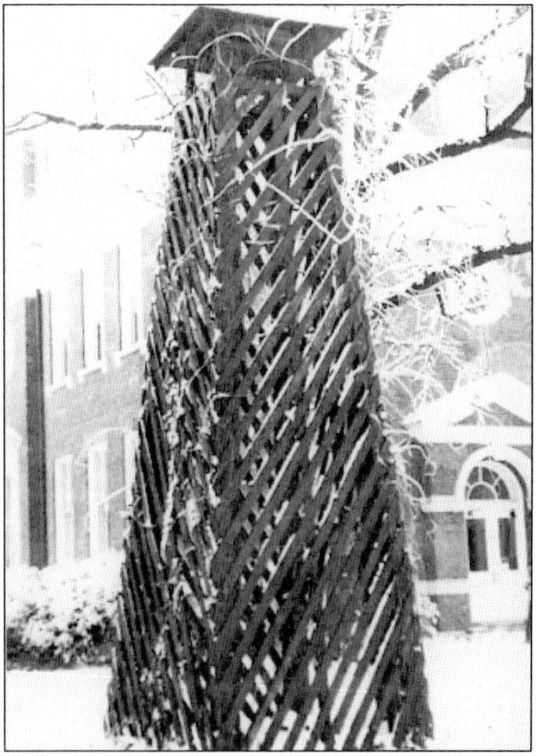

**SPRINGS GYMNASIUM, *c.* 1938.** The original Springs Gymnasium, built in 1924, was named to honor benefactor Leroy Springs. Springs also provided the funds for the addition of a swimming pool in 1929. The building was renovated into a student center in 1985. (Courtesy of Presbyterian College Archives.)

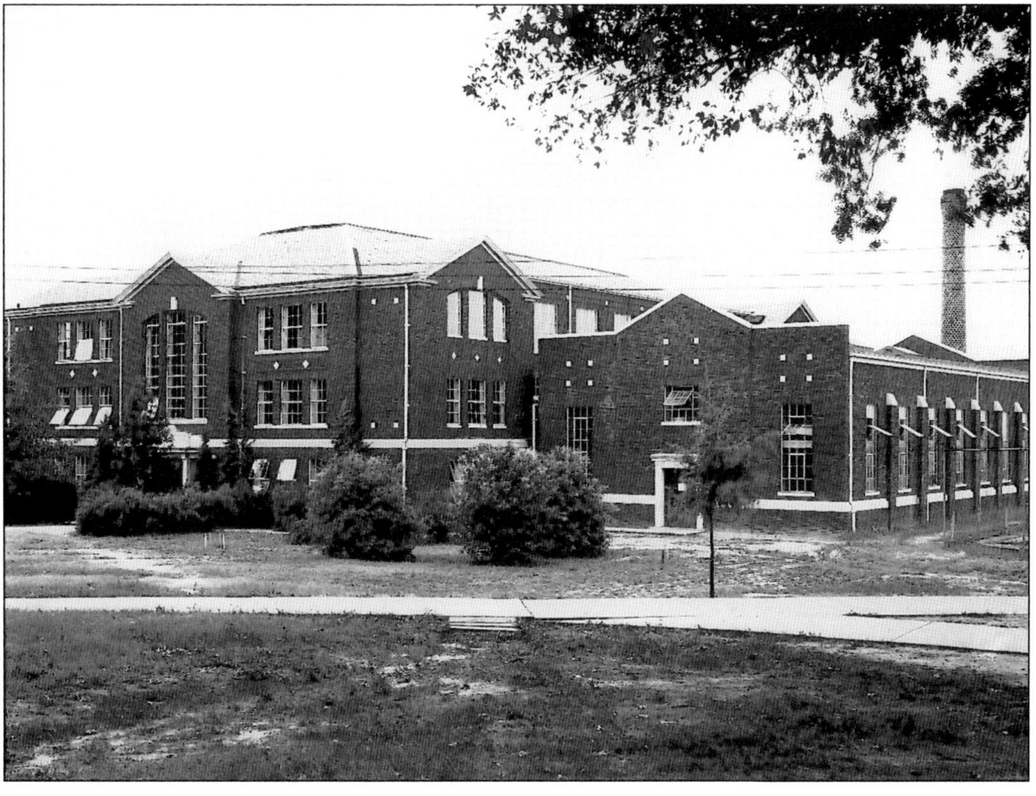

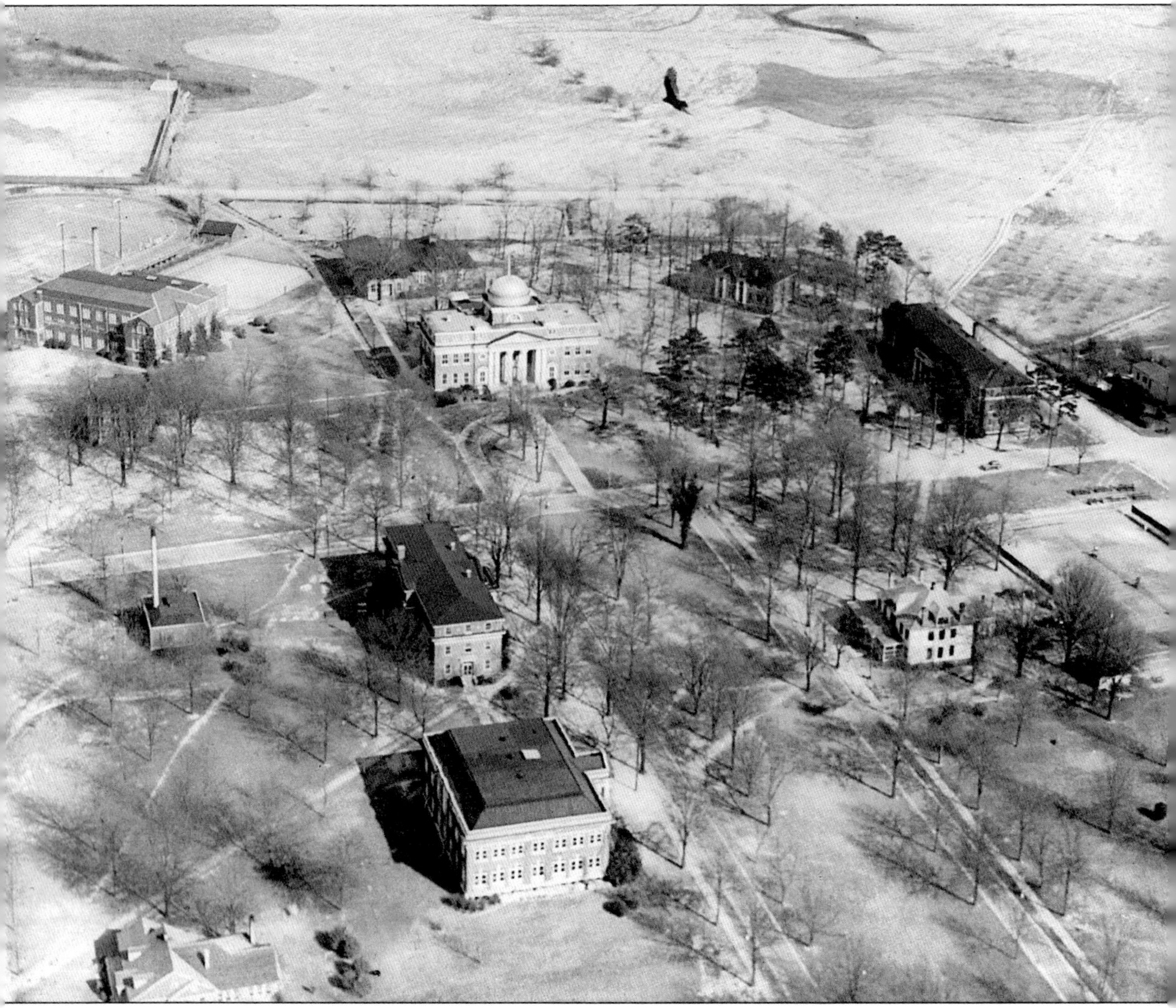

**Aerial View of the Campus, 1939.** As the college had not yet acquired the land for the East Plaza, development at this time was confined to the present–day West Plaza. The heating plant, which appears on the far left, and the President's House, on the far right, no longer exist. (Courtesy of Presbyterian College Archives.)

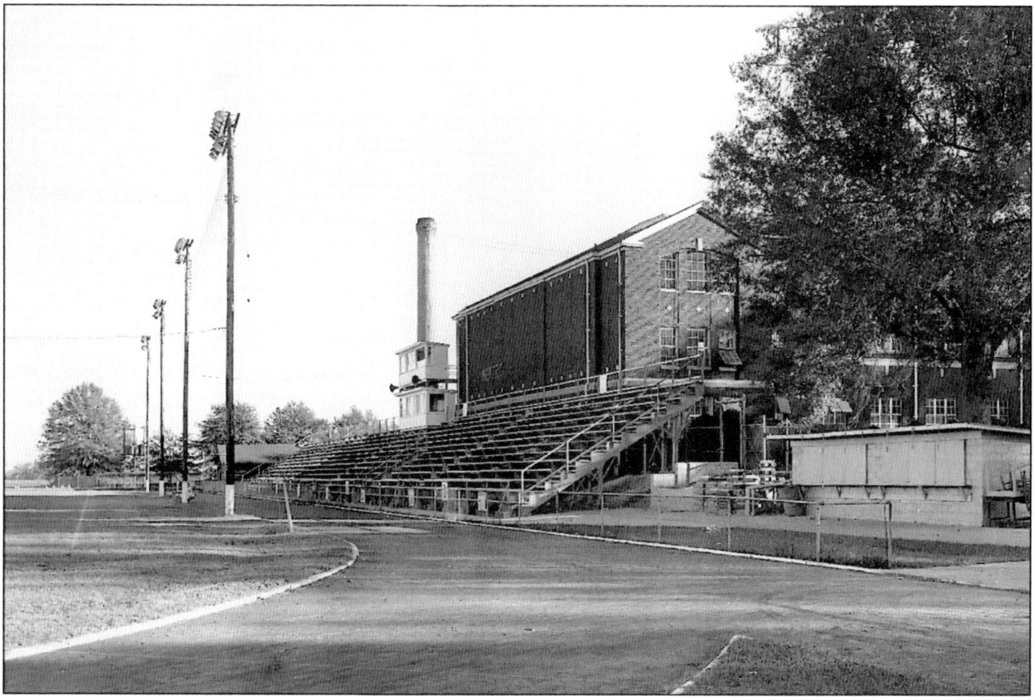

**Bailey Memorial Stadium.** Named for W.J. Bailey, the stadium was dedicated in 1928. It was designed to seat 3,000 spectators; the accompanying Johnson athletic field boasted one of the finest tracks in the South. (Courtesy of Presbyterian College Archives.)

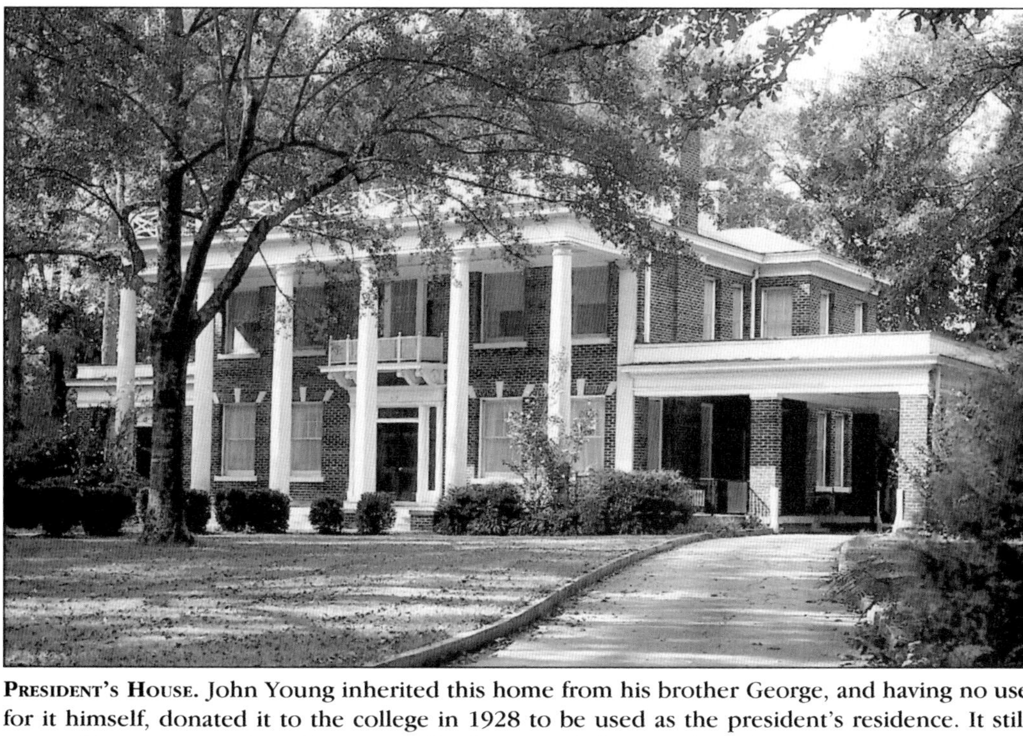

**President's House.** John Young inherited this home from his brother George, and having no use for it himself, donated it to the college in 1928 to be used as the president's residence. It still serves this purpose today. (Courtesy of Presbyterian College Archives.)

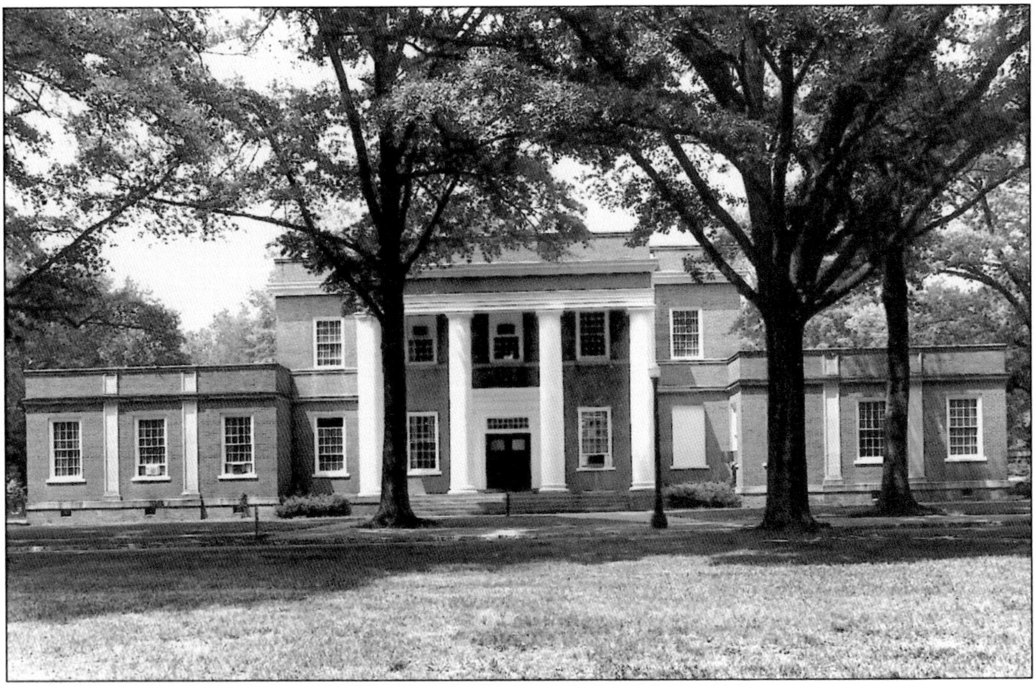

**Smith Administration Building.** Built with Works Projects Administration (WPA) funds and opened in 1942, this building originally served as a library for both the college and the town of Clinton. Following the construction of the Thomason Library, it was remodeled in 1979 to serve as the administration building. The building was named for the parents of John I. Smith of Greenville, who provided a significant gift to underwrite the renovation. (Courtesy of Presbyterian College Archives.)

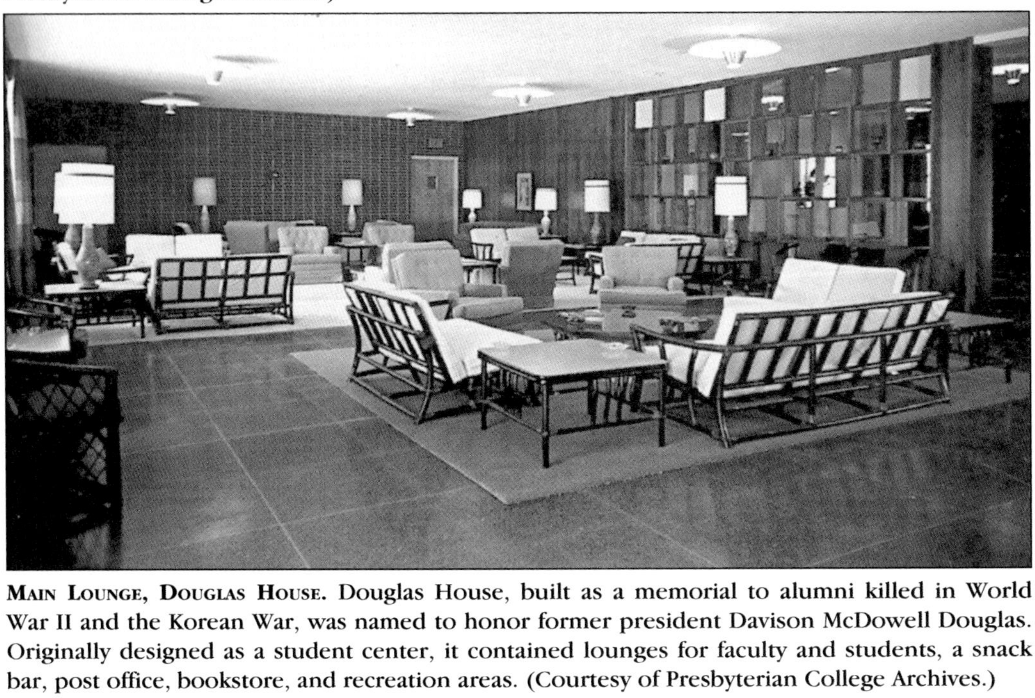

**Main Lounge, Douglas House.** Douglas House, built as a memorial to alumni killed in World War II and the Korean War, was named to honor former president Davison McDowell Douglas. Originally designed as a student center, it contained lounges for faculty and students, a snack bar, post office, bookstore, and recreation areas. (Courtesy of Presbyterian College Archives.)

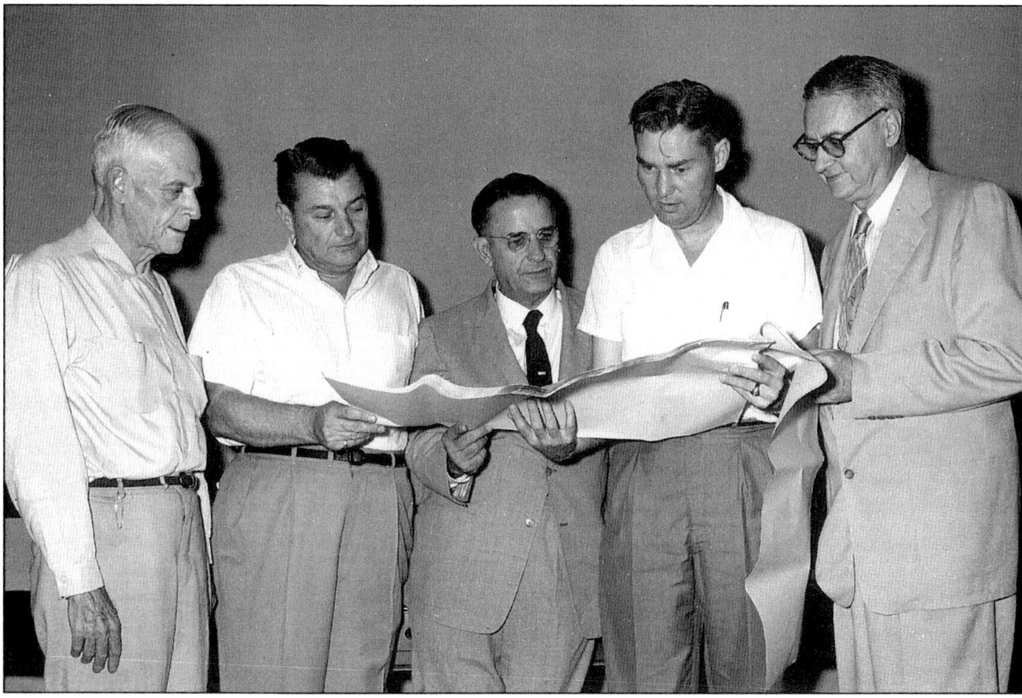

**Building Committee, 1957.** Among those responsible for PC's growth in the 1950s and 1960s were the members of the building committee of the Board of Trustees. Pictured from left to right are James C. Todd, P.S. Bailey, J.F. Jacobs Sr., Robert M. Vance, and Pres. Marshall W. Brown. (Courtesy of Presbyterian College Archives.)

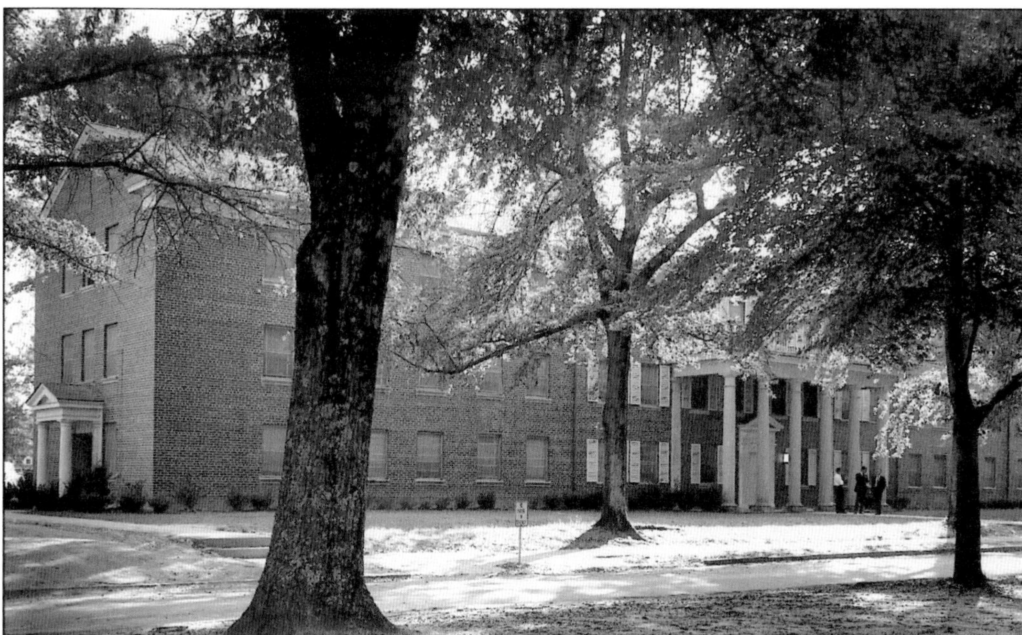

**Bailey Hall.** Built in 1955, this dormitory was named for Clinton business leader and longtime board member William J. Bailey. (Courtesy of Presbyterian College Archives.)

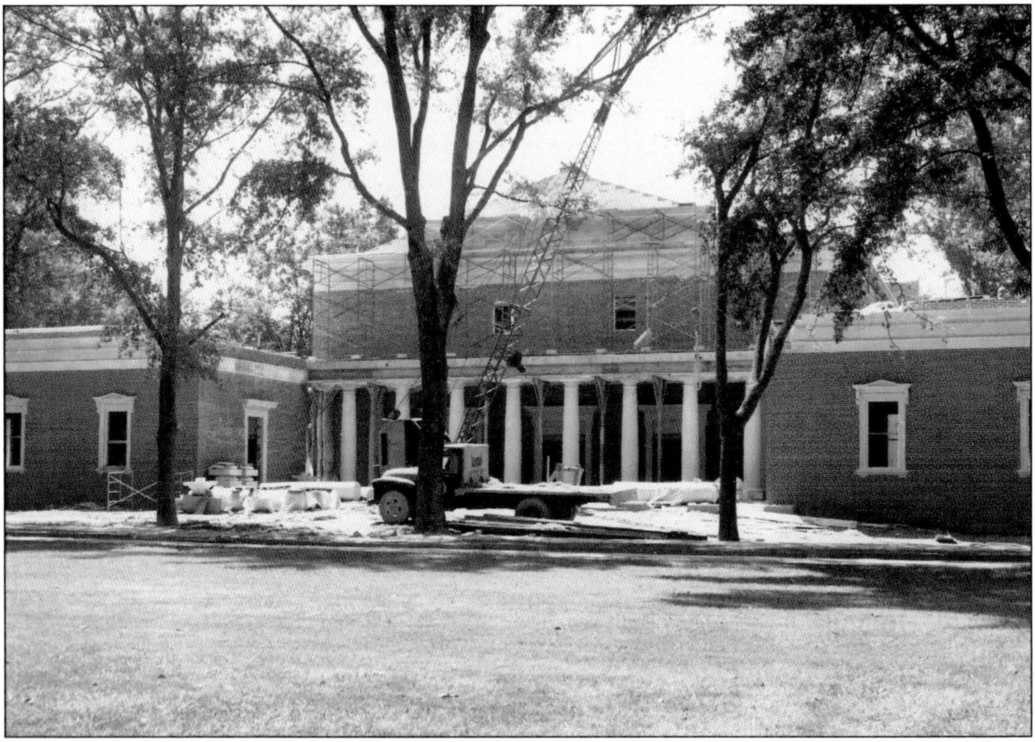

**Belk Auditorium Under Construction.** Built in 1960, this large auditorium cost $500,000. It was named for William Henry Belk, founder of the Belk department stores, and was paid for in part by Belk family members and Belk stores in South Carolina and Georgia. (Courtesy of Presbyterian College Archives.)

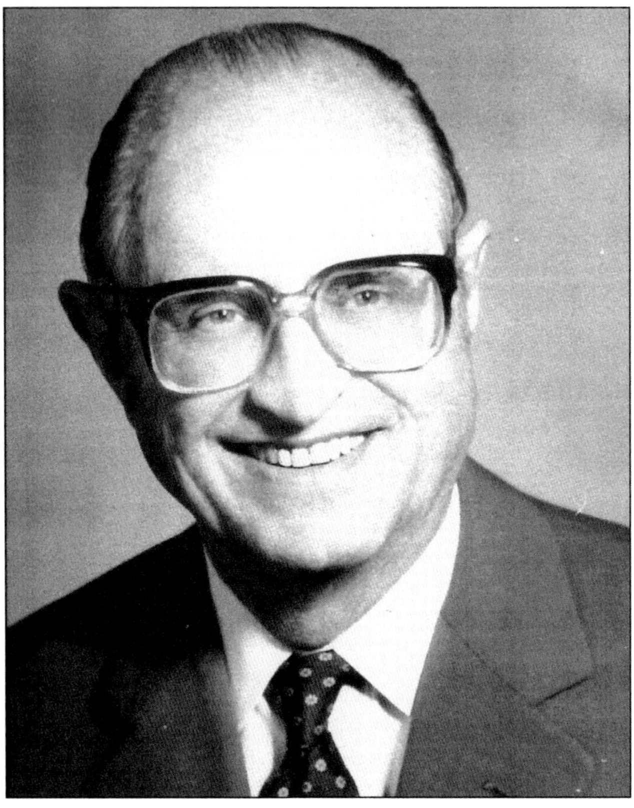

**Irwin Belk.** The generosity of trustee Irwin Belk and other members of the Belk family has made possible several buildings on the PC campus, including Belk Auditorium, Grotnes Hall, Mary Irwin Belk Hall, and Carol International House. (Courtesy of Presbyterian College Public Relations Office.)

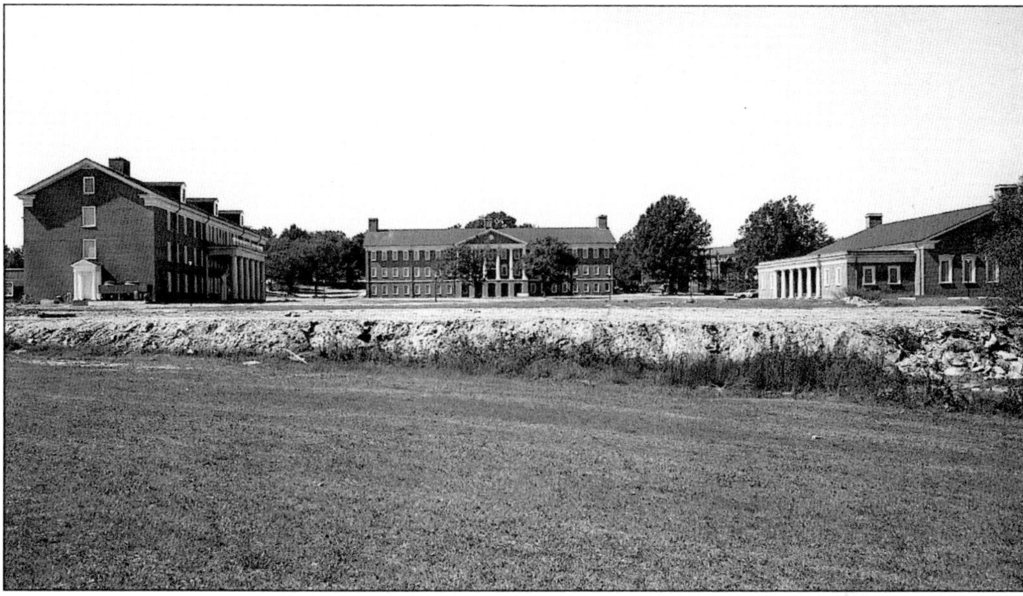

**Clinton Hall, Richardson Hall, and Greenville Dining Hall, 1965.** Clinton Hall, the first dormitory for female students, was financed largely by alumni and friends in Clinton. In addition to housing 125 women, it included a large reception parlor and four "dating parlors." Built at the same time were Greenville Dining Hall and Richardson Hall. Alumni and friends in Greenville funded the construction for Greenville Dining Hall. Construction of Richardson was encouraged by a challenge grant from H. Smith Richardson, president of the Vick Chemical Company. (Courtesy of Presbyterian College Archives.)

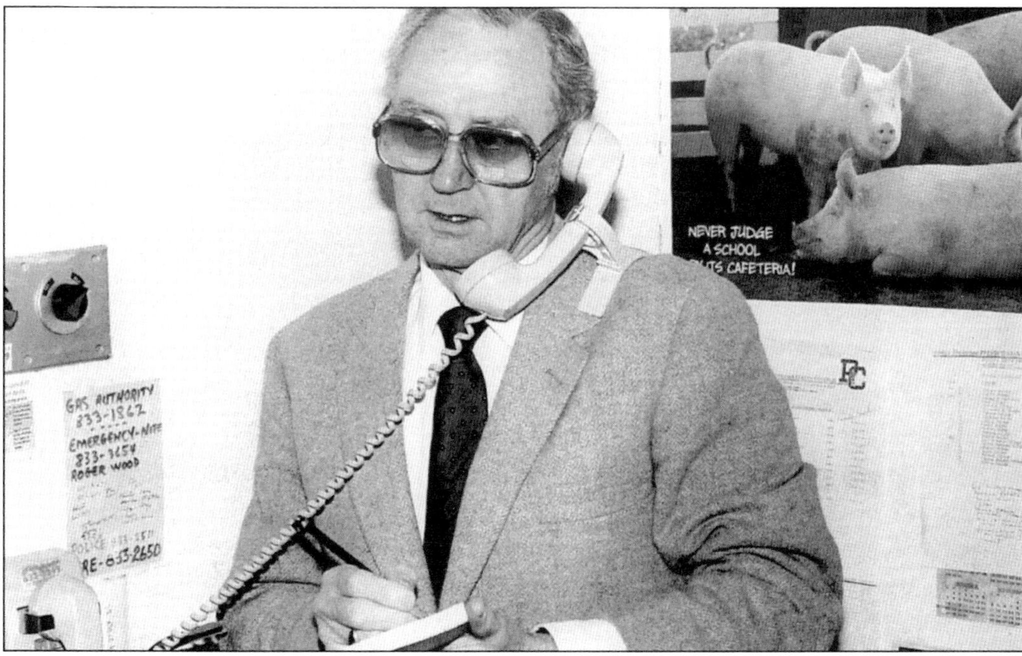


**Vernon Powell.** Vernon Powell presided over the dining hall for many years, serving in Judd Hall from 1947 to 1960, and Greenville Dining Hall from 1977 to 1999. (Courtesy of Presbyterian College Public Relations Office.)

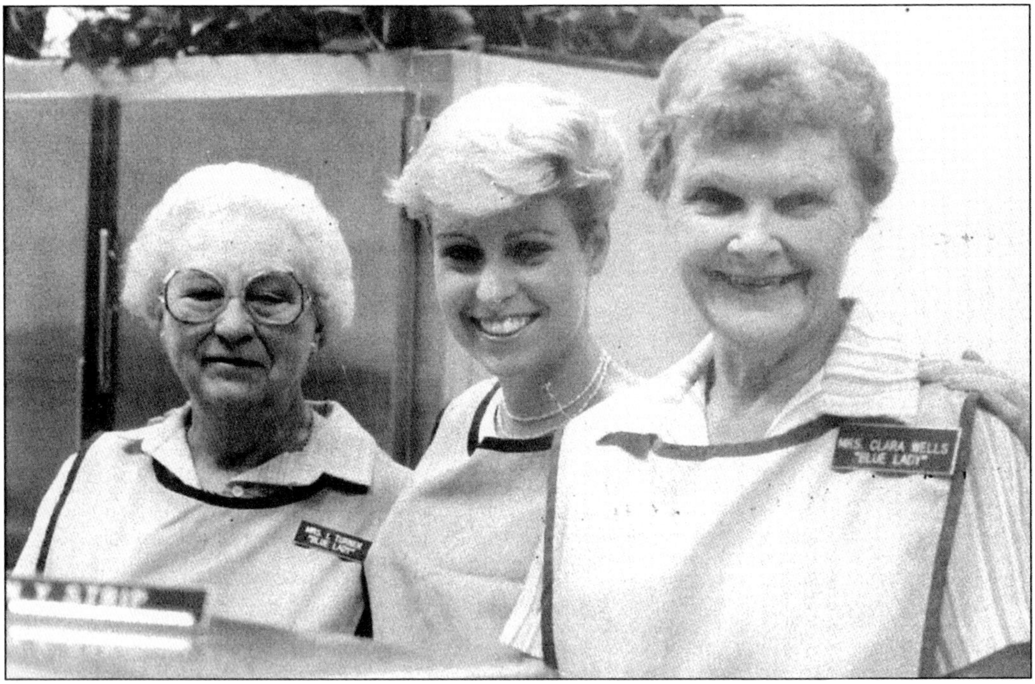


**Blue Ladies.** The friendly faces of the "Blue Ladies" are a familiar sight in the dining hall. One college annual referred to them as "grandmothers with spunk." (Courtesy of Presbyterian College Public Relations Office.)

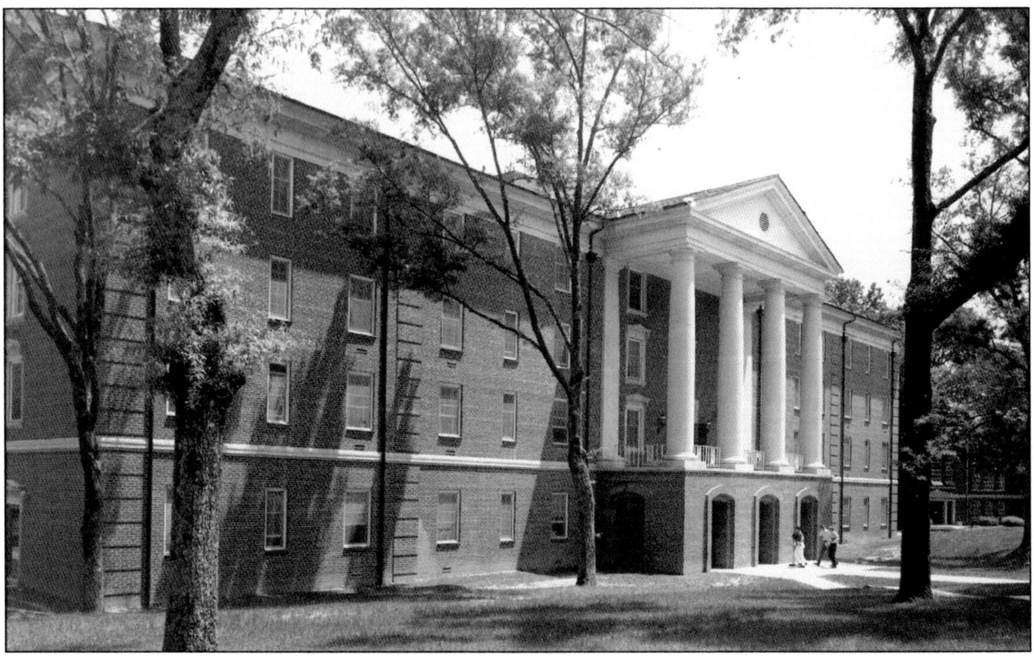

**Georgia Hall.** Georgia Hall dormitory, built in 1968, was largely financed by contributions from the Synod of Georgia. It was the first men's dormitory built at PC since the construction of Bailey Hall in 1955, and included recreation areas and lounges to supplement the overcrowded Douglas House. (Courtesy of Presbyterian College Archives.)

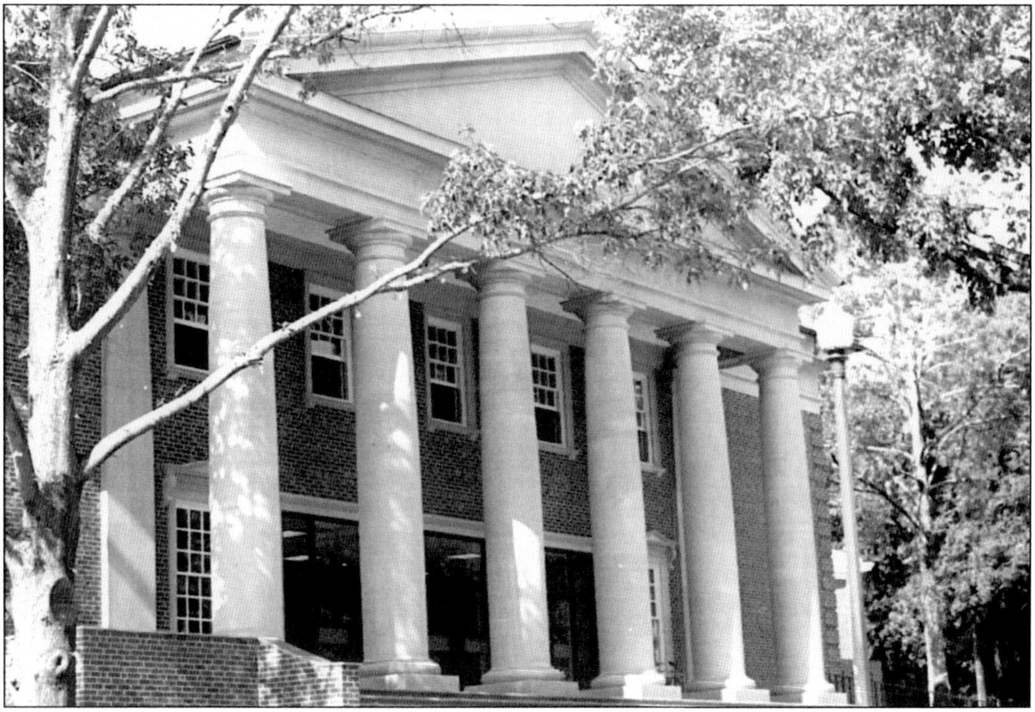

**THOMASON LIBRARY UNDER CONSTRUCTION.** The new library, dedicated in 1974, was named for benefactor James H. Thomason Sr. of Mountville. The 45,000-square-foot building was designed to house 175,000 books, and included the Eugene T. Wilson Learning Center for curriculum materials, and the Dillard-Elliott Room for rare books. (Courtesy of Presbyterian College Archives.)

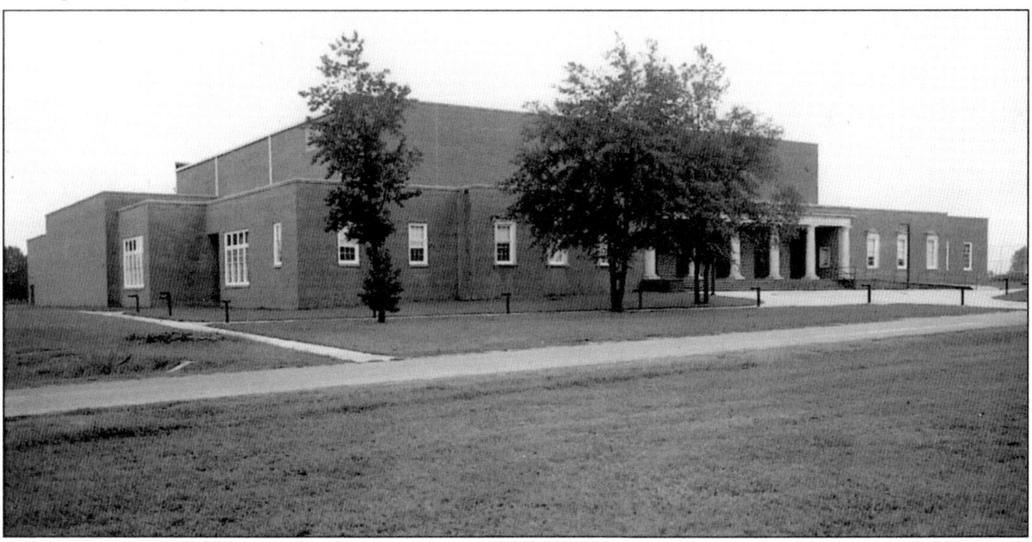

**TEMPLETON GYMNASIUM.** The new gymnasium, which replaced Springs, was dedicated in 1975 and named in honor of alumnus Ross E. Templeton, Class of 1924. In addition to a new basketball arena, the building provided expanded locker room, classroom, office, and exercise space. It was further enlarged by the construction of the Mabry-Smith-Yonce wing, and the later addition of locker rooms, offices, and a sports medicine facility. (Courtesy of Presbyterian College Archives.)

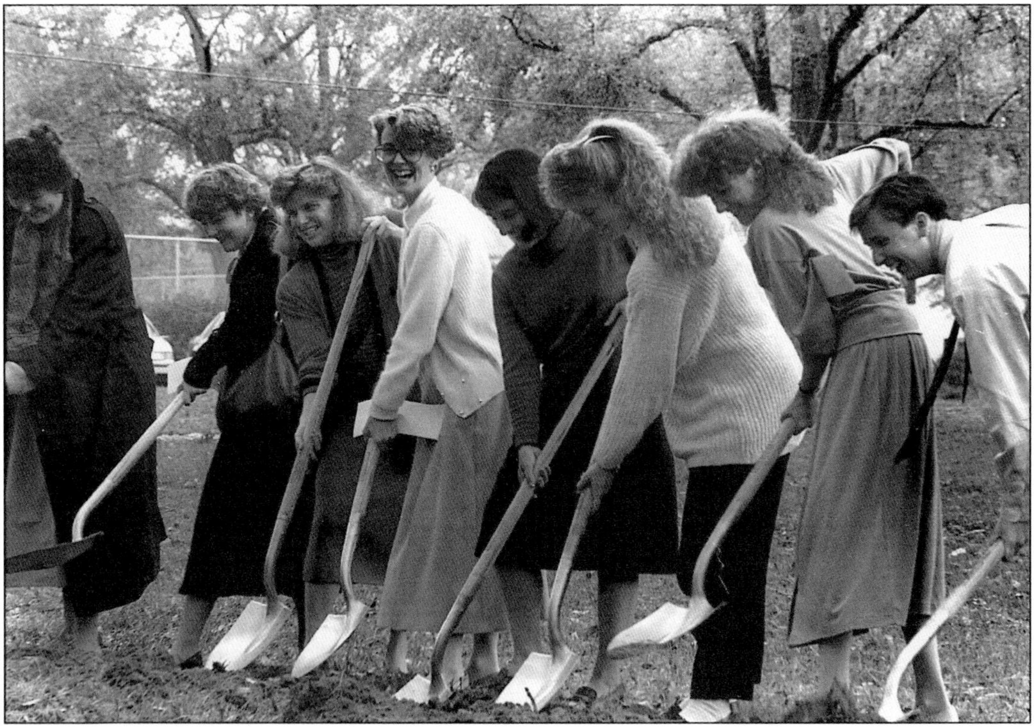

**Groundbreaking for Edmunds Hall.** This recital hall, named in honor of alumnus and trustee deSaussure Davis Edmunds, was dedicated in 1990. Designed to seat 340 people, it was intended to provide a smaller venue for lectures, musical events, and drama presentations. (Courtesy of Presbyterian College Archives.)

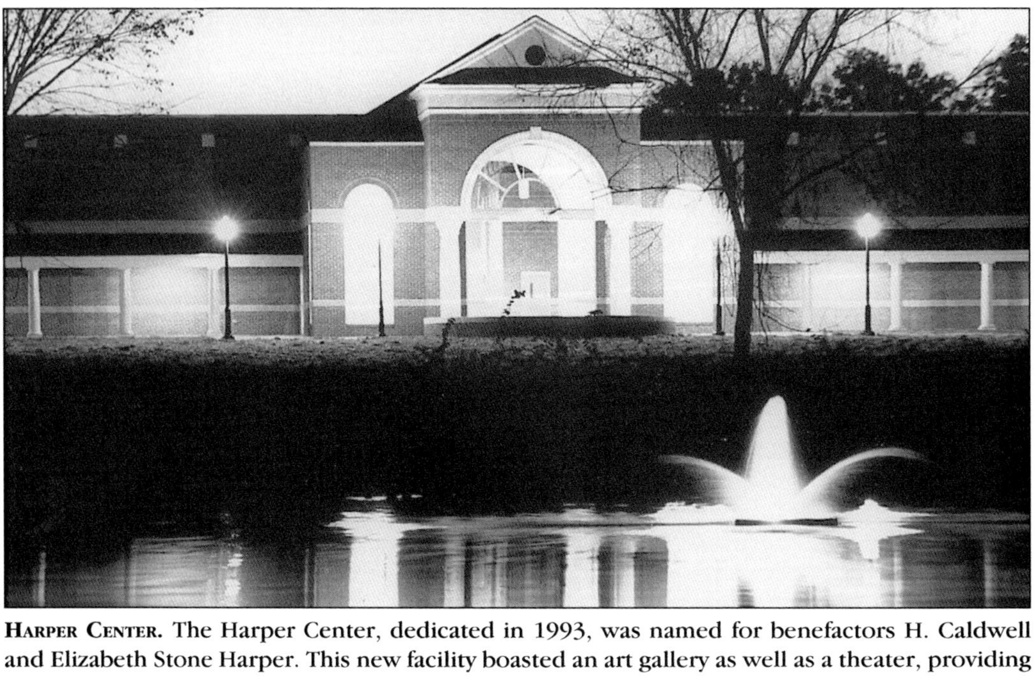

**Harper Center.** The Harper Center, dedicated in 1993, was named for benefactors H. Caldwell and Elizabeth Stone Harper. This new facility boasted an art gallery as well as a theater, providing a permanent home for dramatic presentations. (Courtesy of Presbyterian College Archives.)

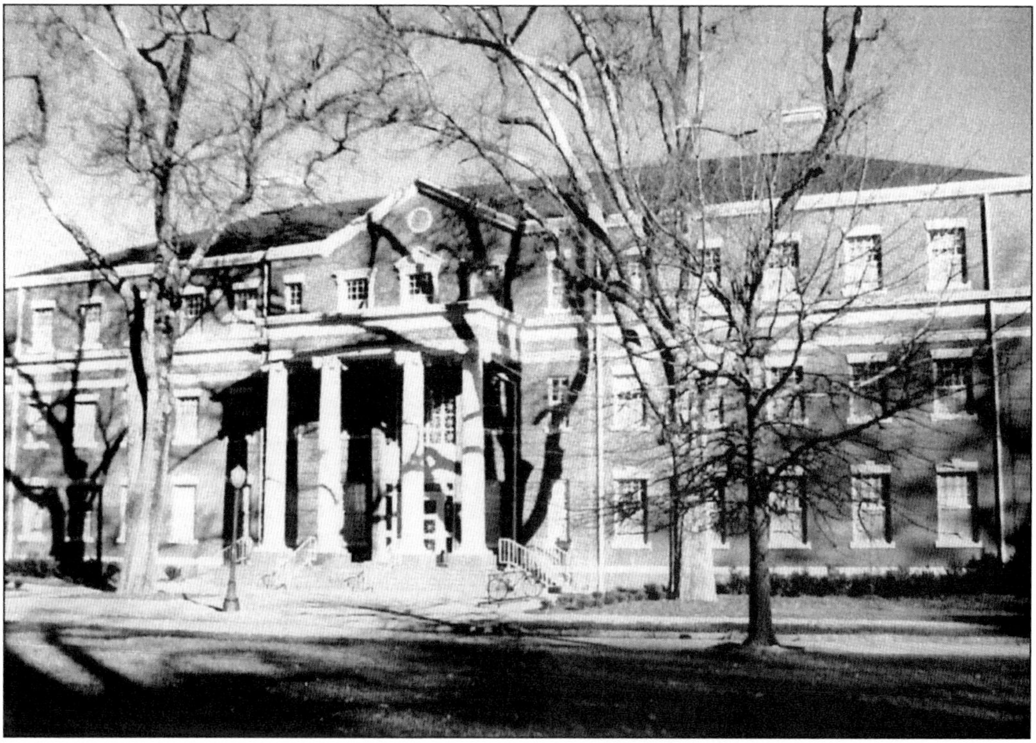

**HARRINGTON PEACHTREE ACADEMIC CENTER.** This building, constructed on the former site of Spencer Hall, was named after alumnus and trustee chairman Frank Harrington, longtime pastor of the Peachtree Presbyterian Church in Atlanta. (Courtesy of Presbyterian College Public Relations Office.)

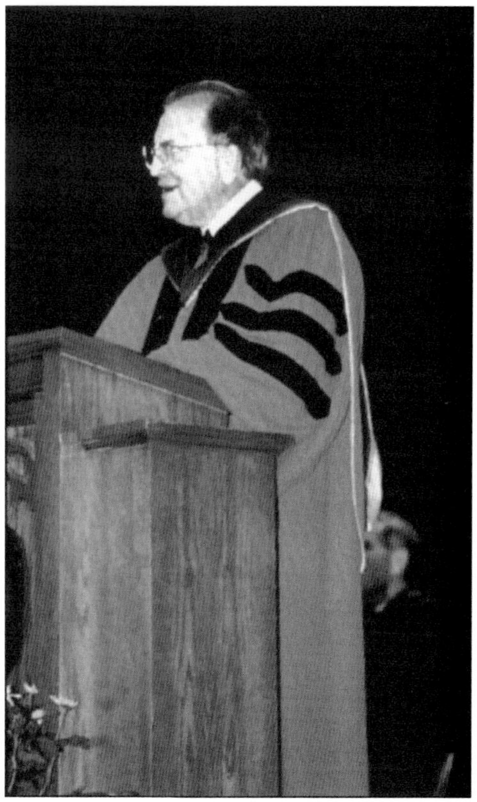

**FRANK HARRINGTON.** Dr. Harrington, who graduated from PC in 1957, served as chairman of the Board of Trustees for 17 years. (Courtesy of Presbyterian College Public Relations Office.)

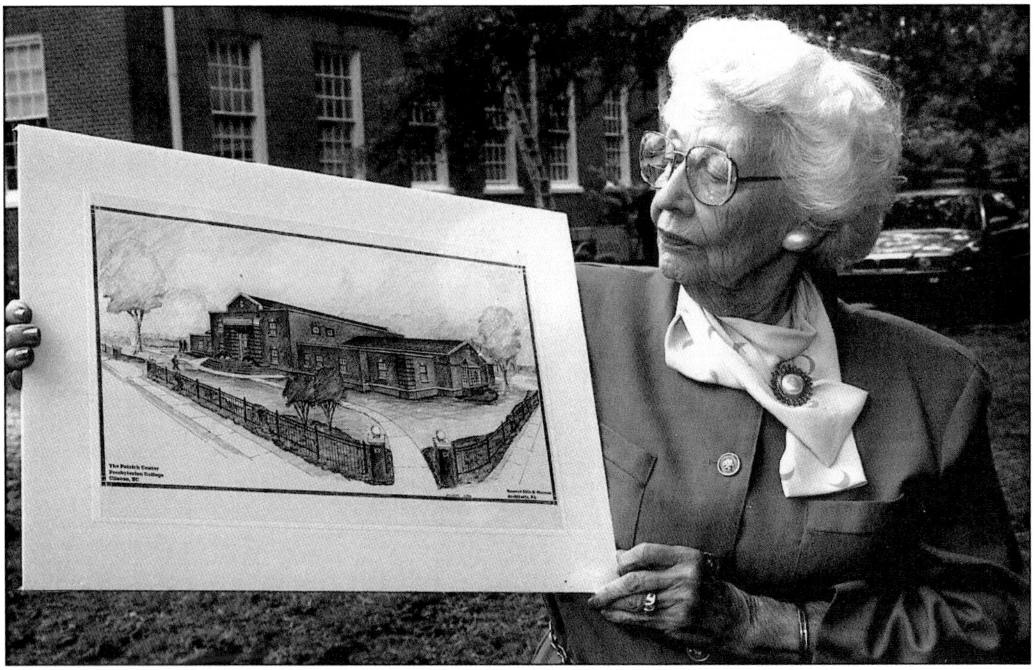

**Patrick Center.** Dedicated in the fall of 2000, this alumni and admissions center is named for alumnus Joe Patrick and his wife Gerry. Joe Patrick graduated from the college in 1937, and the Patrick Family Foundation provided much of the funding for the building. Here, Gerry Patrick displays the plans for the center. (Courtesy of Presbyterian College Public Relations Office.)

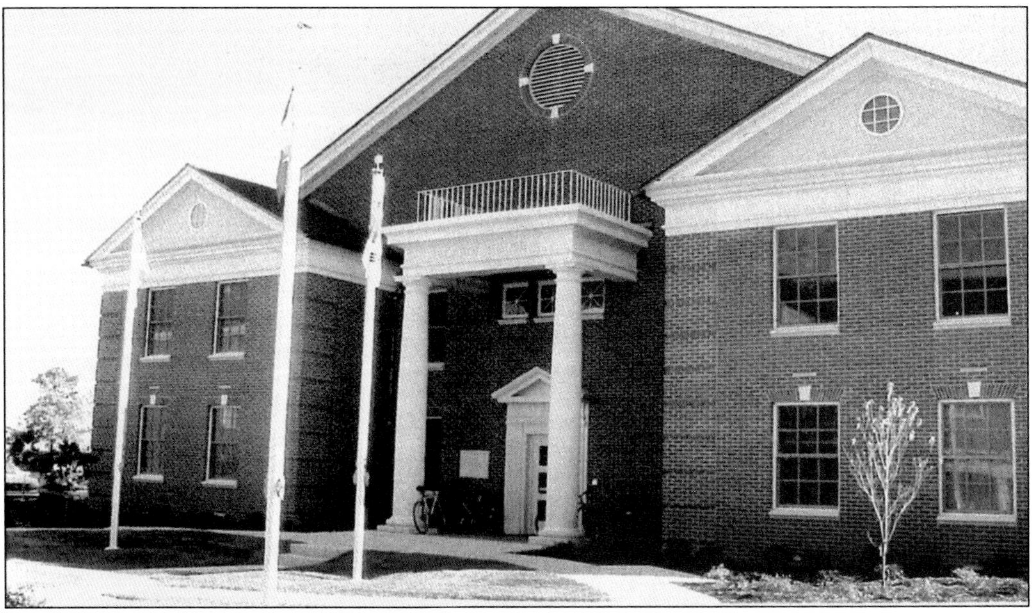

**Carol International House.** Dedicated in the fall of 2000, this living and learning center was named for Carol Grotnes Belk, wife of Irwin Belk. It is designed to house 33 students, and includes both international students and American students, many of whom have studied abroad. In addition to the traditional dormitory accommodations, it contains a classroom and a computer lab. (Courtesy of Presbyterian College Public Relations Office.)

# *Three*

# THE CLASSROOM

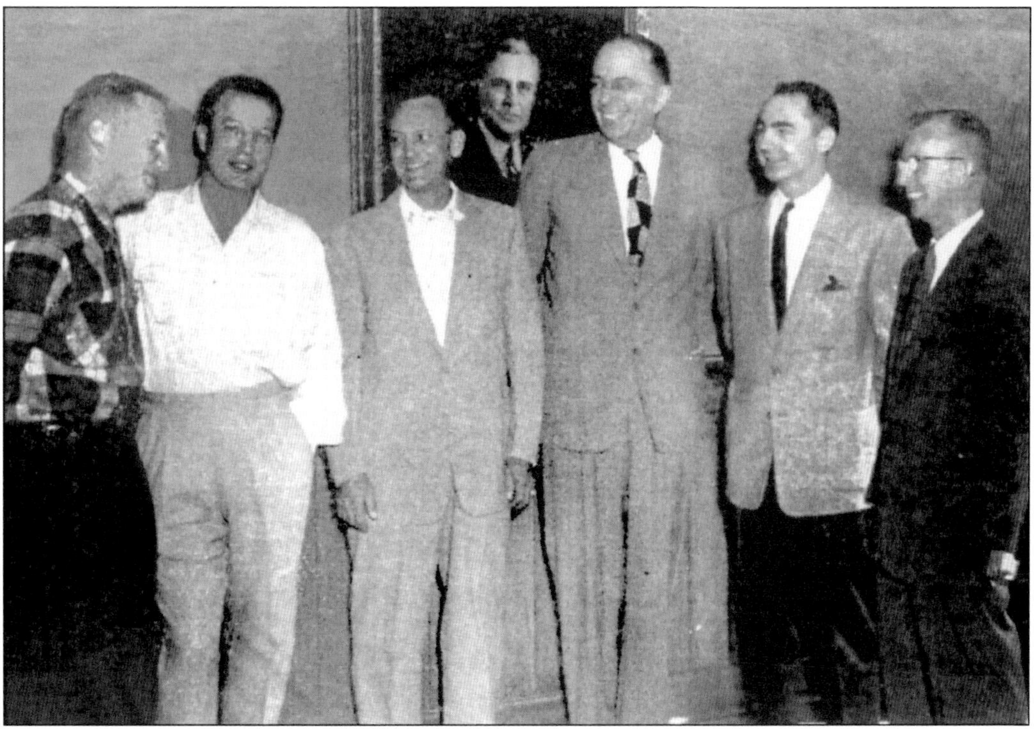

**NEW FACULTY, 1954.** New members of the faculty in 1954 included, from left to right, Edward Schembechler (assistant football coach); Norman MacLeod (English); Kenneth Porter (math); Clarence Thayer (vocational guidance and psychology); Lloyd Davis (English); and Aurel Erwin (French). (Courtesy of Presbyterian College Alumni News.)

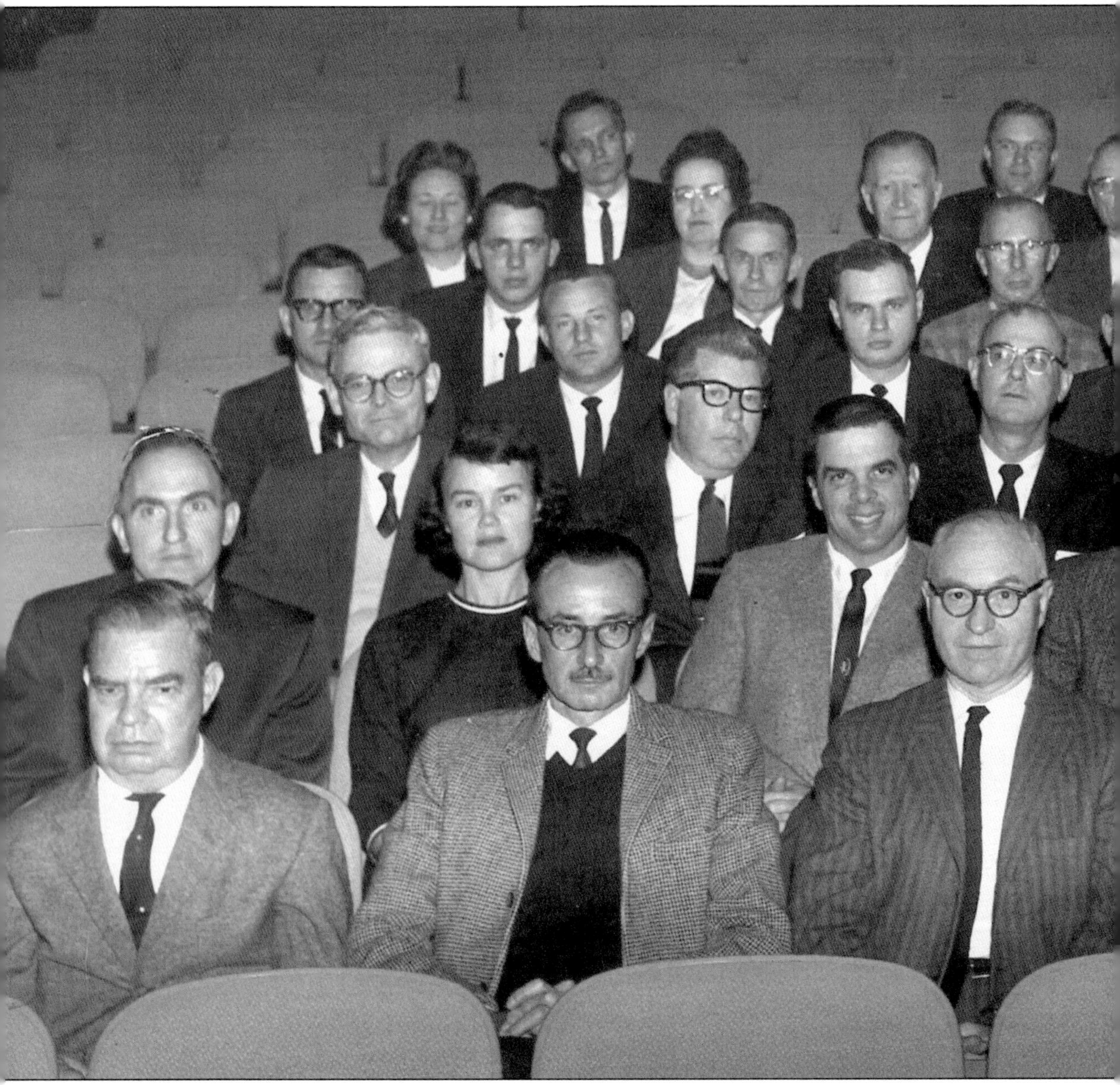

**FACULTY, 1964.** Among the faculty at this time, a large number went on to serve the college for many years. Pictured from left to right are (first row) Whitelaw, Glover, Dean Gettys, President Weersing, Hay, and Adams; (second row) N. Carter, E. Carter, Gault, Burnside, Anderson, and Freeman; (third row) Stump, Halsall, Baker, Patte, Harris, and Gunn; (fourth row) Cate, P.

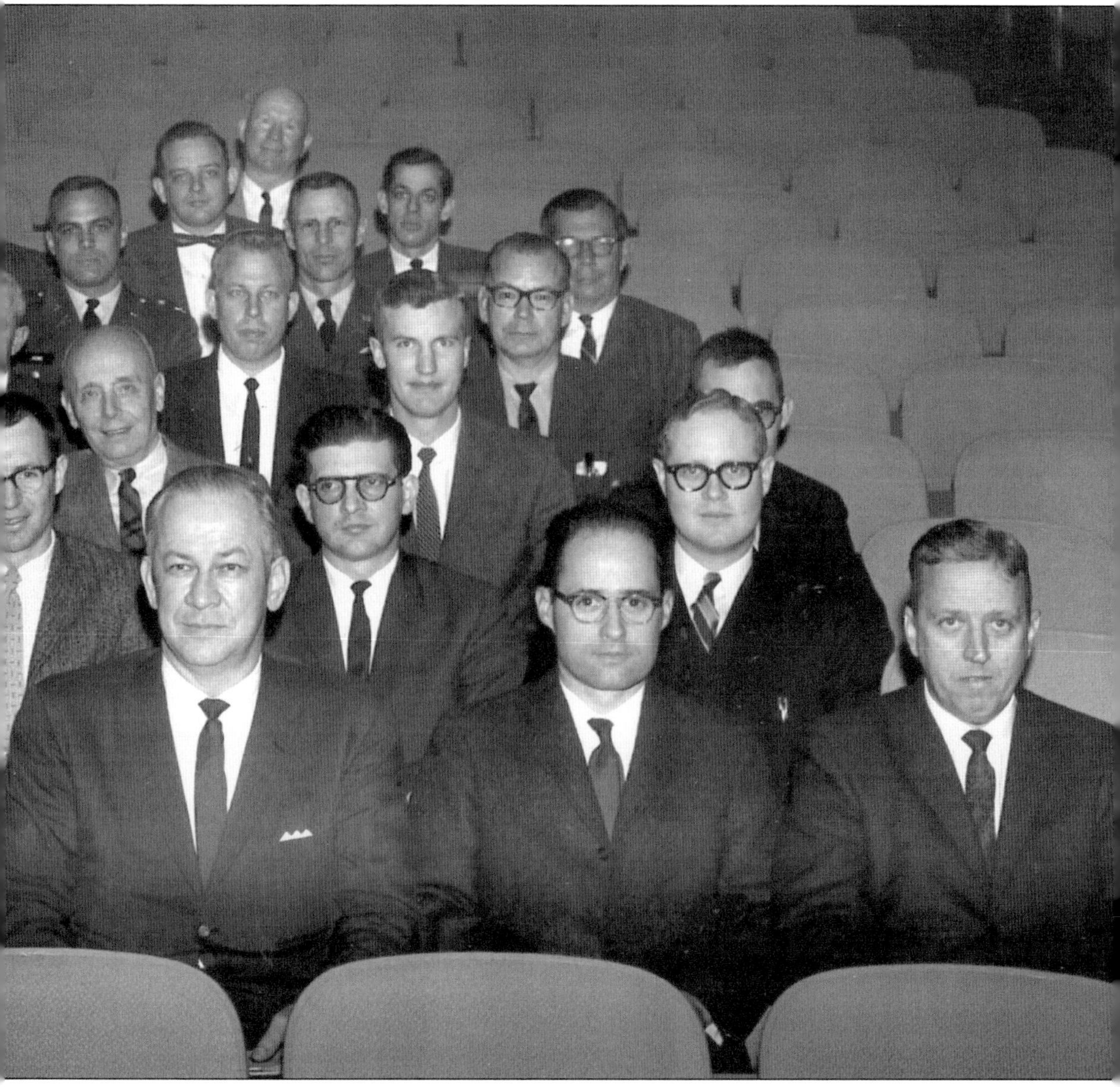

Campbell, Prater, King Moorefield, and Riggs; (fifth row) Connelly, Clark, Erwin, Howe, Ulrich, and T. Martin; (sixth row) R. Martin, Burts, Fraser, Cooler, Cannon, and Brown; (seventh row) Hammet, E. Campbell, and Thackston.

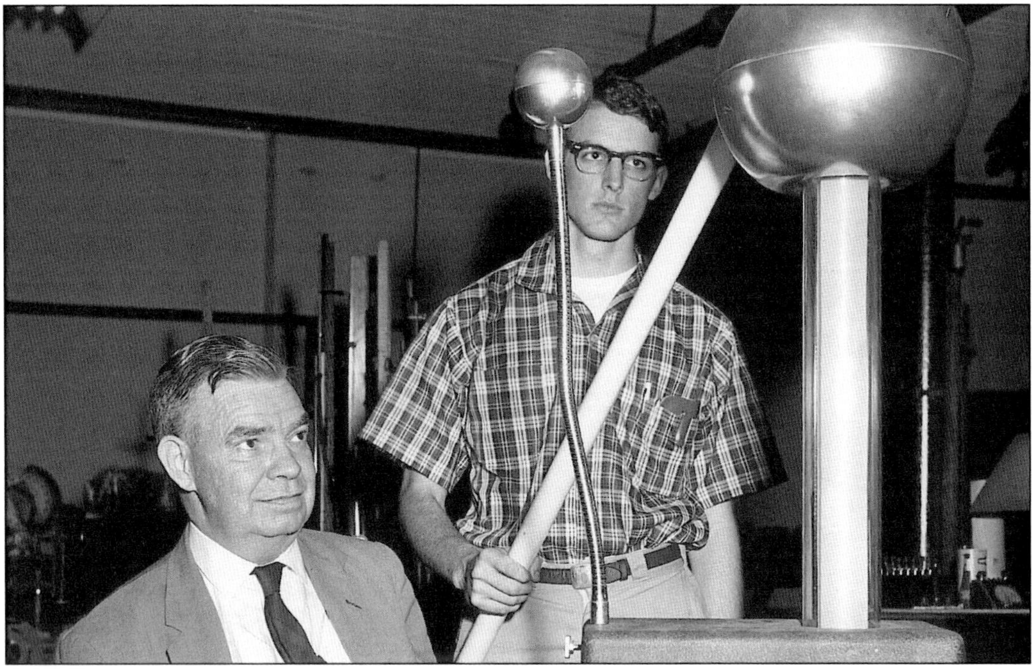

**Dr. Neill G. Whitelaw Supervises a Student, 1960.** Dr. Whitelaw taught physics at PC from 1935 to 1967. In the photo above he is seen supervising a student. (Courtesy of Presbyterian College Archives.)

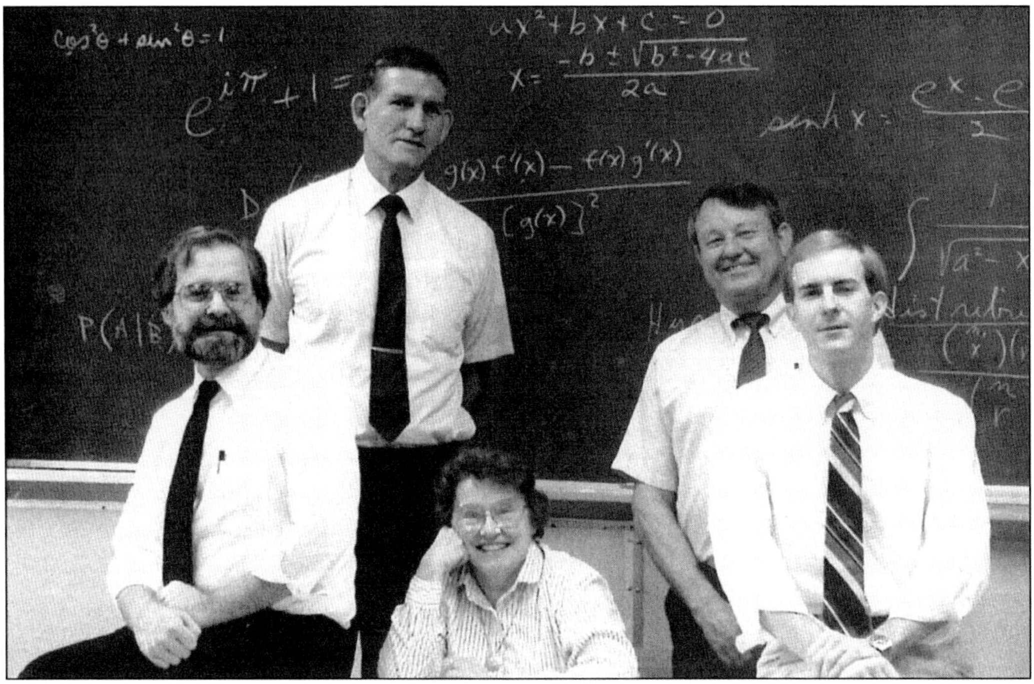


**Math Faculty.** PC's math faculty is pictured above. From left to right are Joel Jones, Eugene Womble, Lutrecia Hunter, Paul Campbell, and Brian Beasley. (Courtesy of Presbyterian College Archives.)

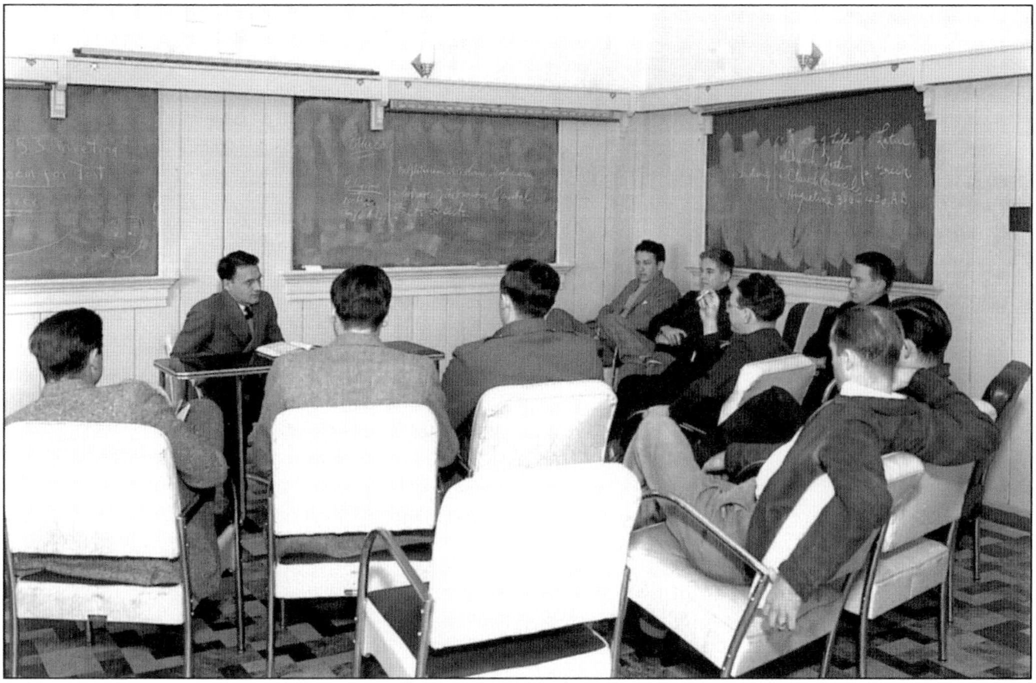

**CLASSROOM SCENE, 1938.** Dress codes and smoking policies have surely changed since this photo was taken in the late 1930s. Note the coats and ties on the students, and the cigarettes in some hands. (Courtesy of Presbyterian College Archives.)

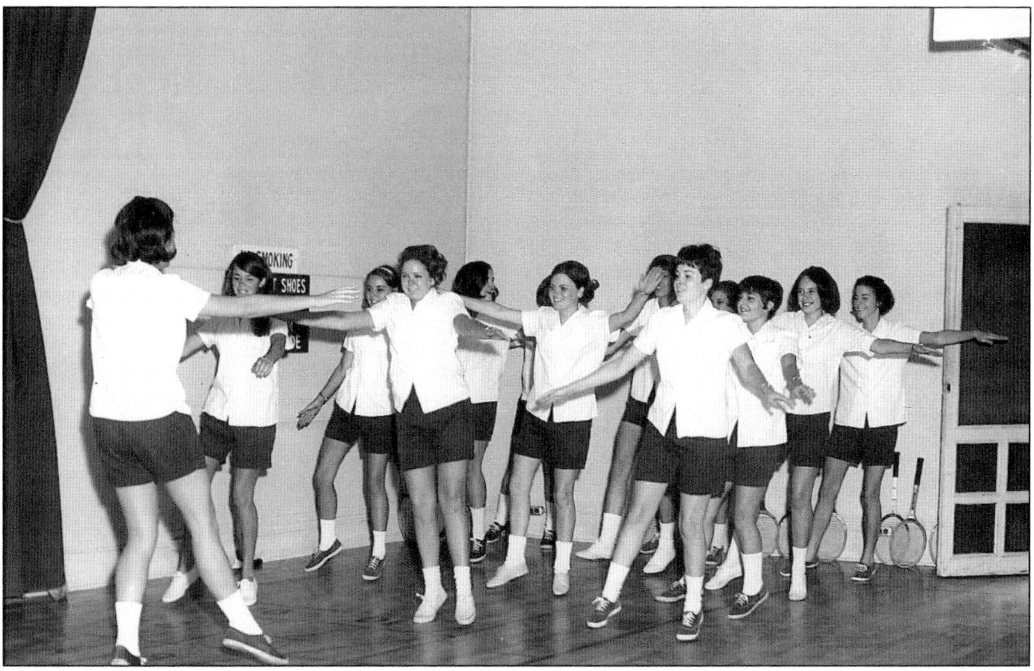

**WOMEN'S PHYSICAL EDUCATION CLASS IN JUDD HALL, *c.* 1965.** With the advent of full co-education, a one-year course in physical activities became a requirement for all women. (Courtesy of Presbyterian College Archives.)

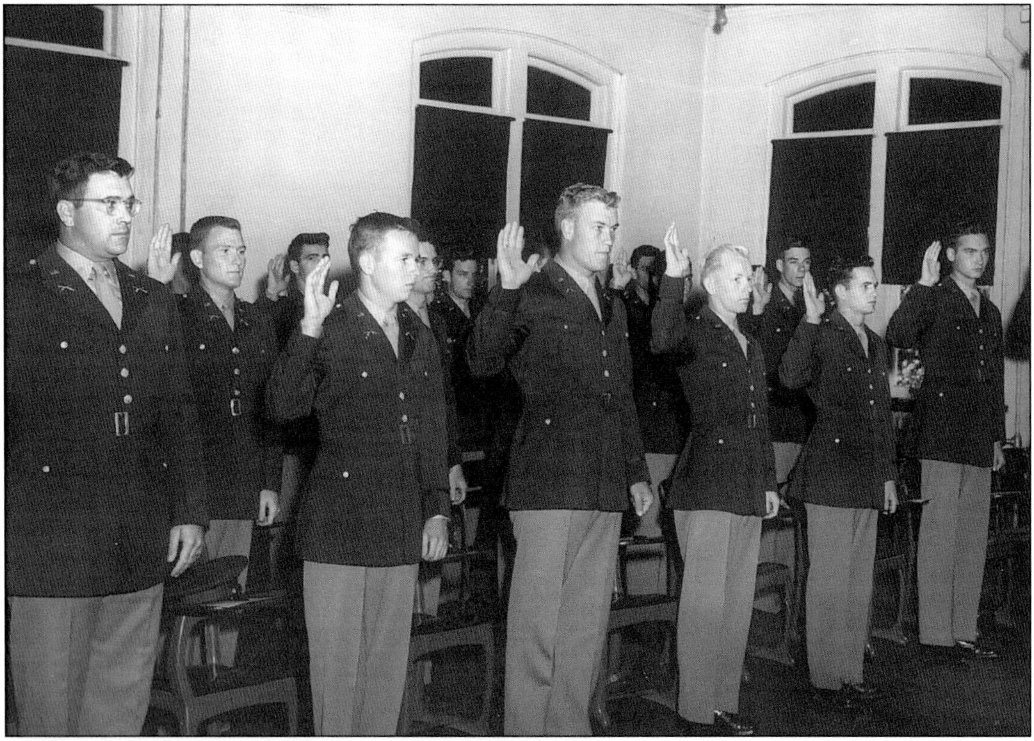

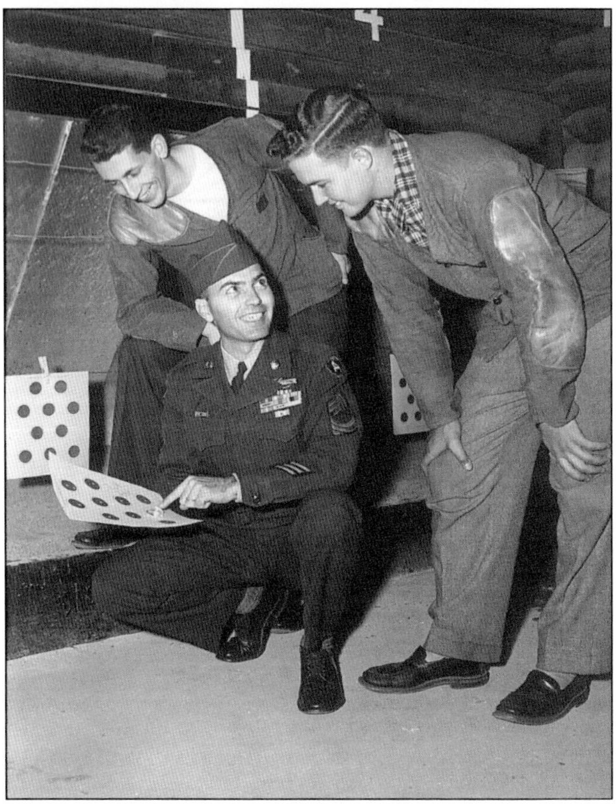

**ROTC Swearing-In, Commencement 1950.** ROTC has been a part of the college program since 1919, one of the first units to be organized in the country. Originally required of all male students, it later became a voluntary program. (Courtesy of Presbyterian College Archives.)

**Rifle Team Members, 1953–1954.** Here, Sgt. Wayne Wood, coach of the team, compares scores with Will Neville and Horace Walpole. (Courtesy of Presbyterian College Archives.)

**SUMMER CAMP, 1954.** Cadets William Tiller (left) and Dick Ropp engage in mortar training during summer training at Fort Bragg. (Courtesy of Presbyterian College Archives.)

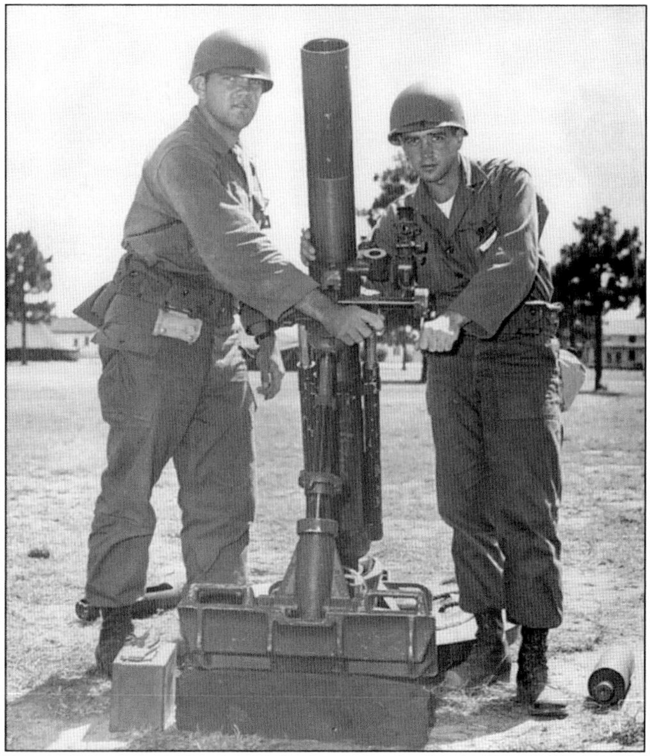

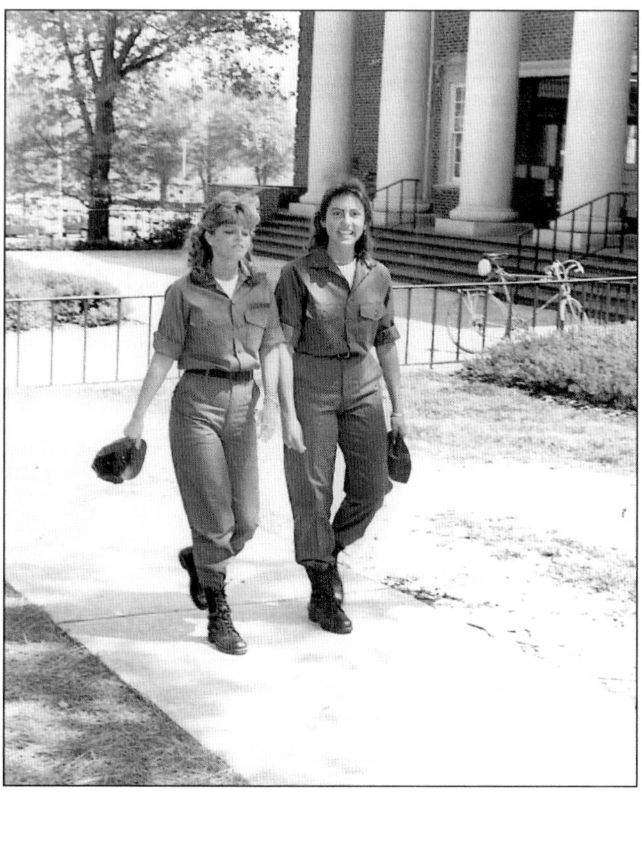

**CADETS ELANA GOURLEY AND SIMONE CLARK.** Limited enrollment of women in the College's ROTC program began in the fall of 1974. (Courtesy of Presbyterian College Archives.)

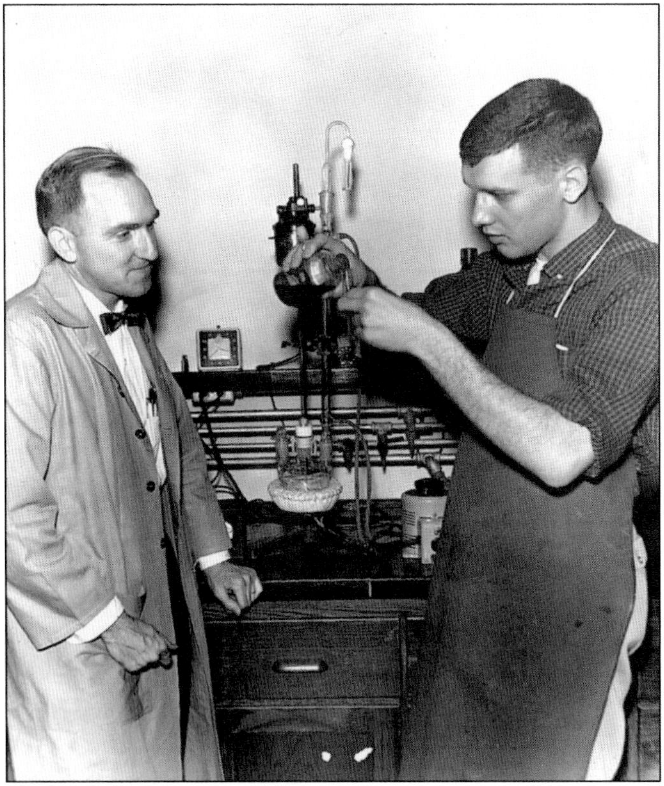

**Dr. K. Nolon Carter, 1961.** Dr. Carter began his work as a chemistry teacher at PC in 1951 and retired in 1987. Here he instructs Maurice Schwartz in chemistry lab. (Courtesy of Presbyterian College Archives.)

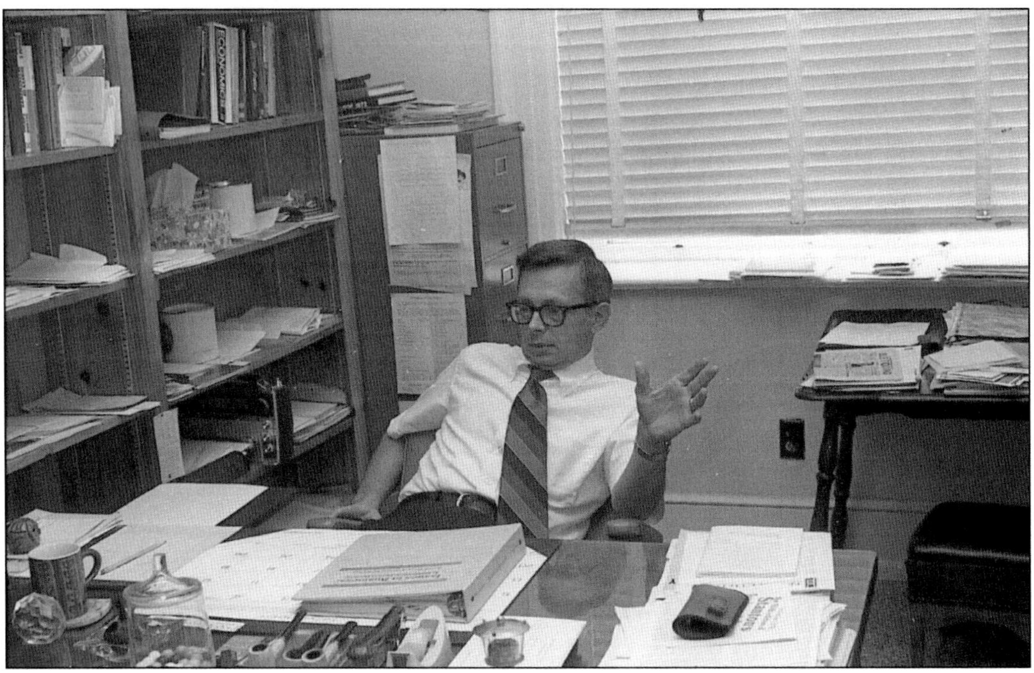

**Dr. Carl Arnold.** Dr. Arnold joined the economics faculty in 1969 and retired in 1991. He was known as a tough but caring teacher whose door was always open to students. (Courtesy of Presbyterian College Archives.)

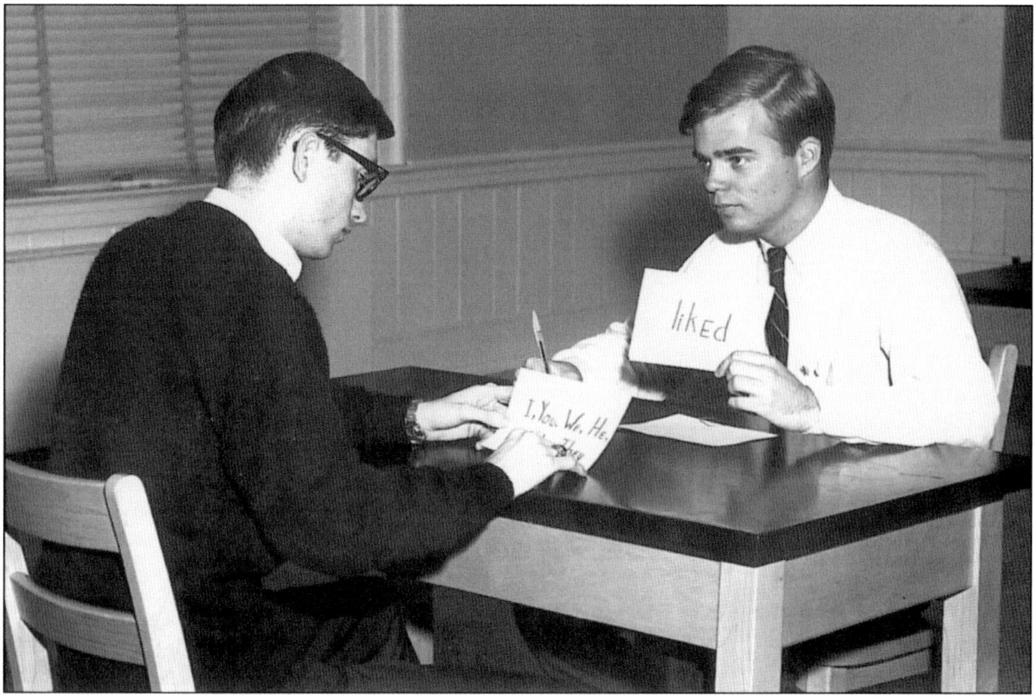


**Psychology Lab.** Students Skip Taylor and Carter Jones experiment with verbal reinforcement and conditioning in 1967. (Courtesy of Presbyterian College Archives.)

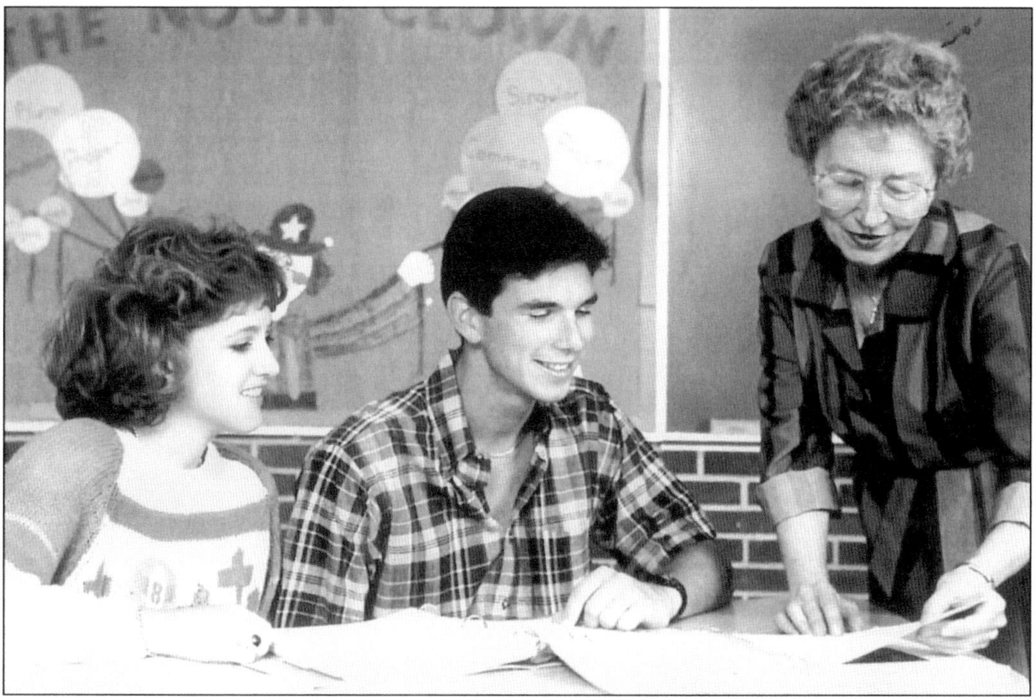

**Dr. Dottie Brandt Advises Students, 1992.** Dr. Brandt joined the education faculty in 1967 and retired in 1998. She established the teacher training program in elementary education. (Courtesy of Presbyterian College Public Relations Office.)

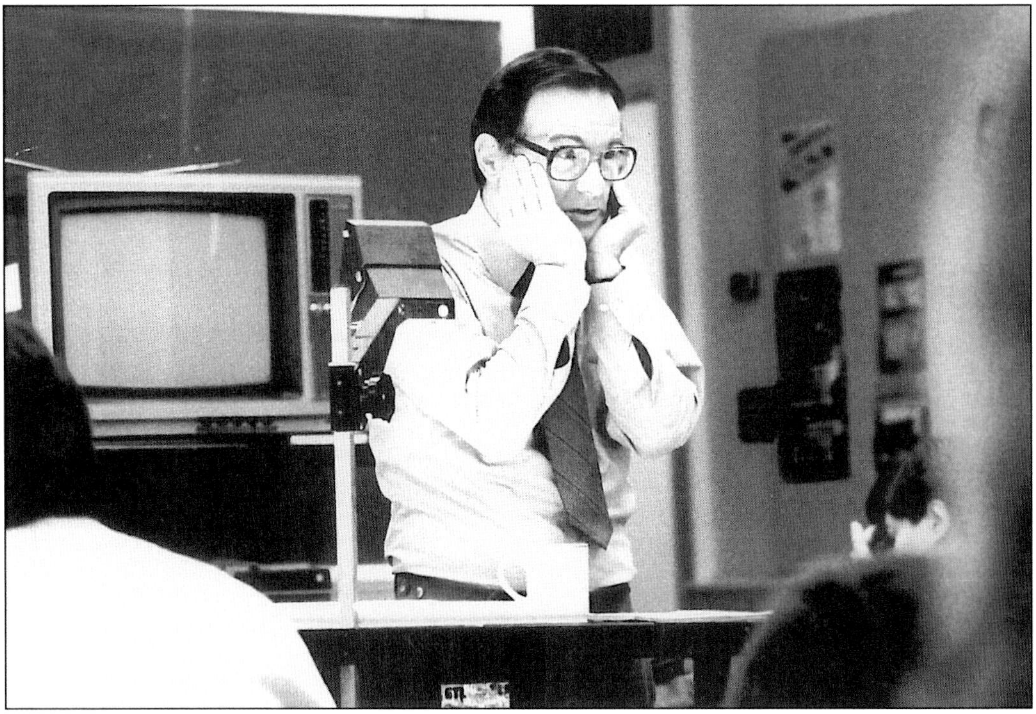

**Dr. Jim Skinner Strikes a Characteristic Pose.** Dr. Skinner has been emoting for his English classes since 1965. (Courtesy of Presbyterian College Public Relations Office.)

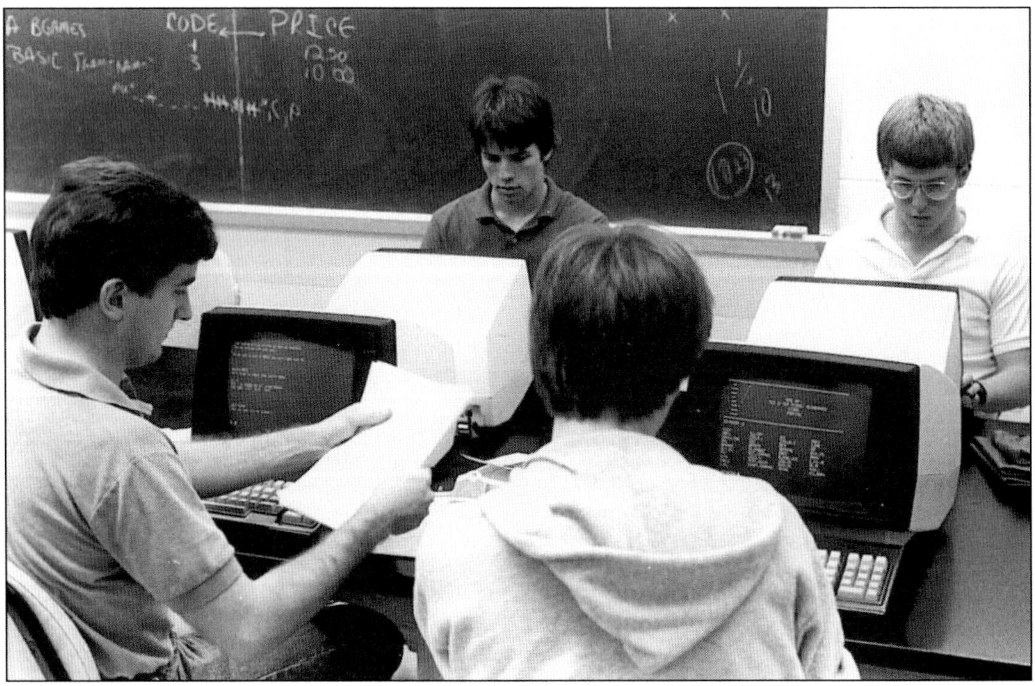


**Computer Lab, 1985.** Administrative computers to deal with registration and scheduling were in use at the college by 1969. Soon after, they became available for library research and classes in computer science. (Courtesy of Presbyterian College Archives.)

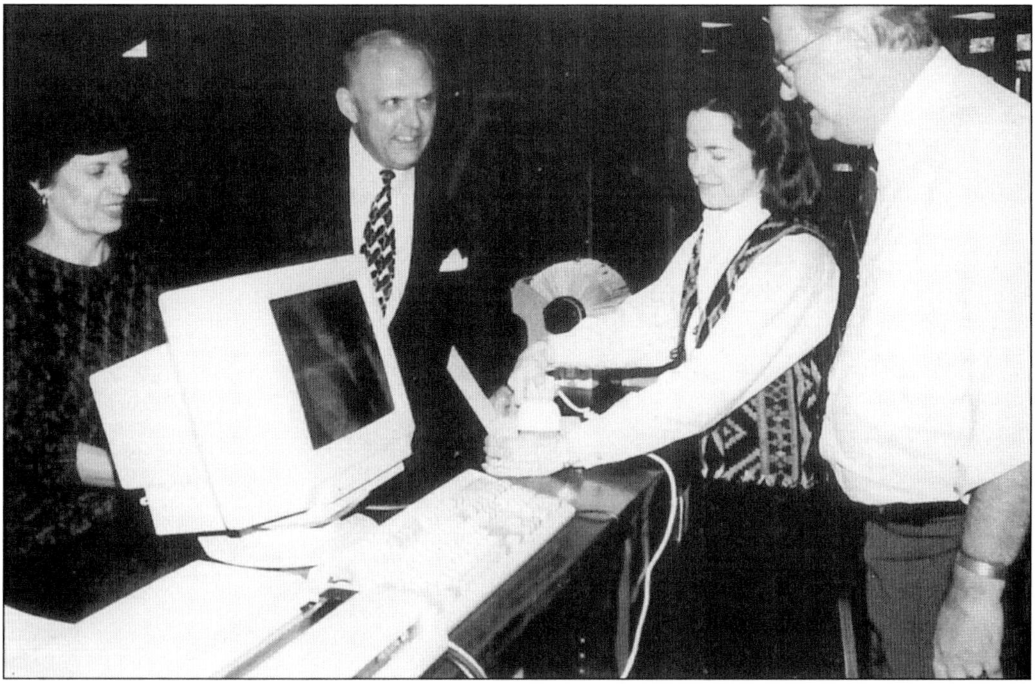

**Library Technology.** Librarians Diane Yarborough, Teresa Inman, and Lennart Pearson demonstrate new library technology to Pres. Kenneth B. Orr. (Courtesy of Presbyterian College Public Relations Office.)

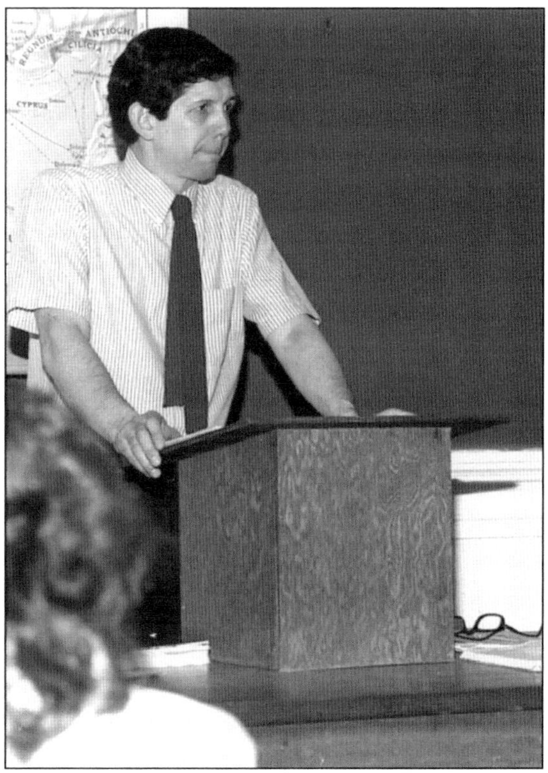

**Dr. George Ramsey.** Dr. Ramsey joined the religion department in 1968, specializing in the Bible and world religions. (Courtesy of Presbyterian College Archives.)

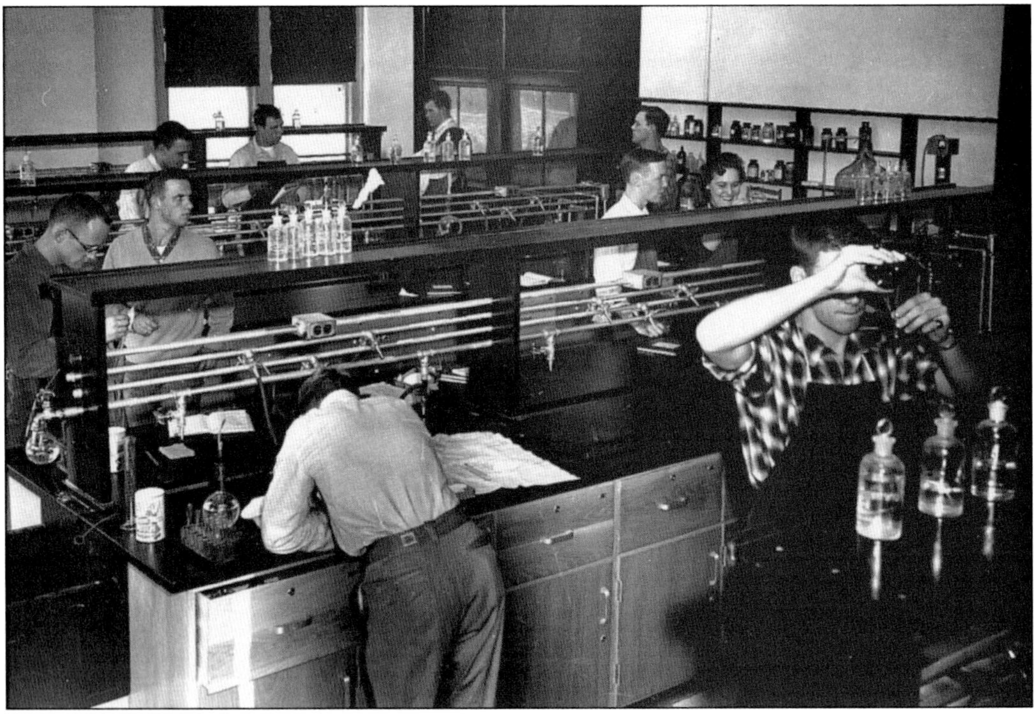

**SCIENCE LAB IN JACOBS HALL, 1955–1956.** Before the construction of Richardson Hall in 1965, science laboratories were located in Jacobs Hall. (Courtesy of Presbyterian College Archives.)

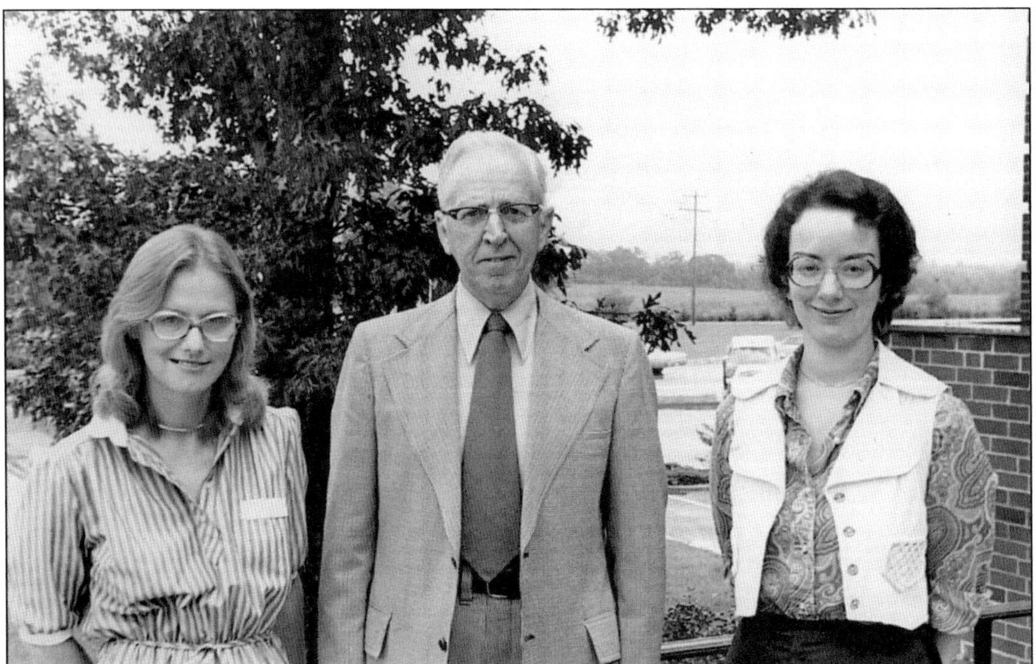

**LANGUAGE FACULTY.** Pictured above from left to right are Yvonne King (French, 1967–1985); Richard Adams (Spanish, 1950–1981); and Connie Colwell (German and French, 1977–present). (Courtesy of Presbyterian College Archives.)

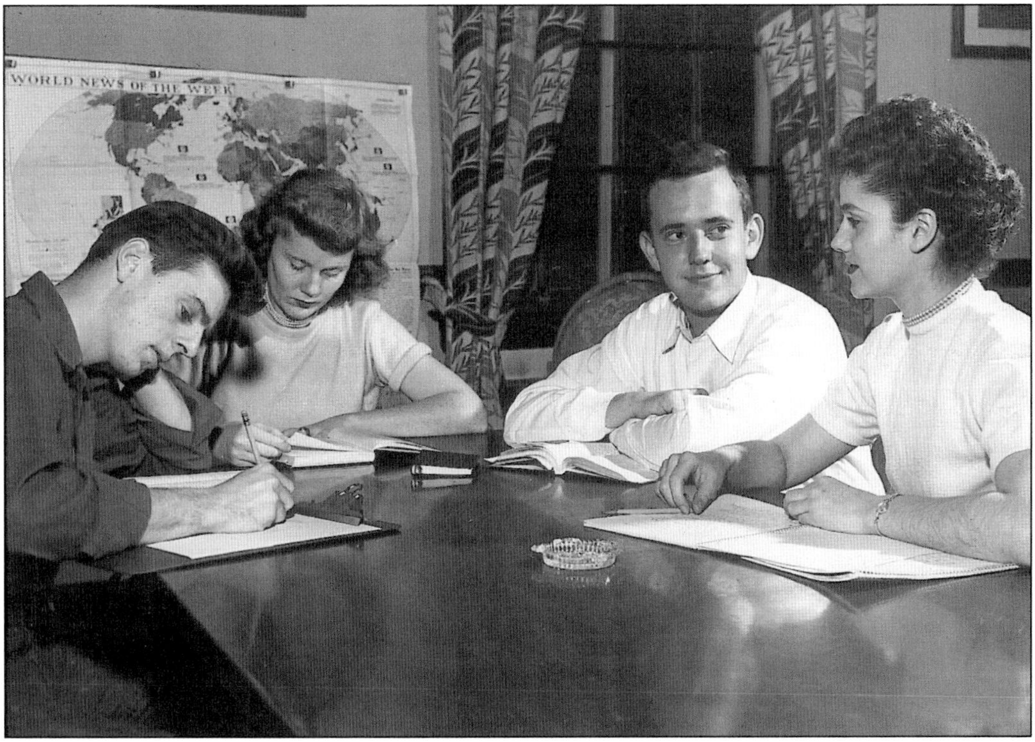


**HARD AT WORK.** Pictured in this 1953 photograph are Billy Sprouse, Barbara Allen, Roy Williams, and Gene Lanier as they study in the library. (Courtesy of Presbyterian College Archives.)

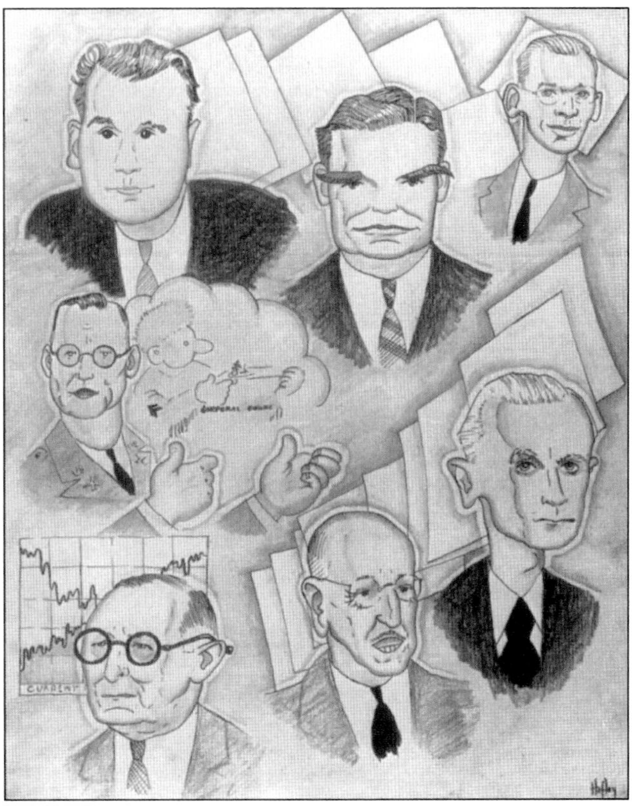

**FACULTY CARICATURES, 1939.** Among those pictured in this entertaining drawing are Neill Whitelaw, J. Boyd Kennedy, and F. Dudley Jones. (Courtesy of 1939 *PaC SaC*.)

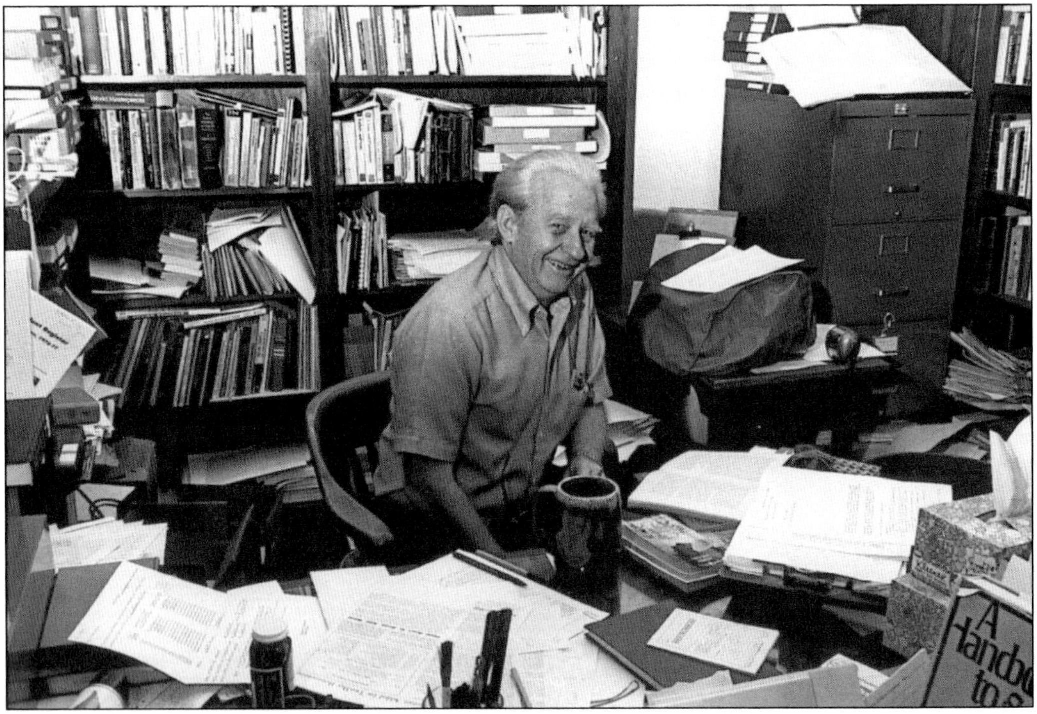

**Prof. S. Allen King.** Professor King joined the English faculty in 1959, and retired in 1985. He was an expert on grammar and modern literature. (Courtesy of Presbyterian College Archives.)

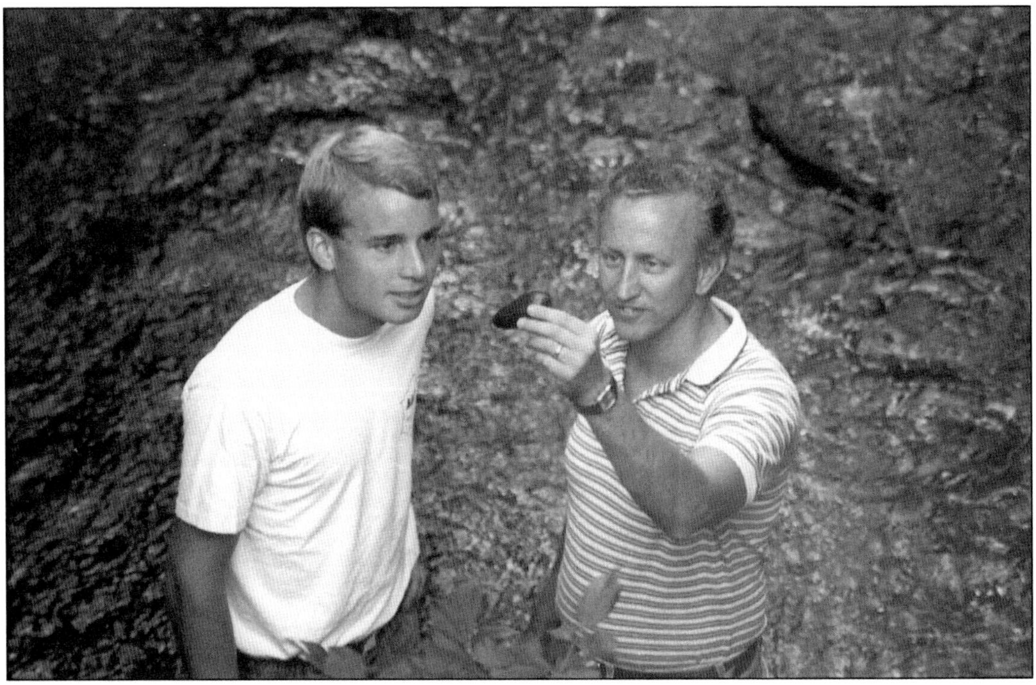

**Field Work.** Dr. Robert Hudson and student assistant Courtney Shelbourne examine juvenile mussels during the summer of 1990. Hudson's research focuses on artificial cultivation of freshwater mussels. (Courtesy of Presbyterian College Archives.)

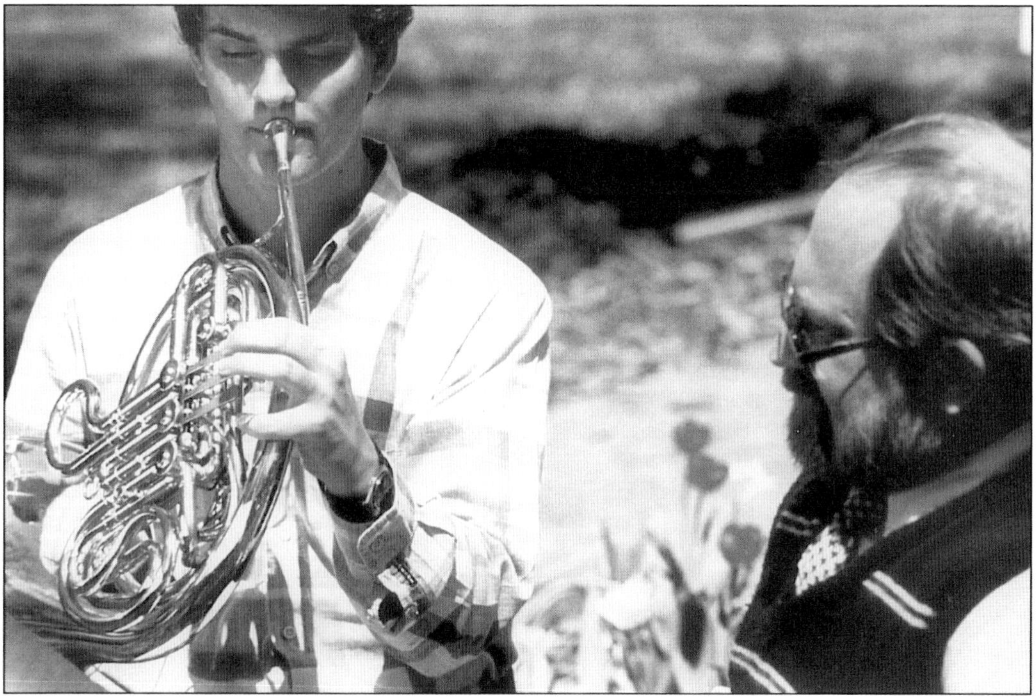

**Instruction in Music, *c.* 1990.** A fine arts department was added in 1965 to increase course offerings in art, music, and drama. Here, Orval Oleson, who joined the faculty in 1983, instructs a student. (Courtesy of Presbyterian College Archives.)

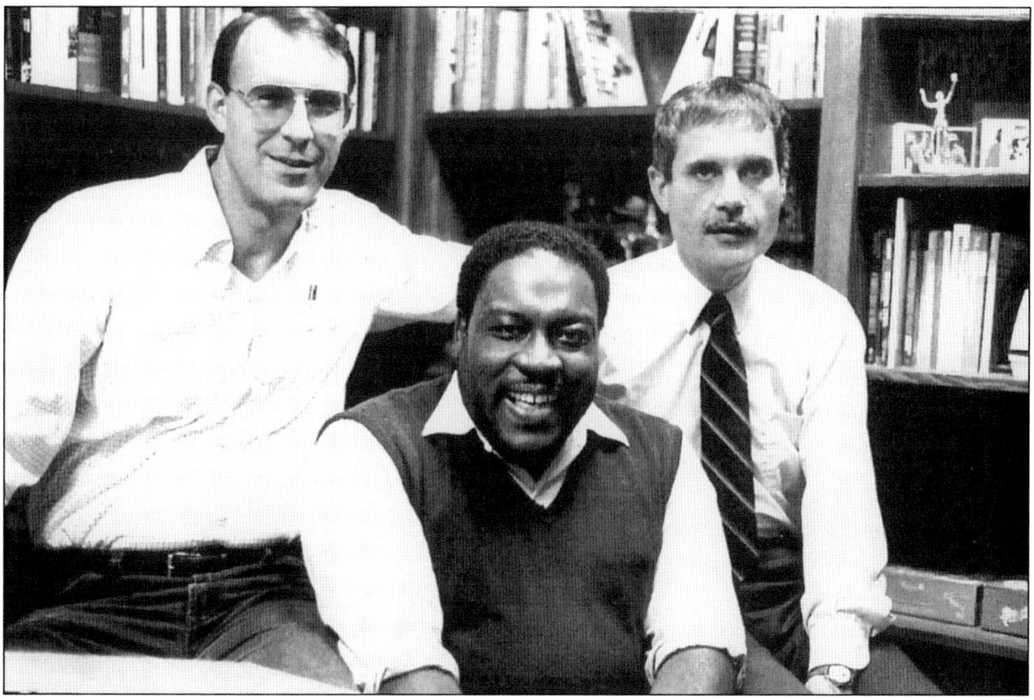

**Members of Political Science Faculty, 1990.** From left to right are Thomas Weaver, Booker Ingram, and David Gillespie. (Courtesy of Presbyterian College Public Relations Office.)

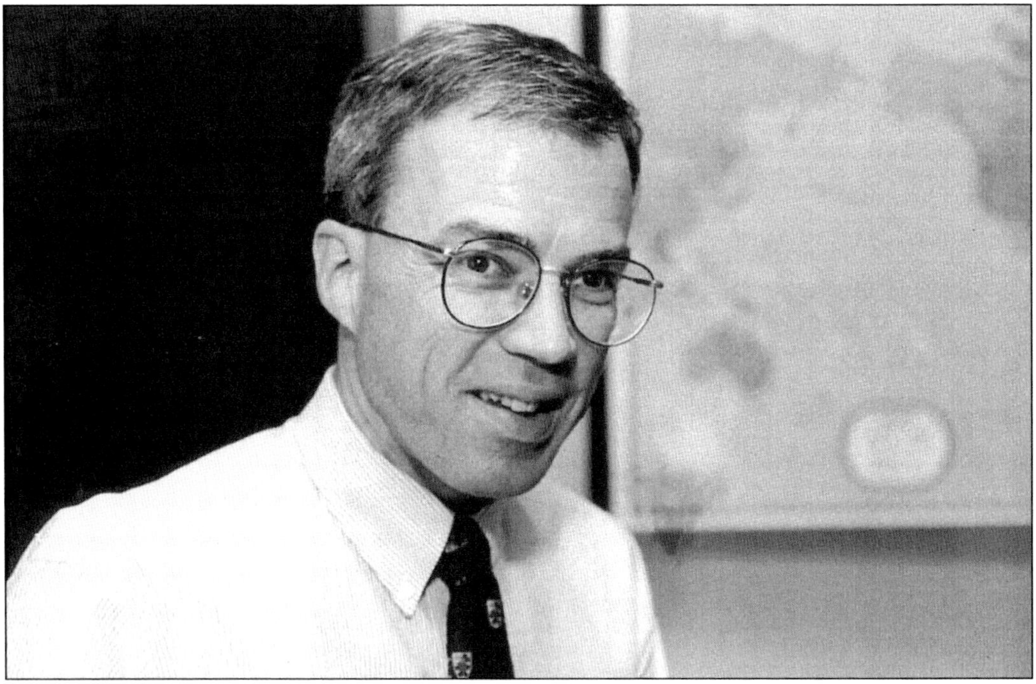

**Dr. Peter Hobbie.** Dr. Hobbie joined the religion faculty in 1990. His classes have instilled a love of learning in many students. (Courtesy of Presbyterian College Public Relations Office.)

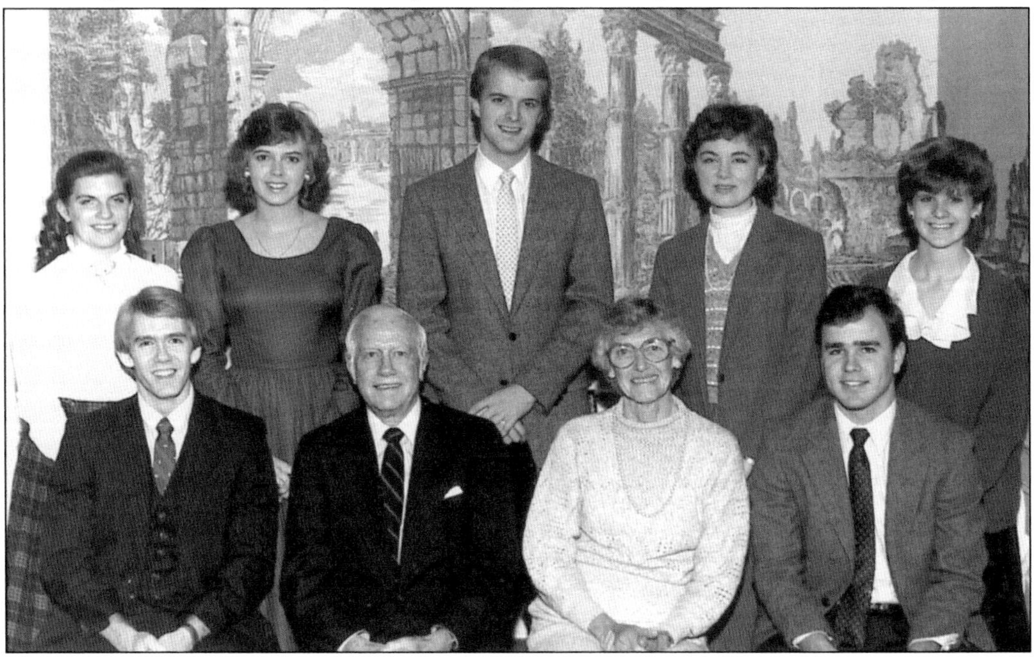

**Quattlebaum Scholars, 1986.** Mr. and Mrs. Alexander Quattlebaum established this program of full honor scholarships in 1980. Shown seated with the program's founders are scholarship recipients Jeff Gee (left) and Brett Armstrong (right). Standing from left to right are Sara Robertson, Kim Whidden, Jonathan Hicklin, Ansley Belcher, and Cathy Roach. (Courtesy of Presbyterian College Archives.)

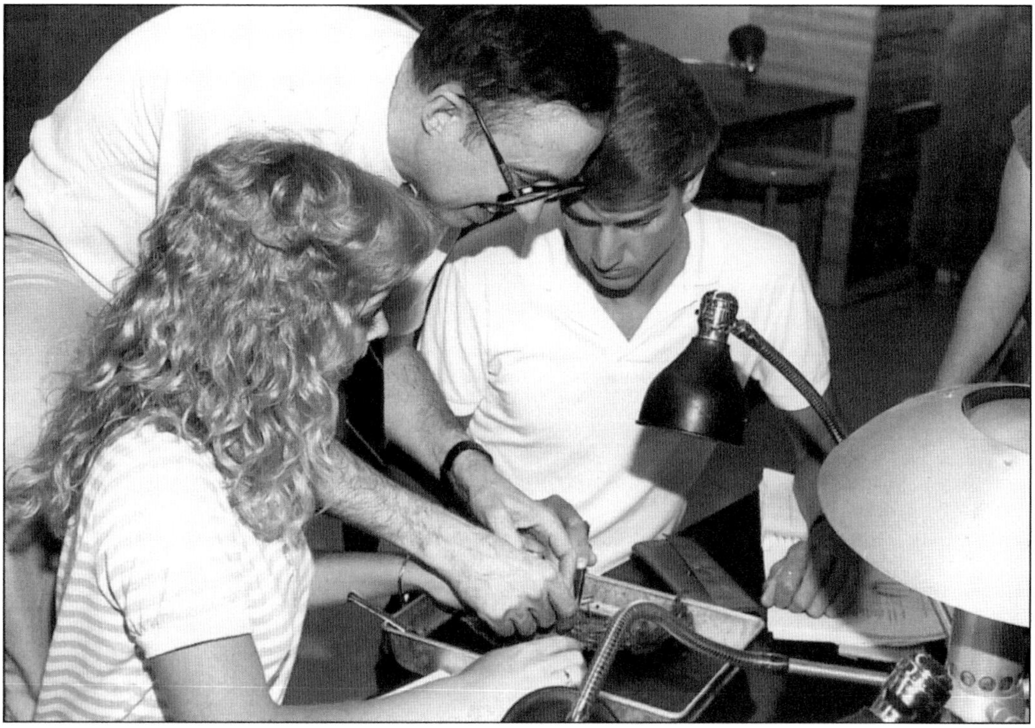

**Biology Lab.** Dr. Fred James, who joined the faculty in 1971, supervises students in biology lab in 1986. (Courtesy of Presbyterian College Archives.)

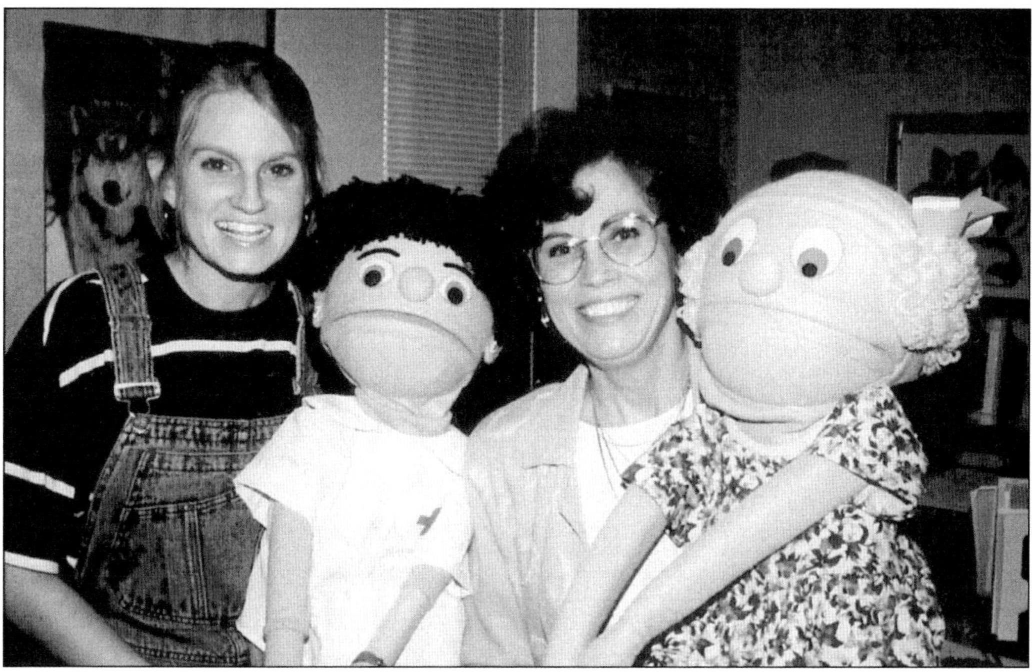

**Education Professor Sheryl Bair and Friends.** Dr. Bair began teaching special education at PC in 1994. She is pictured here with a student and two of her "Kids on the Block" puppets. (Courtesy of Presbyterian College Public Relations Office.)

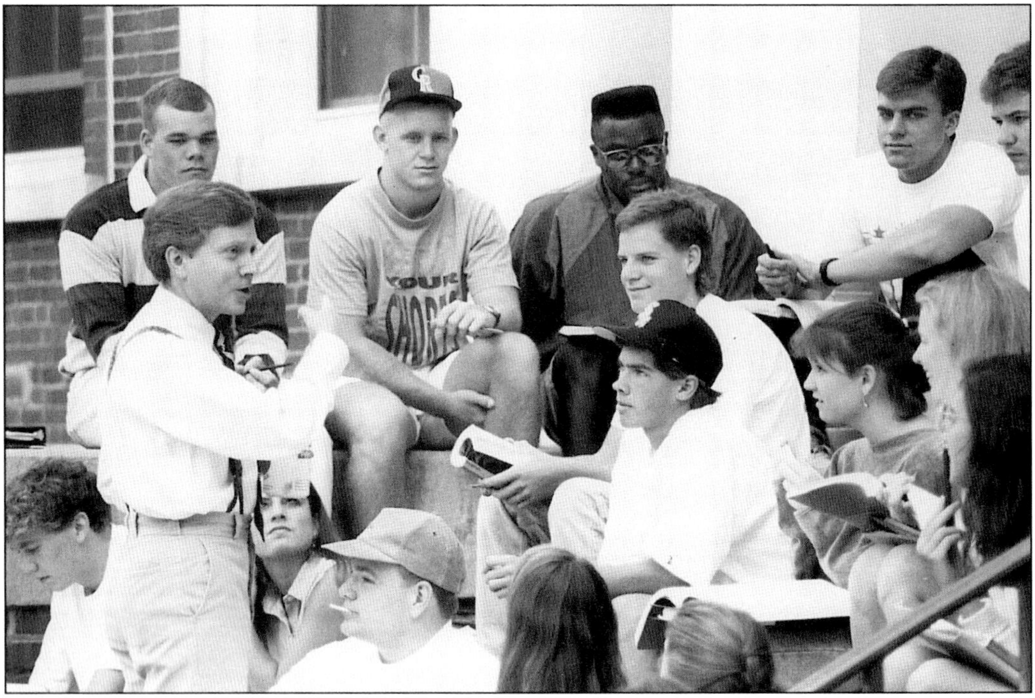

**English Class, 1992.** Dr. Dean Thompson is a familiar sight as he teaches class on the steps of Neville Hall. (Courtesy of Presbyterian College Archives.)

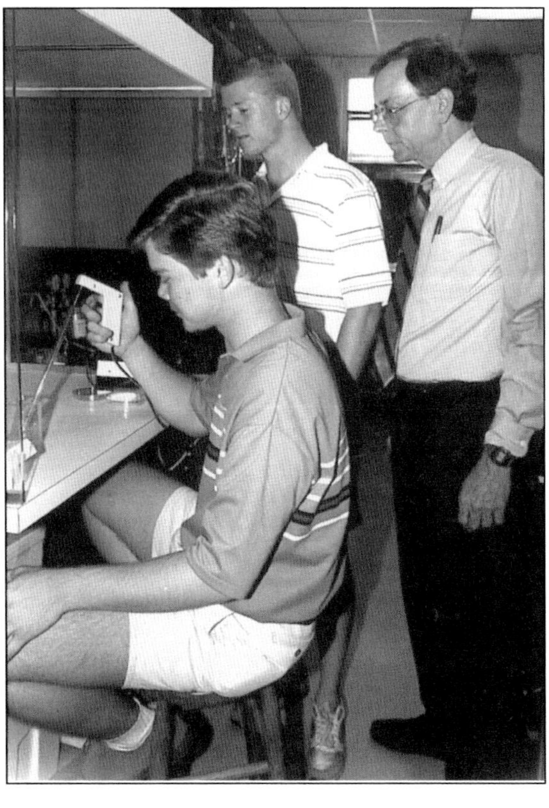

**Summer Fieldwork in Maine.** Dr. James Stidham supervises Andy McCraw (seated) and David Nelson in marine biomedical research at Mt. Desert Island in 1992. (Courtesy of Presbyterian College Archives.)

# *Four*

# ORGANIZATIONS

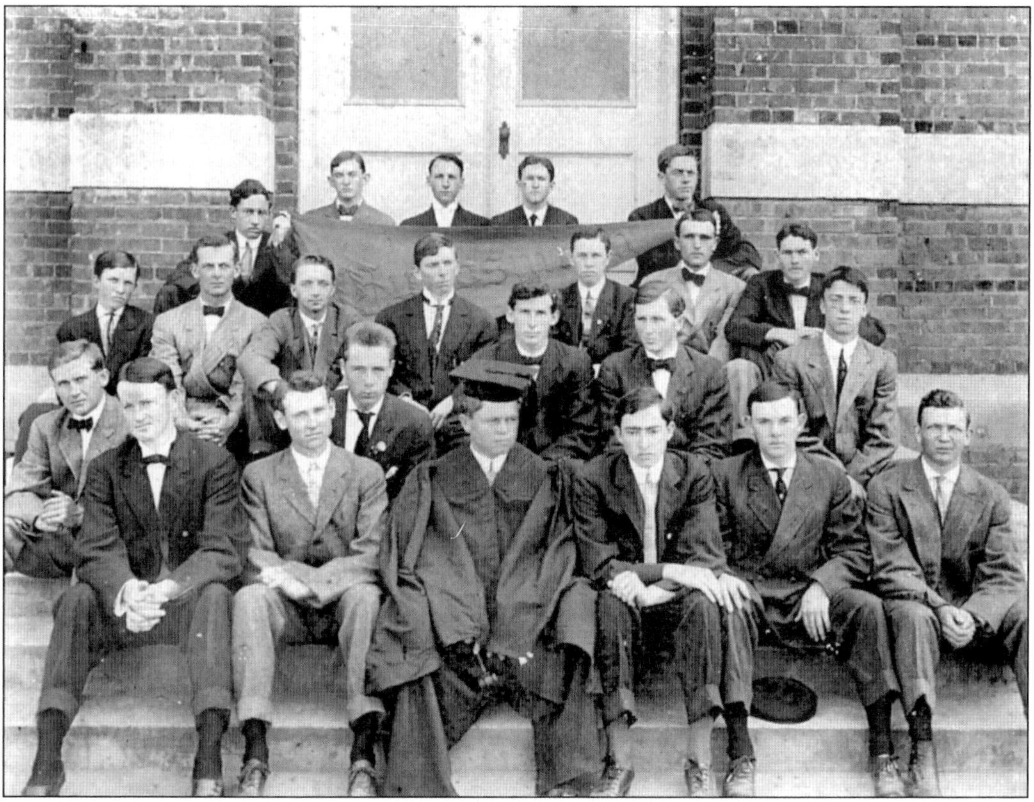

**EUKOSMIAN LITERARY SOCIETY, 1912.** Although all the members have not been identified, it is known that Ellis Fuller is in the front row in cap and gown, and Frank Coleman Young is third from the left in the third row. (Courtesy of Presbyterian College Archives.)

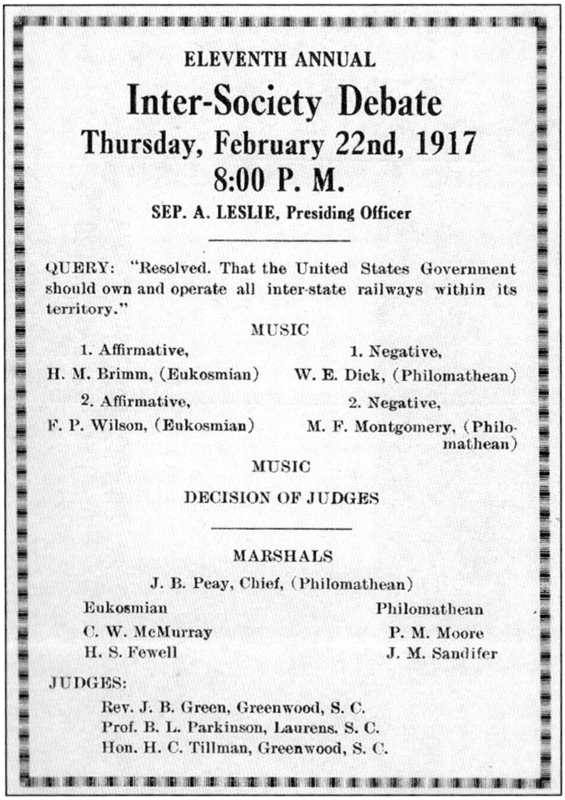

ELEVENTH ANNUAL

**Inter-Society Debate**

**Thursday, February 22nd, 1917**

**8:00 P. M.**

SEP. A. LESLIE, Presiding Officer

QUERY: "Resolved. That the United States Government should own and operate all inter-state railways within its territory."

MUSIC

| 1. Affirmative, | 1. Negative, |
|---|---|
| H. M. Brimm, (Eukosmian) | W. E. Dick, (Philomathean) |
| 2. Affirmative, | 2. Negative, |
| F. P. Wilson, (Eukosmian) | M. F. Montgomery, (Philomathean) |

MUSIC

DECISION OF JUDGES

MARSHALS

J. B. Peay, Chief, (Philomathean)

| Eukosmian | Philomathean |
|---|---|
| C. W. McMurray | P. M. Moore |
| H. S. Fewell | J. M. Sandifer |

JUDGES:

Rev. J. B. Green, Greenwood, S. C.
Prof. B. L. Parkinson, Laurens. S. C.
Hon. H. C. Tillman, Greenwood, S. C.

**INTER–SOCIETY DEBATE PROGRAM.** Literary societies were organized early in the college's history, with Eukosmian being founded in 1883 and Philomathian in 1894. They held frequent debates, as well as oratorical and debating contests at commencement. (Courtesy of Presbyterian College Archives.)

**PI KAPPA ALPHA AROUND 1891.** Pi Kappa Alpha, organized in 1890, was among the first social fraternities to be established at the college. Due to concerns about hazing, fraternities were banned from the campus in 1909. They were reinstated, however, in 1921, and the chapter was re-established. (Courtesy of Presbyterian College Archives.)

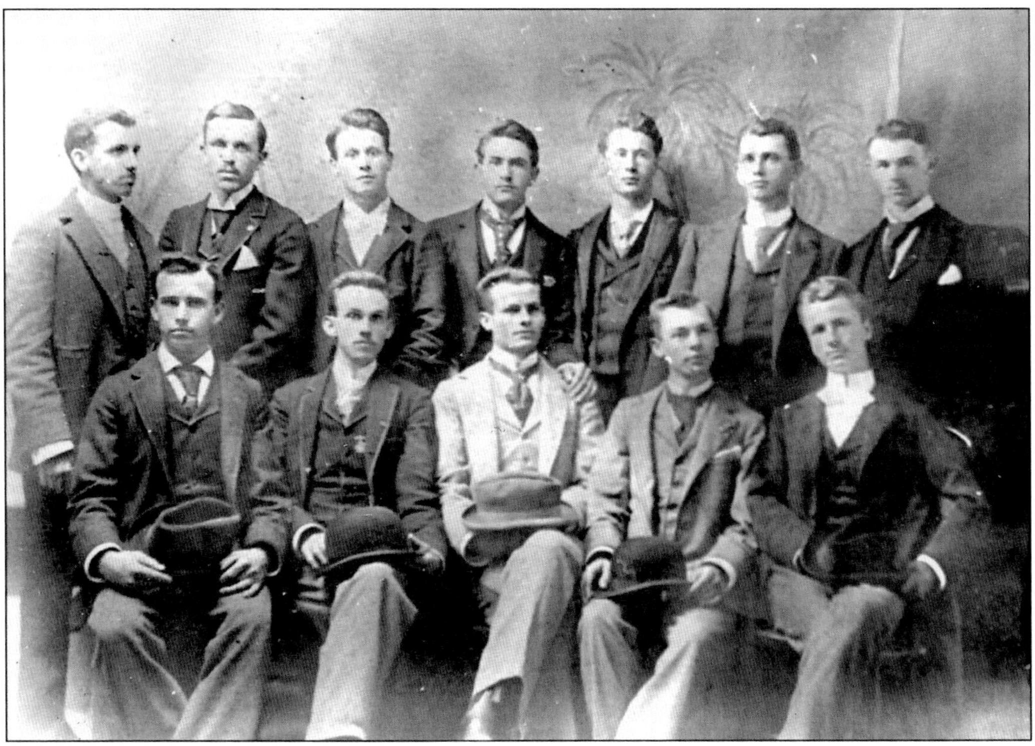

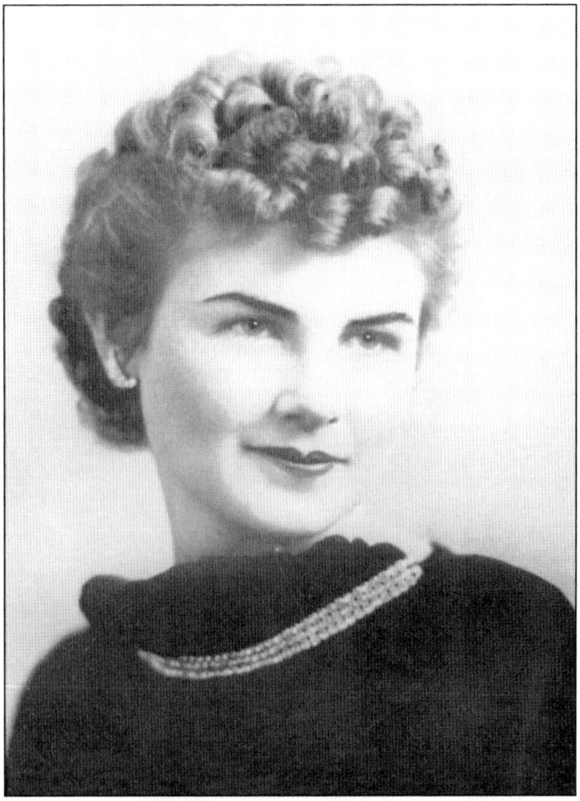

"**Sponsors.**" Prior to full co-education, most organizations on the campus had female "sponsors." Pictured here is Bebe Dillard, 1936 *PaC SaC* Advertising Sponsor. (Courtesy of 1936 *PaC SaC*.)

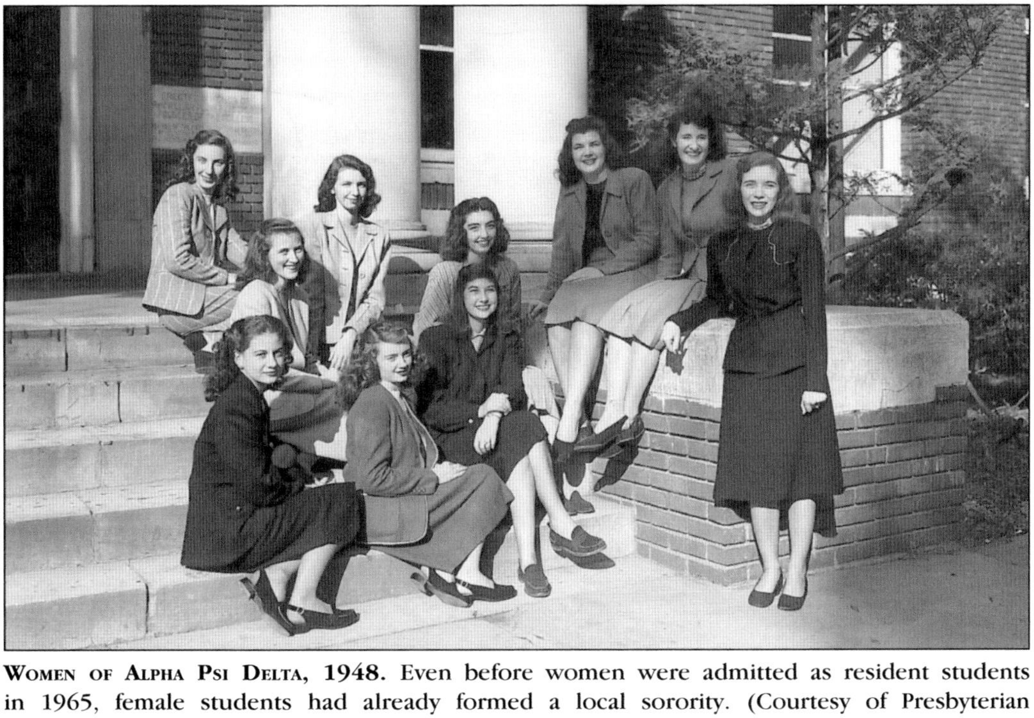

**Women of Alpha Psi Delta, 1948.** Even before women were admitted as resident students in 1965, female students had already formed a local sorority. (Courtesy of Presbyterian College Archives.)

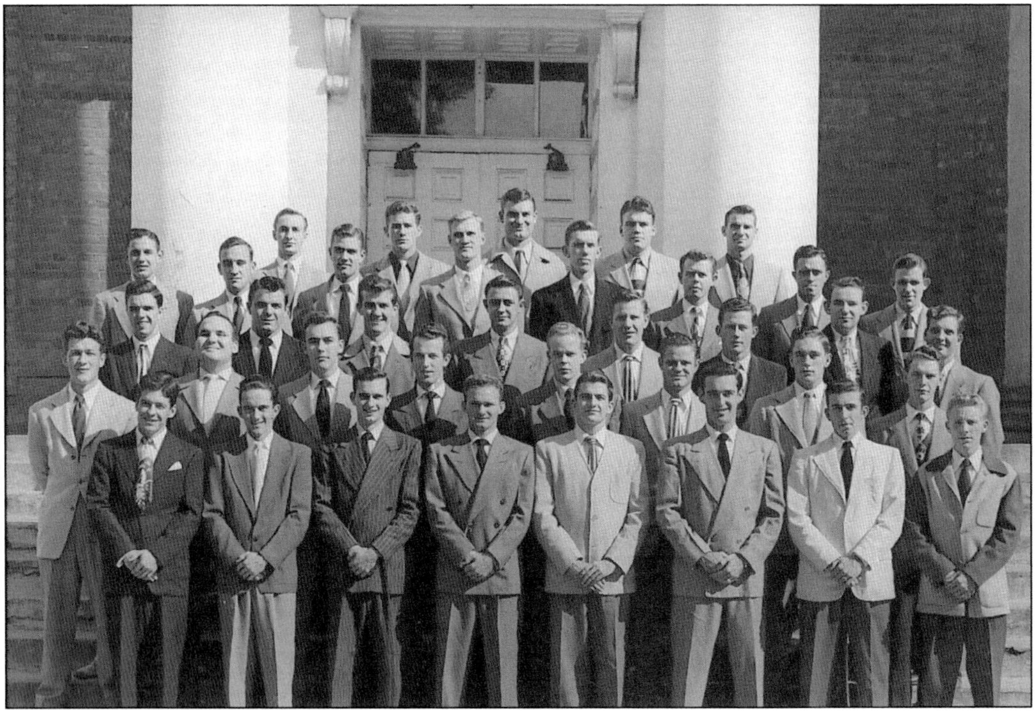

**ALPHA LAMBDA TAU FRATERNITY, 1948–1949.** Pictured from left to right are (front row) Cunningham, McKinney, Mundy, Gibbs, Copley, Cutchin, Gilbert, and Swope; (second row) Allred, Kenner, Ozmint, Banks, Wallace, Roberts, B. Ivey, and Seawright; (third row) Logan, Yarborough, M. Ivey, Campbell, Davis, McCutcheon, McGregor, and Harper; (fourth row) Greene, McGregor, McPhaul, McMillan, Wilkinson, Currie, Berry, and MacIntyre; (fifth row) McLeod, Bowles, Riddle, Copley, and Lindsay. (Courtesy of Presbyterian College Archives.)

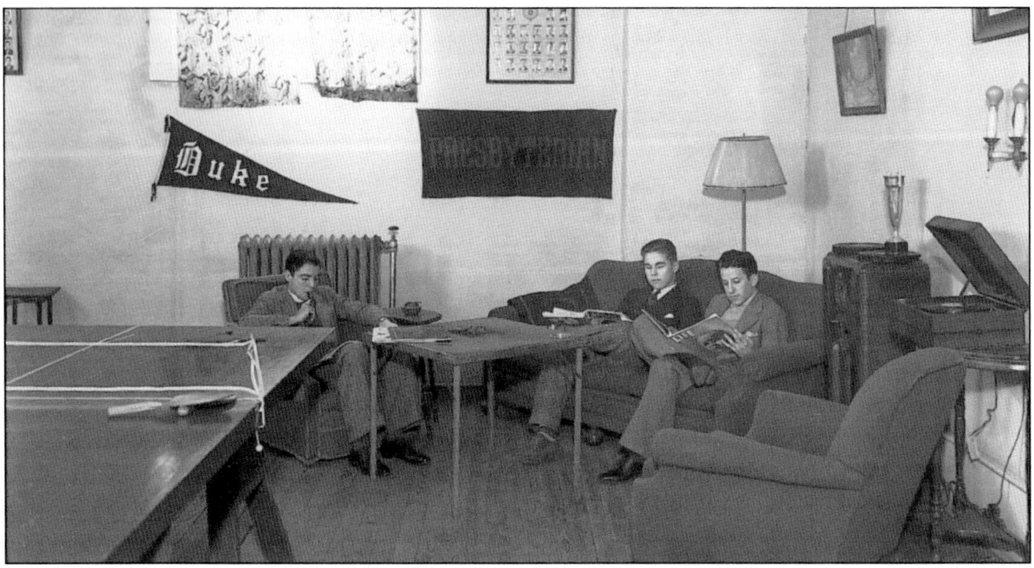


**FRATERNITY ROOM.** Most social fraternities used rooms on the third floor of Neville Hall for meetings and social events. Other rooms were located on Broad Street and behind Laurens Hall. (Courtesy of Presbyterian College Archives.)

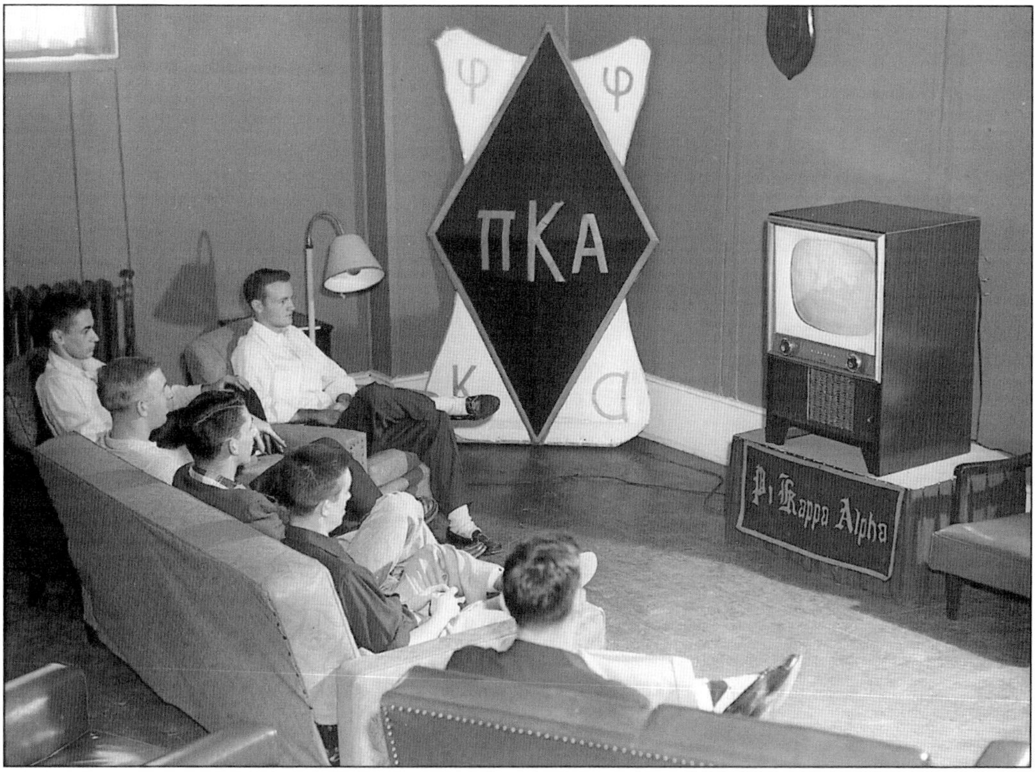


**PIKA ROOM, 1955.** The PIKA room at this time was located on the third floor of Neville Hall. (Courtesy of Presbyterian College Archives.)

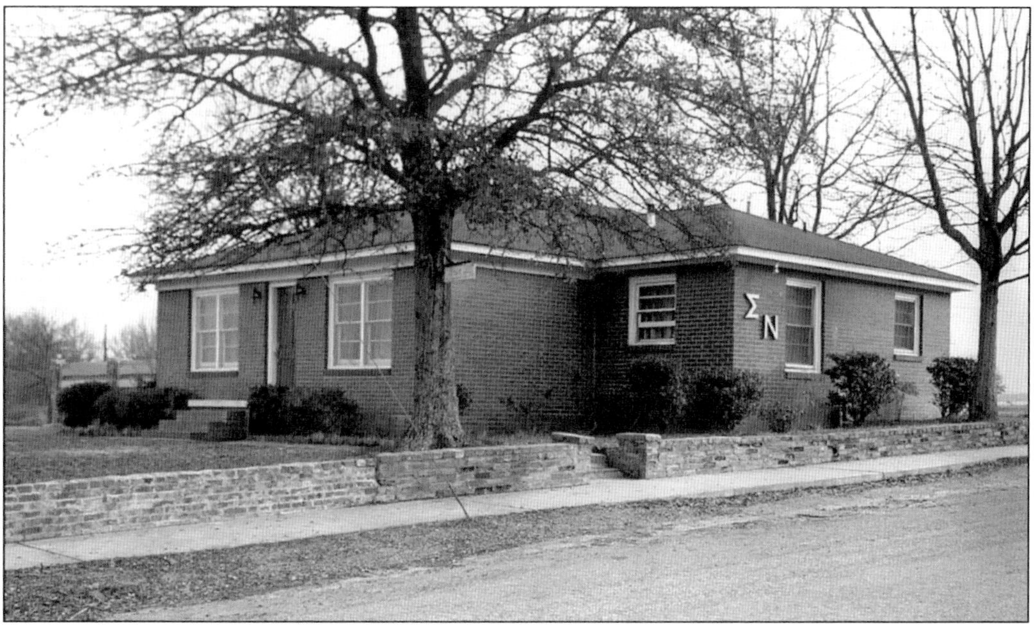


**SIGMA NU LODGE, 1950S.** The Sigma Nu Lodge was built as the first of a planned series of fraternity houses. It was the only one built at the time, and the current fraternity court replaced the original concept in the 1970s. (Courtesy of Presbyterian College Archives.)

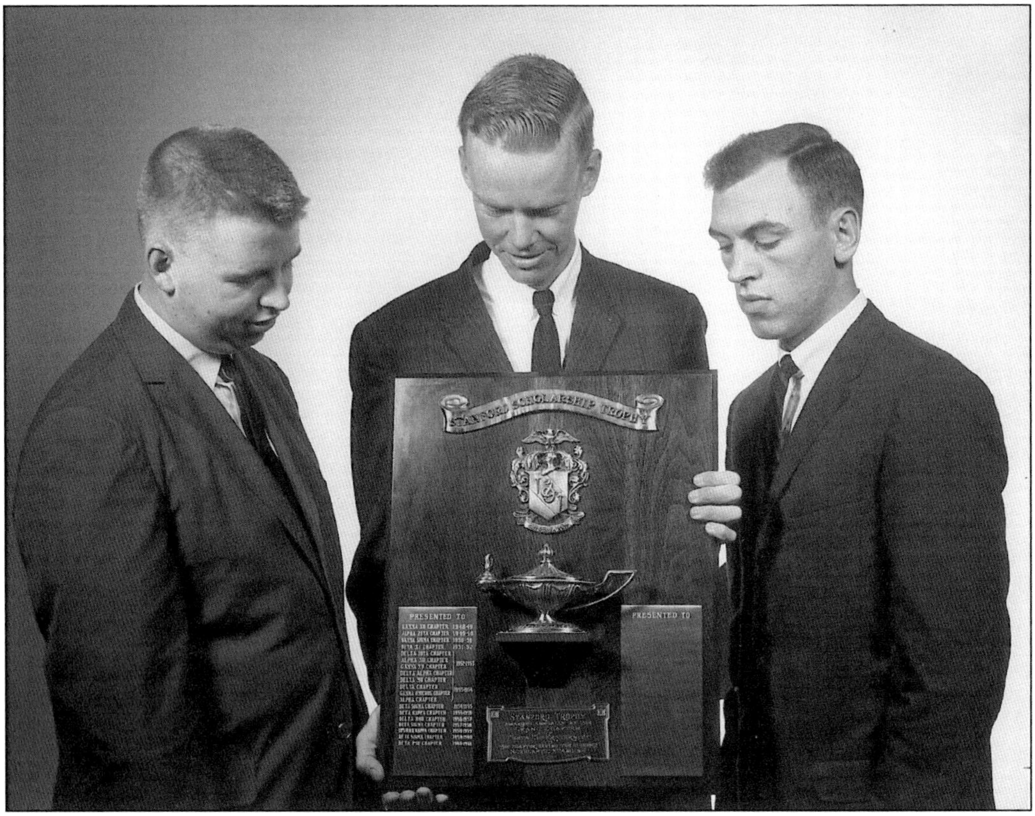


**Award Winners.** Theta Chi officers Ted Elders, Arthur DeYoung, and David Worth are seen in this photograph with the trophy for highest scholastic standing in 1963. (Courtesy of Presbyterian College Archives.)

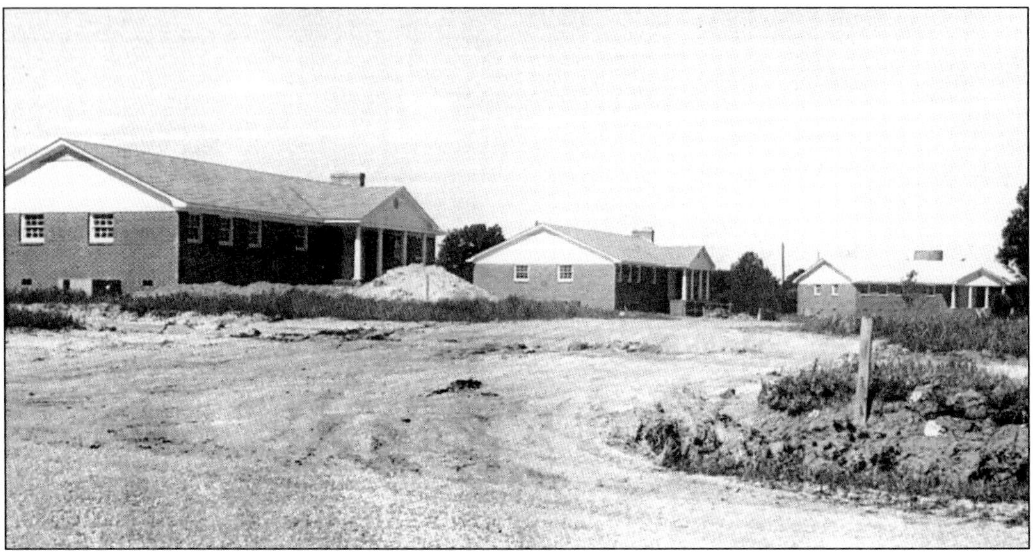

**Fraternity Court Under Construction, 1973.** When completed, these six houses included space for meetings and social events, as well as two bedrooms apiece. (Courtesy of 1973 *PaC SaC*.)

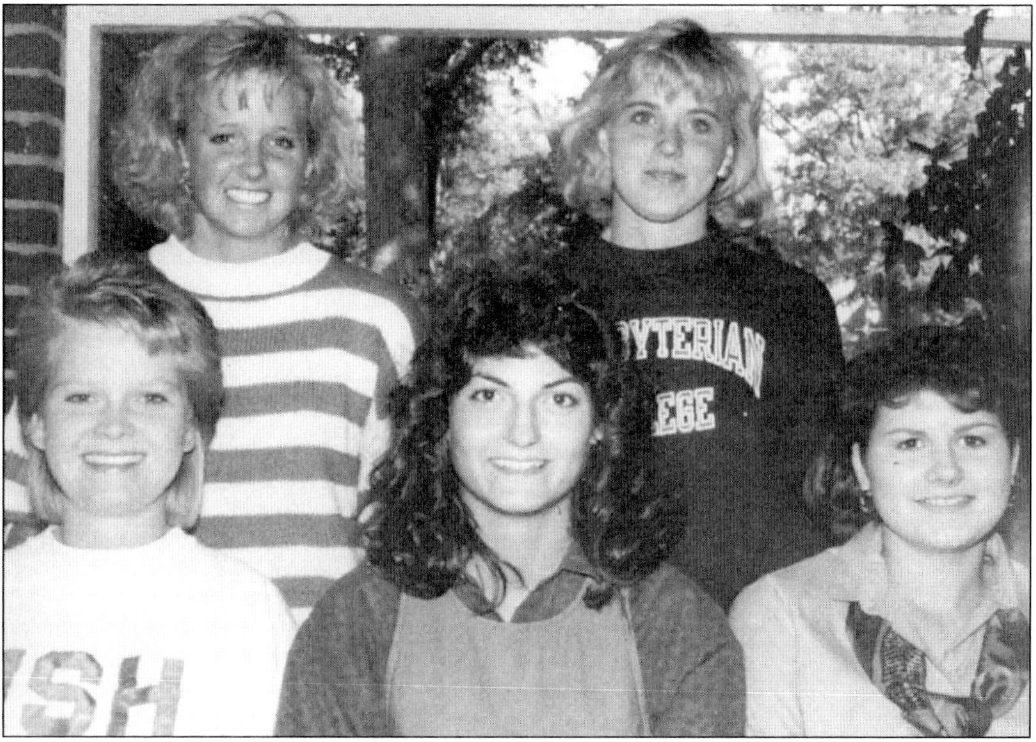

**Women's Social Hall.** After women were admitted as residential students, and before the advent of sororities in 1990, the Women's Social Hall provided a social organization for women, and sponsored numerous events on campus. Pictured above are the WSH officers from 1988. (Courtesy of 1988 *PaC SaC*.)

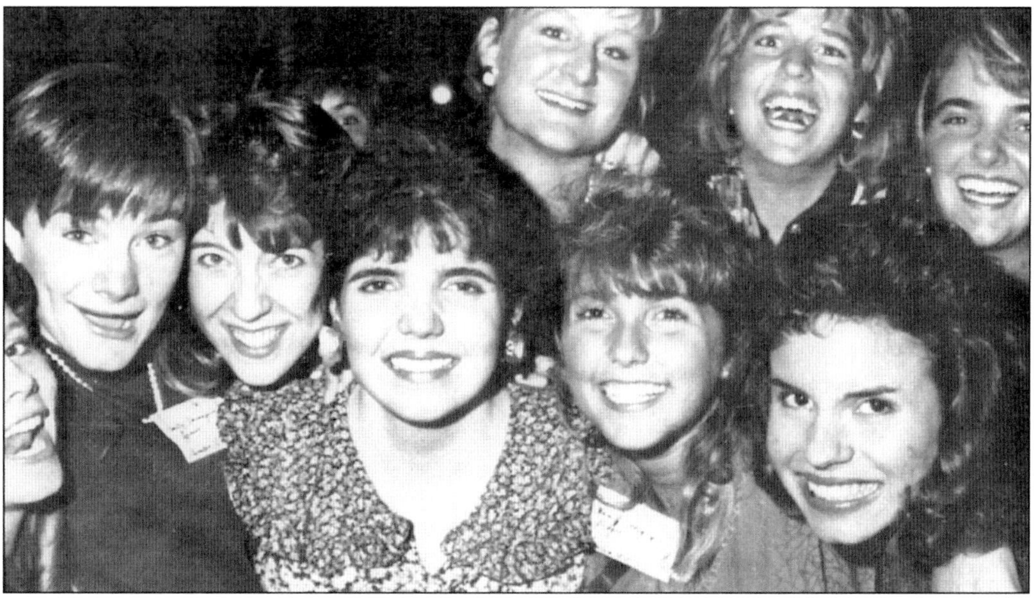

**Sorority Bids, 1989–1990.** Martha Rowlings, Sally Davenport, Kim Kroeger, Ana Parajon, Nancy Cottigny, Maya Vicente, Malinda Morris, Kris Bostwick, and Amy Ashfield as they celebrate their Alpha Delta Pi bids. (Courtesy of 1990 *PaC SaC*.)

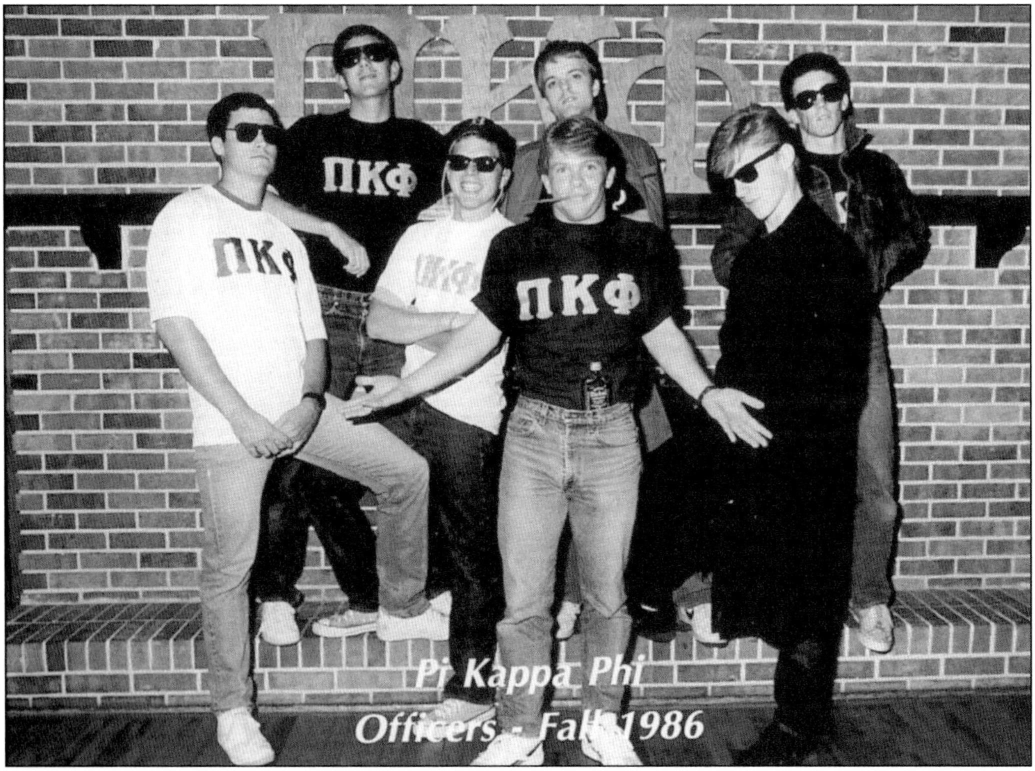


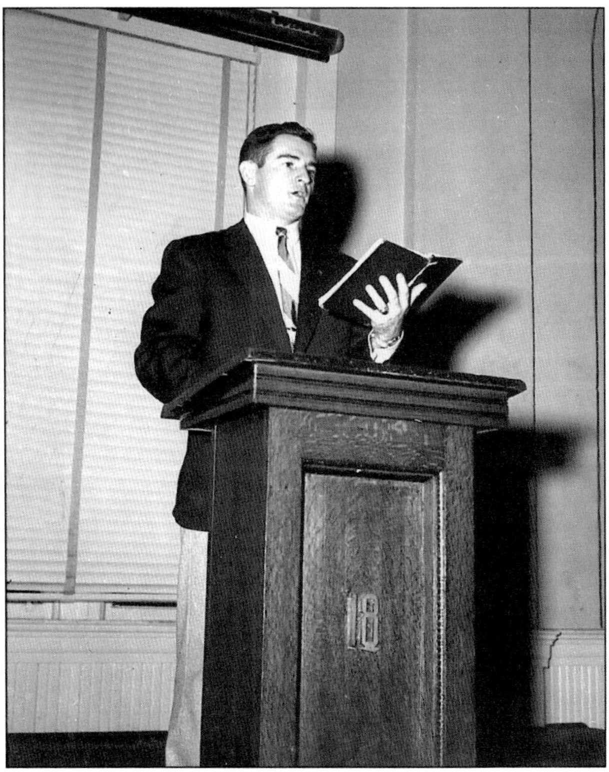

**OFFICERS OF PI KAPPA PHI, 1986.** From left to right are the following: (front row) Wayne Hutchings, historian; Will Deavor, vice-archon; Tim Foster, archon; Jeff McIntyre, secretary; (back row) Jeff Ray, treasurer; Jonathan Hicklin, chaplain; and James Whipple, warden. (Courtesy of Presbyterian College Public Relations Office.)

**STUDENT CHRISTIAN ASSOCIATION.** The Student Christian Association functioned as the governing board for a number of student activities, including intramurals and freshman orientation, and sponsored the annual Religious Emphasis Week. President Tom Stallworth, shown here in 1955, went on to serve as professor, dean of students, alumni director, and even soccer coach at the college. (Courtesy of Presbyterian College Archives.)

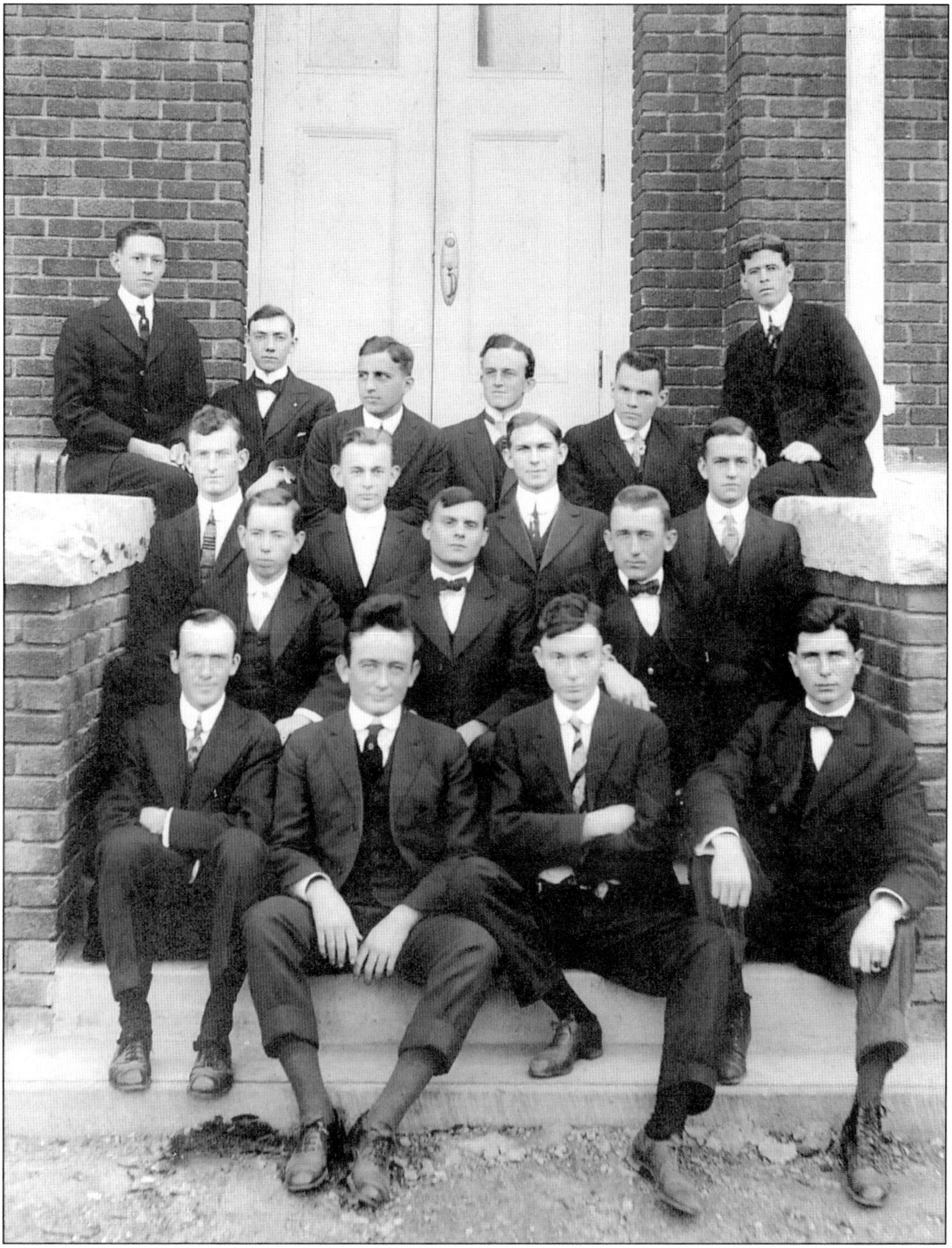

**Ministerial Band, 1915–1916.** The Ministerial Band, which existed as early as 1913, was reorganized in 1936 as the Ministerial Club. It gave aspiring ministers a chance to prepare by preaching, teaching Sunday school, and leading prayer meetings in local churches. (Courtesy of Presbyterian College Archives.)

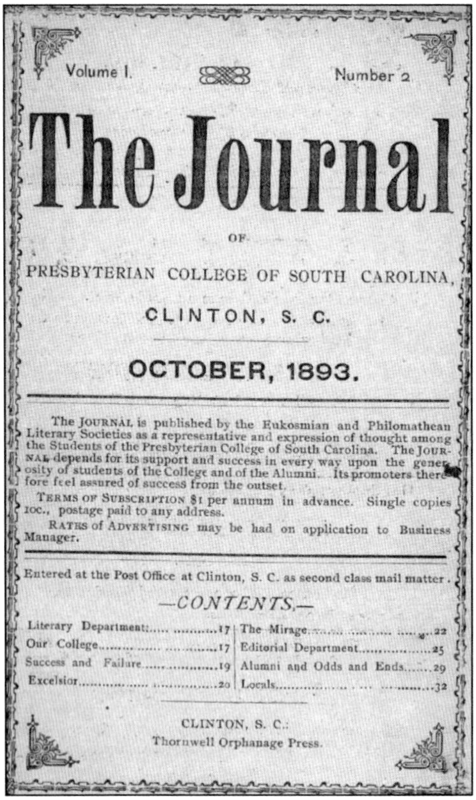

Volume I. Number 2

# The Journal

OF

PRESBYTERIAN COLLEGE OF SOUTH CAROLINA,

CLINTON, S. C.

OCTOBER, 1893.

The JOURNAL is published by the Eukosmian and Philomathean Literary Societies as a representative and expression of thought among the Students of the Presbyterian College of South Carolina. The JOURNAL depends for its support and success in every way upon the generosity of students of the College and of the Alumni. Its promoters therefore feel assured of success from the outset.

TERMS OF SUBSCRIPTION $1 per annum in advance. Single copies 10c., postage paid to any address.

RATES of ADVERTISING may be had on application to Business Manager.

Entered at the Post Office at Clinton, S. C. as second class mail matter.

—CONTENTS.—



CLINTON, S. C.:
Thornwell Orphanage Press.

***THE JOURNAL*, 1893.** *The Journal* and *The Palladium* were two of the early publications produced by the literary societies. (Courtesy of Presbyterian College Archives.)

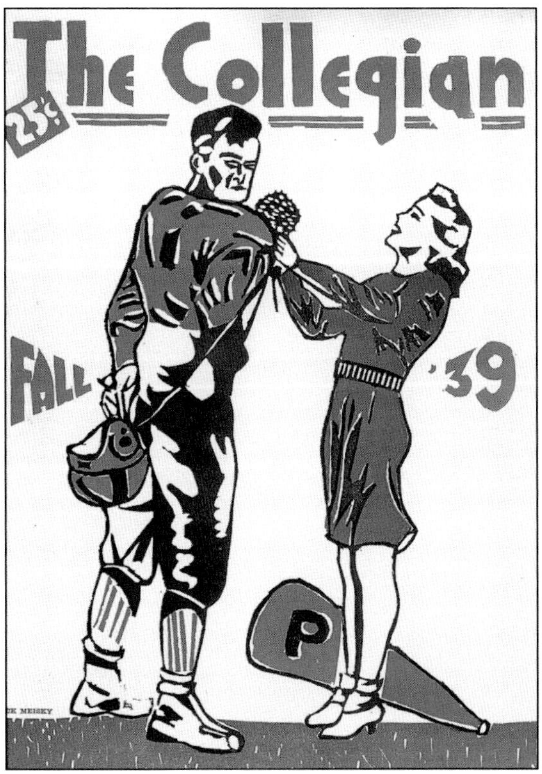


**THE COLLEGIAN.** The Collegian was published longer than the earlier college magazines. Founded in 1902, it continued to be published until the 1950s. Its "commencement number" pre-dated the *PaC SaC*, and served as a kind of early yearbook. (Courtesy of Presbyterian College Archives.)

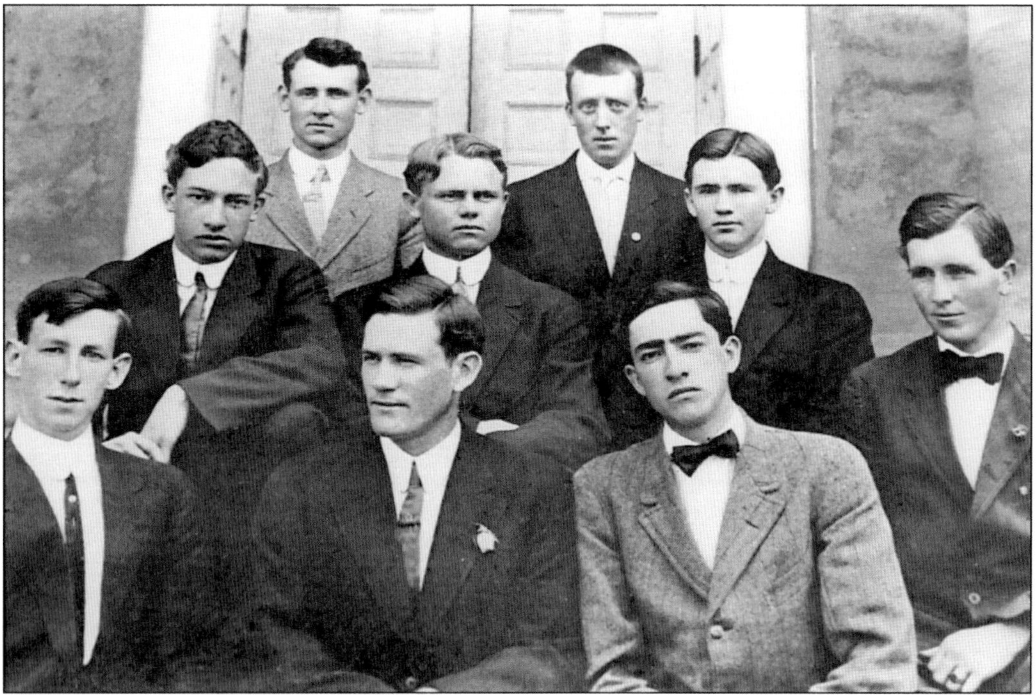

***Collegian* Staff, 1910–1911.** Although staffers in this photograph have not been specifically identified, members of the organization that year included T.W. Simpson, C.D. Fulton, J.M. Fewell, J.M. Lemmon, H.W. Baker, G.W. Taylor, W.S. Fewell, T.C. Brown, E.A. Fuller, and B.M. Schlotter. (Courtesy of Presbyterian College Archives.)

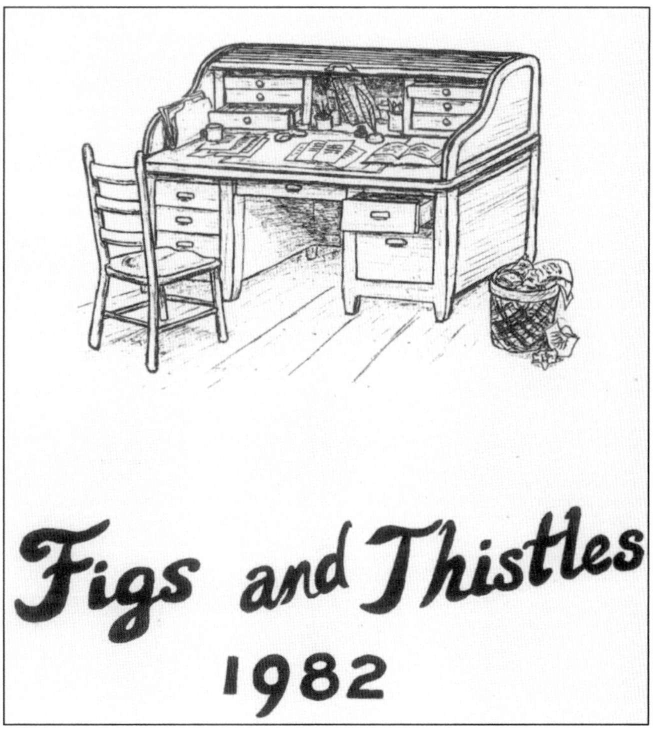


***Figs and Thistles*.** This annual literary magazine, which is still published today, first appeared in 1967. (Courtesy of Presbyterian College Archives.)

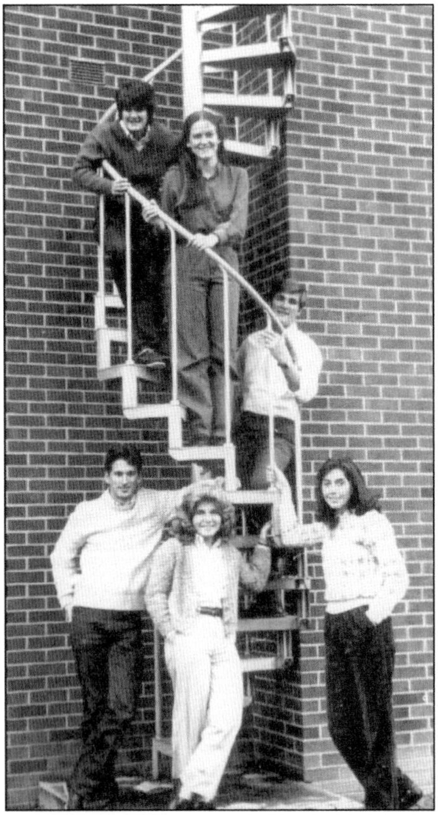

***Figs and Thistles* Staff, 1983.** Pictured are Lisa Vierra (editor), Grey Mason, Tim Cowsert, Rebecca Stiles, Jill Reid, Karen Reetz, Cheri Jones, Jane Rogers, and Cheryl Thomas. (Courtesy of 1983 *PaC SaC*.)

***PaC SaC* Staff at Work, 1914.** The college annual, the *PaC SaC* (named for the initials of the Presbyterian College of South Carolina), was started in 1914. It served as the successor to the commencement issue of *The Collegian* literary magazine, and to a short-lived yearbook entitled the *Garnet and Blue*. Although the people in this photograph cannot be specifically identified, staffers that year included H.D. Smith, E.S. Bennett, H.M. Byrd, W.E. Davis, W.P. Jacobs Jr., J.F. Jacobs Jr., J.S. Land, E.C. King, M.Petty, L.M. Simpson, W.P. Anderson, J.F. Winters, P.N. Gresham, and A.H. Miller. (Courtesy of 1914 *PaC SaC*.)

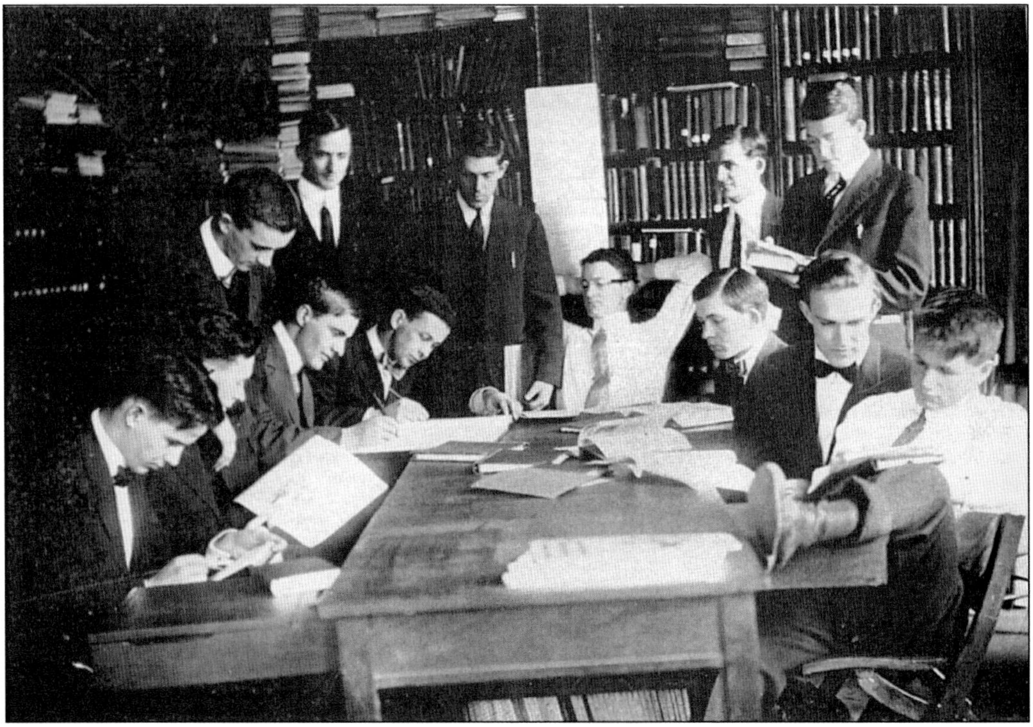

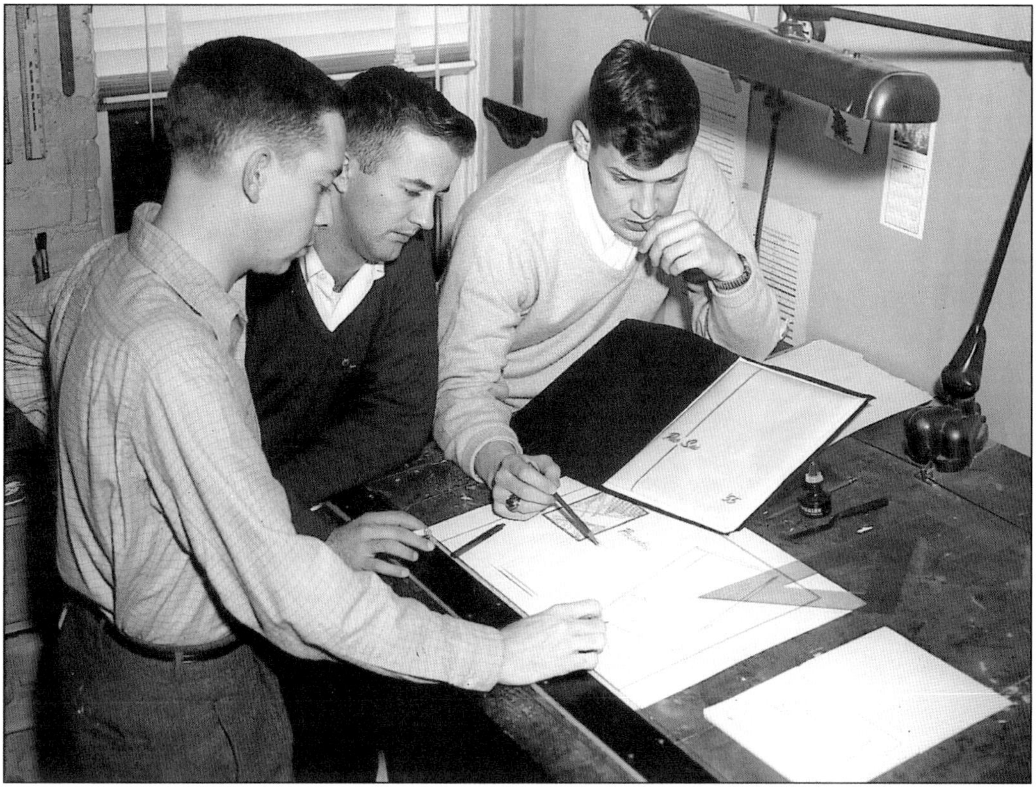

**Staff of the *PaC SaC* at Work, 1954–1955.** The staff of the campus annual works diligently on the layout of the yearbook. (Courtesy of Presbyterian College Archives.)

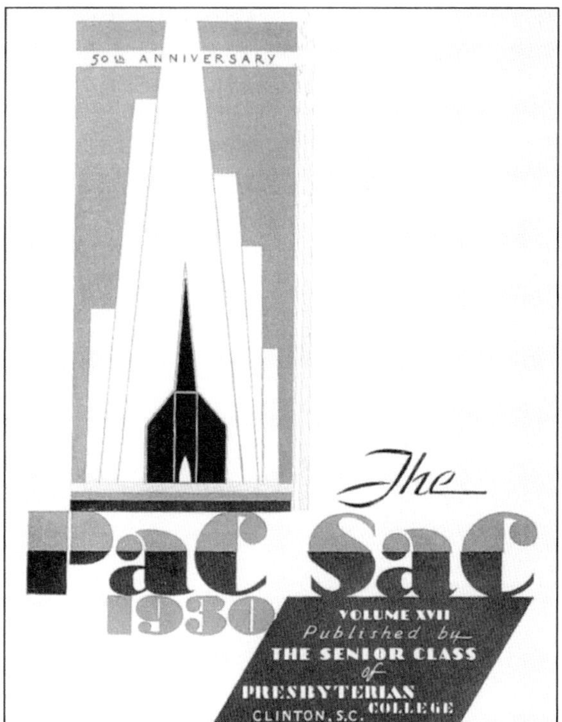


**Fiftieth Anniversary Issue of the *PaC SaC*, 1930.** This special issue was published to celebrate the 50th anniversary of the college. (Courtesy of Presbyterian College Archives.)

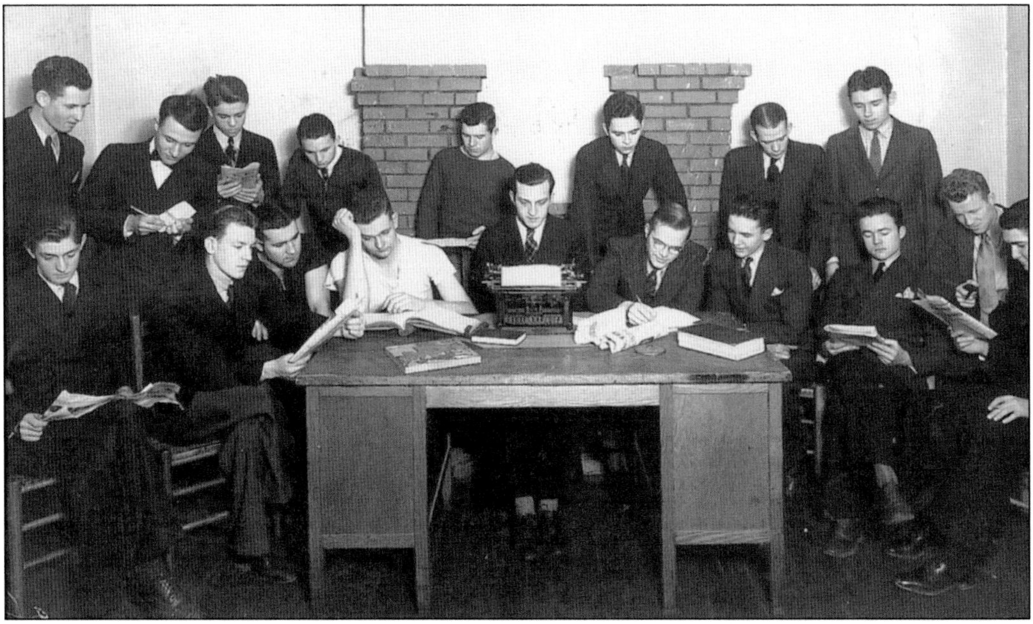

**Bluestocking Staff, 1935–1936.** The student newspaper was first published in 1920, and has won many awards over the years. Among the members of the staff in 1935–1936 were Hugh Holman (editor), Hudson, Patrick, McLees, Charles, Penland, A. Johnson, Stanton, Potter, Ratchford, Darby, Chapman, and MacLeod. (Courtesy of Presbyterian College Archives.)

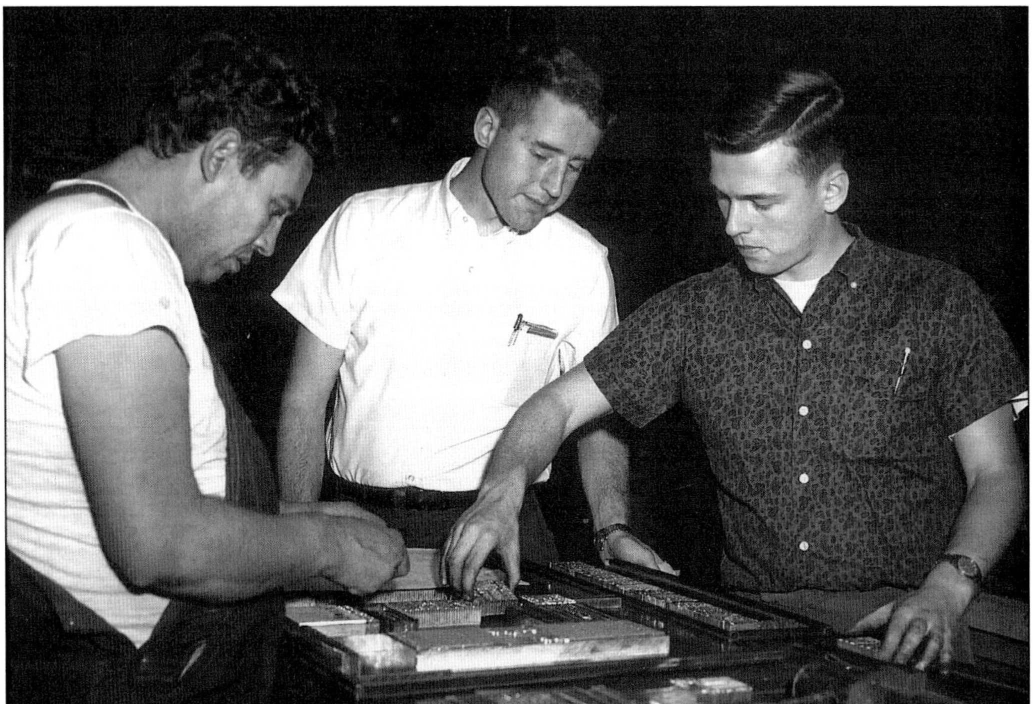

***Bluestocking*, 1962–1963.** Editor DuPont Smith lays the type for an issue of the student newspaper as Phifer and James assist him. (Courtesy of Presbyterian College Archives.)

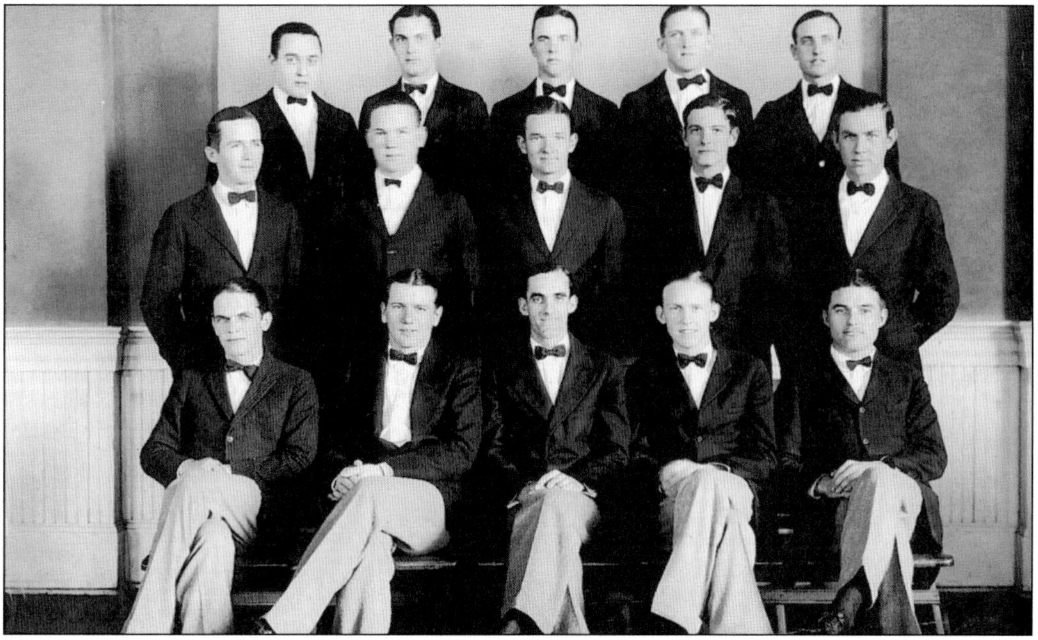

**Glee Club, 1924–1925.** The choir has always been an important part of college life, beginning with the early organization of a glee club. Although the individual members of this glee club are not identified, members that year included W.H. Dendy, Y.A. Montgomery, H.G. Prince, L.D. Stribling, E.G. Beckman, J.E. Dendy Jr., J.K. Roberts, E.L. Wilds, G.L. Cunningham, D.D. Edmunds, W.O. Player, J.M. Stokes, J.P. Brown, J.D. McInnis, E.T. Wilson, and G.L. Wilson. (Courtesy of Presbyterian College Archives.)

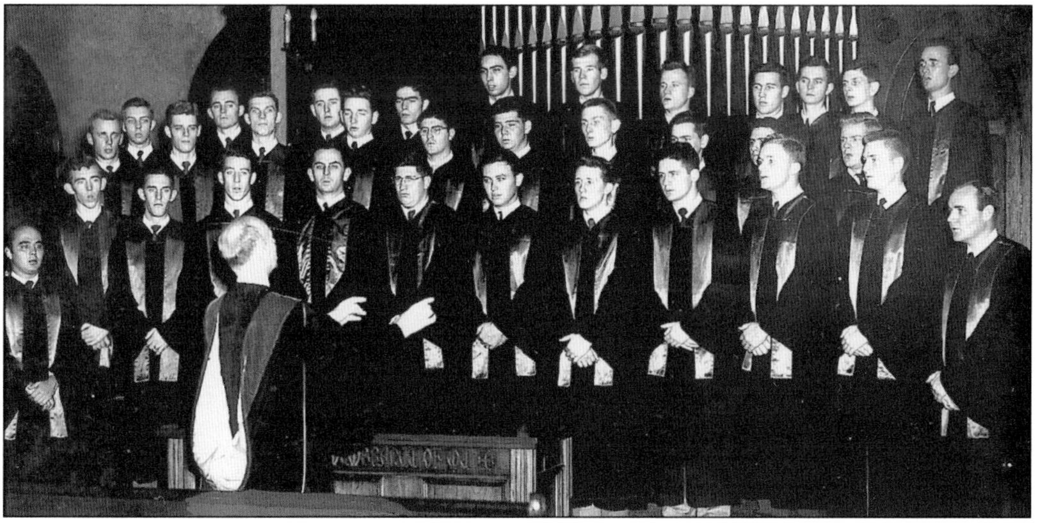

**Choir, 1949.** For many years the all-male choir, under the direction of longtime director Edouard Patte, was well known for its tours and recordings. Members of the choir in 1949 included C. Patte, Kiker, L'heureux, Ivey, Wood, Galloway, McCarter, Engleman, Whitson, Campbell, Collins, Fesperman, Byrum, Daniel, Jackson, Bullock, Penter, Mallard, Kaiser, Dowling, Ford, Neville, Link, Brearley, Beale, Hay, DuBose, Burton, Wheeler, Wardlaw, D. Maxwell, Denham, Cole, Skinner, Floyd, Hollandsworth, Wilder, Smith, Kirven, and S. Maxwell. (Courtesy of Presbyterian College Archives.)

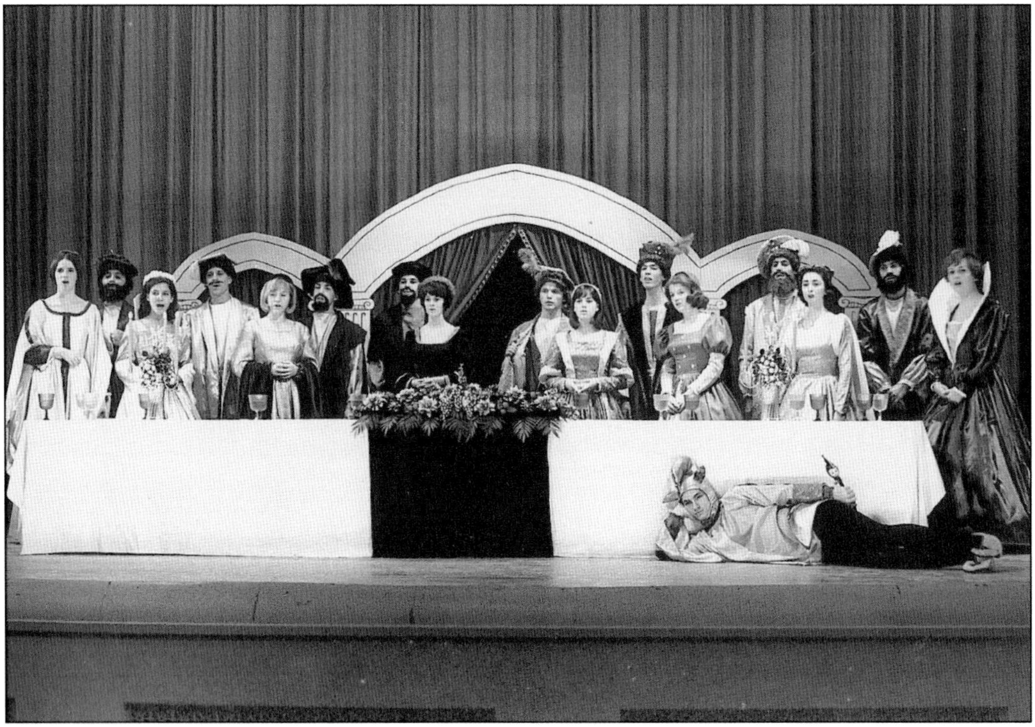

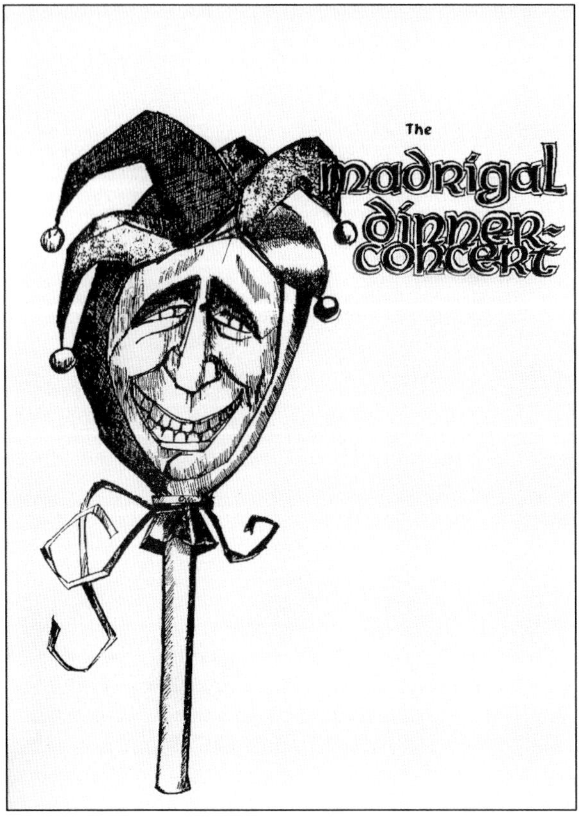


**MADRIGAL DINNER, 1966.** Following the admission of women in 1965, the choir became co-educational under director Charles Gaines. For many years, they presented a popular series of madrigal dinners during the Christmas season. At left is a program for one of the madrigal dinners. (Courtesy of Presbyterian College Archives.)

**BROADWAY CABARET.** A spring highlight for a number of years was the Broadway Cabaret staged by the PC Choir. (Courtesy of Presbyterian College Archives.)

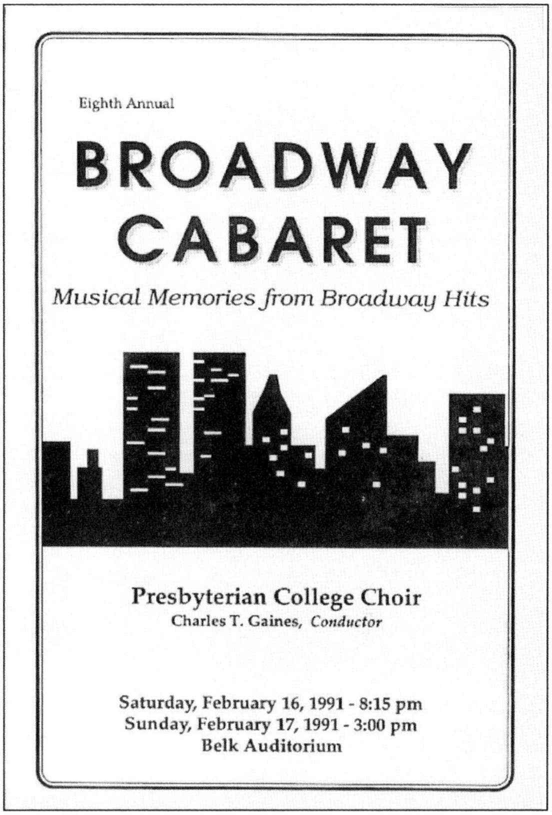


***PHANTOM OF THE OPERA.*** Pictured below is a performance in 1990. (Courtesy of Presbyterian College Archives.)

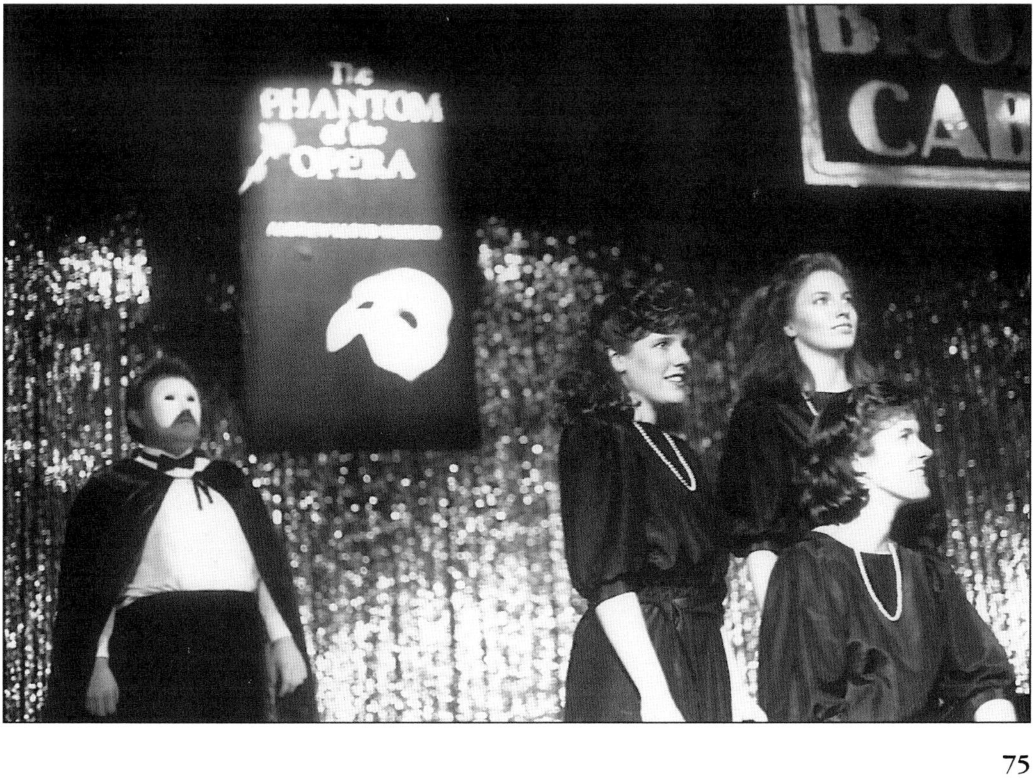

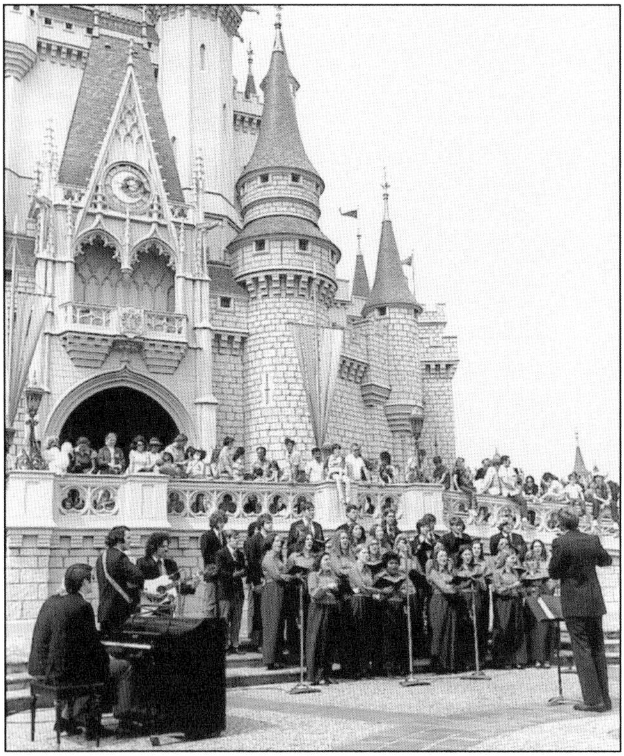

**PC Choir at Disney World.** For many years, the PC choir has gone on tour during spring break, performing throughout the region. (Courtesy of Presbyterian College Archives.)

**Choir Tour in Israel, 1976.** Occasionally, tours took the choir abroad to Europe and the Mideast. (Courtesy of Presbyterian College Archives.)

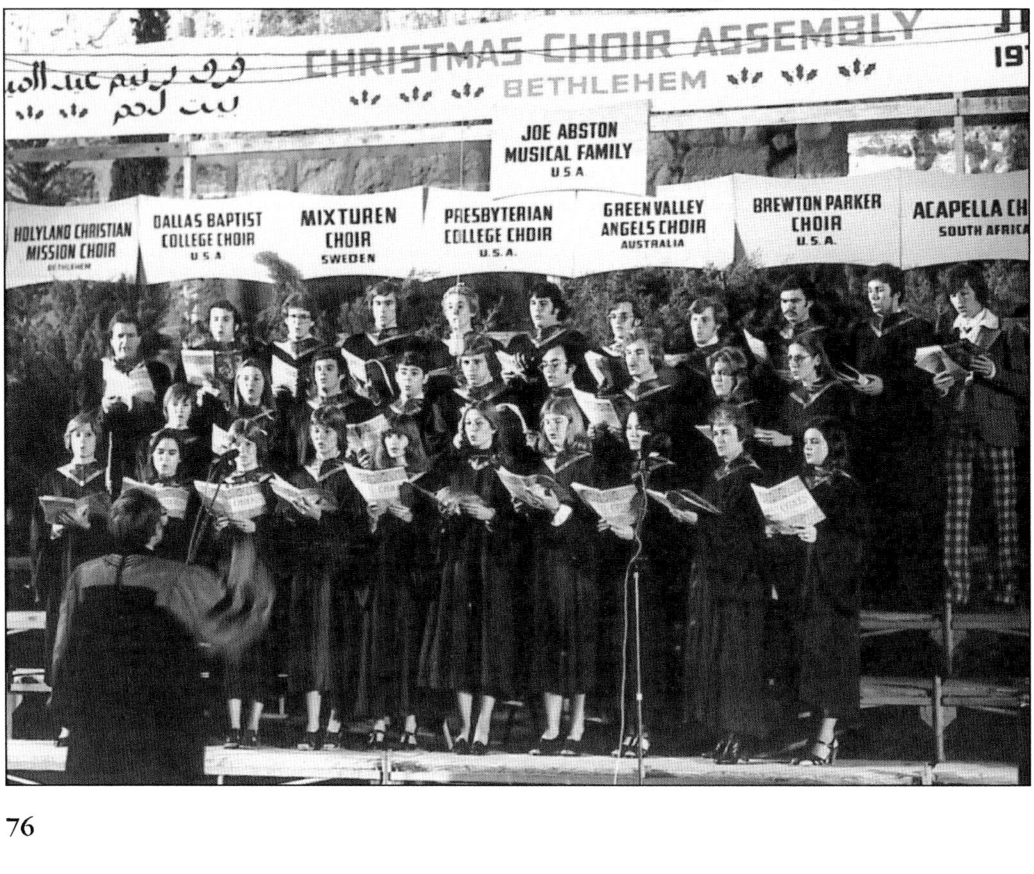

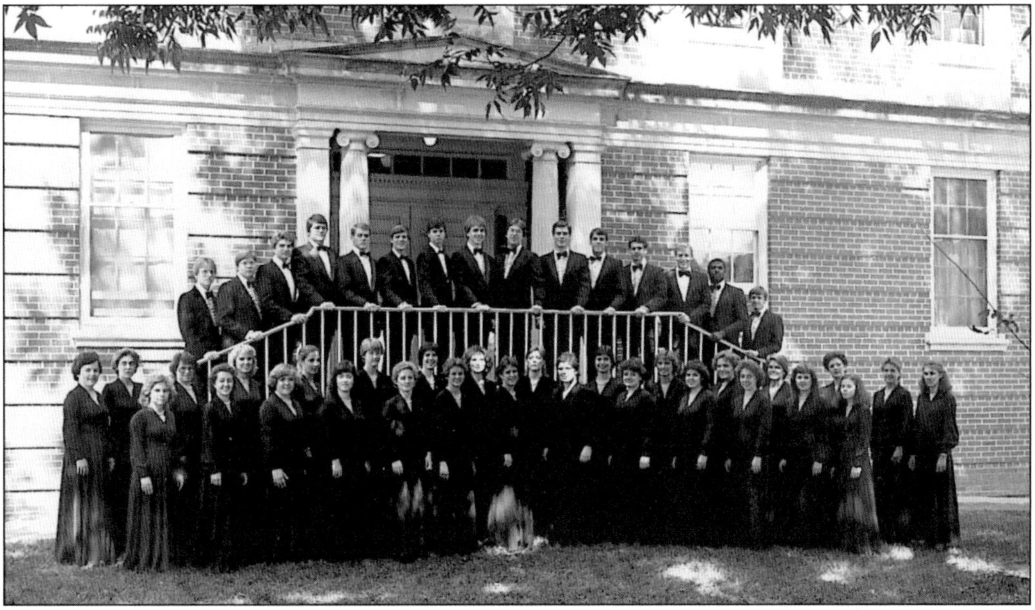

**PC Choir, 1983.** The choir's schedule in 1983 included mini-tours to Atlanta and Spartanburg as well as a spring break tour through North and South Carolina. (Courtesy of Presbyterian College Archives.)

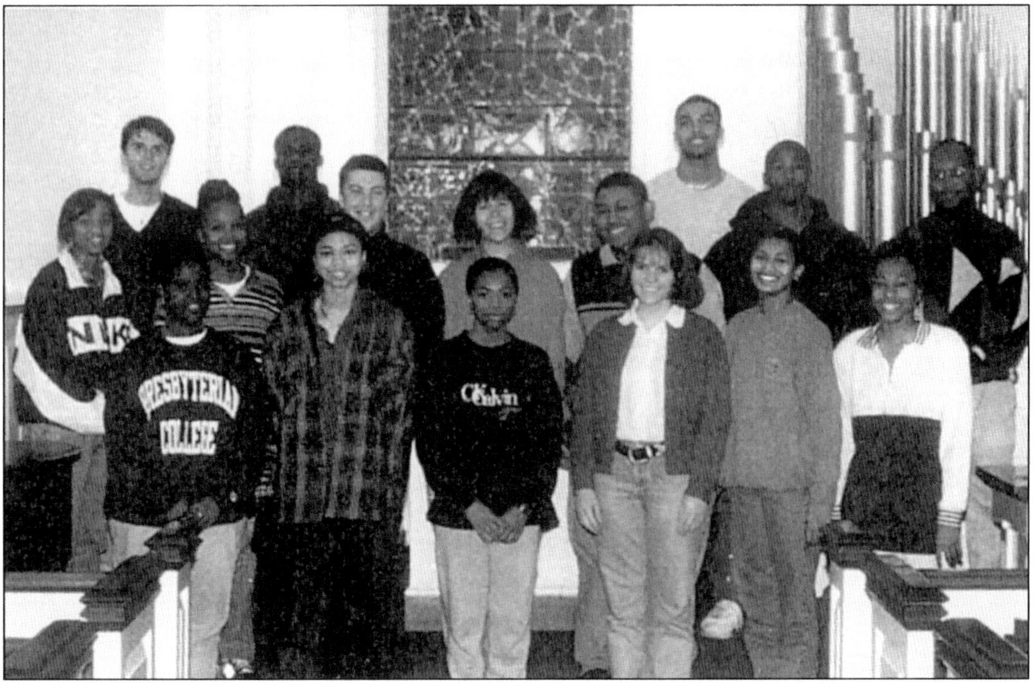


**Student Fellowship Choir, 1997–1998.** In recent years, the Student Fellowship Choir has contributed much to the cultural life of the campus. Pictured from left to right are the following: (front row) T. Jenkins, C. Choice, V. Wright, C. Thomas, C. Shands, and A. Sarratt; (second row) A. Rigdill, D. Cates, M. Charrier, C. Clasen, M. Adams, J. Pearson, and B. Hampton (director); (third row) C. McCallum, R. Sullivan, and K. Brown. (Courtesy of 1998 *PaC SaC*.)

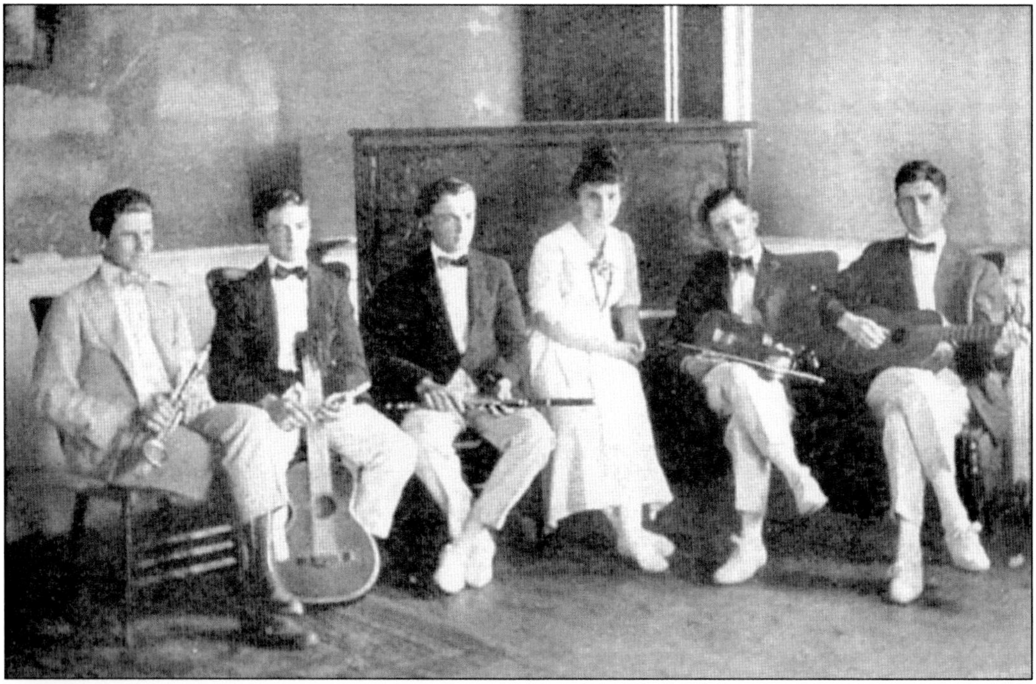

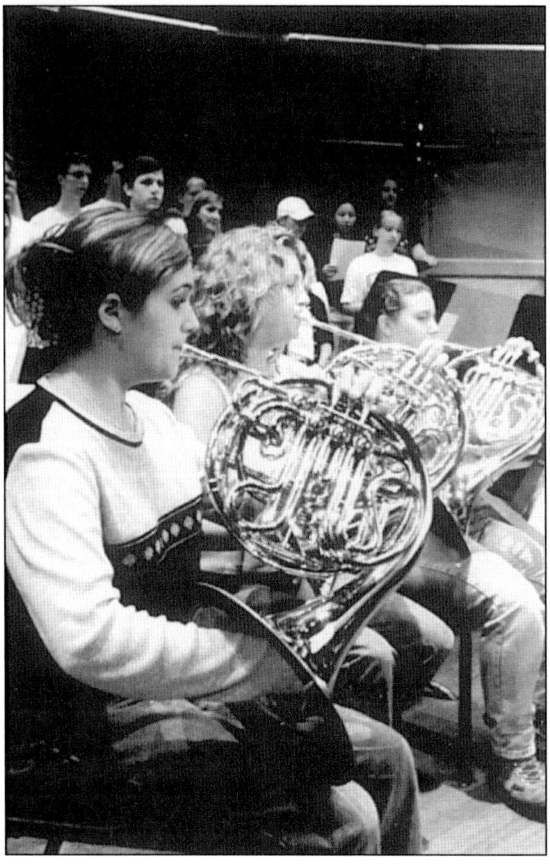

**Orchestra, 1917.** Instrumental music was quite an early feature of college life. Pictured here from left to right are H.K. Neely, clariphone (director); H.M. Brimm, flute; W.W. Brimm, piccolo; Essie Copeland, piano; S.W. Dendy, violin; and C.S. Evans, guitar. (Courtesy of 1917 *PaC SaC*.)

**Wind Ensemble, 1998.** Instrumental music continues to play a prominent part in campus life. The wind ensemble's schedule in 1998 included three concerts, featuring hymns, folk music, and pop music. (Courtesy of Presbyterian College Public Relations Office.)

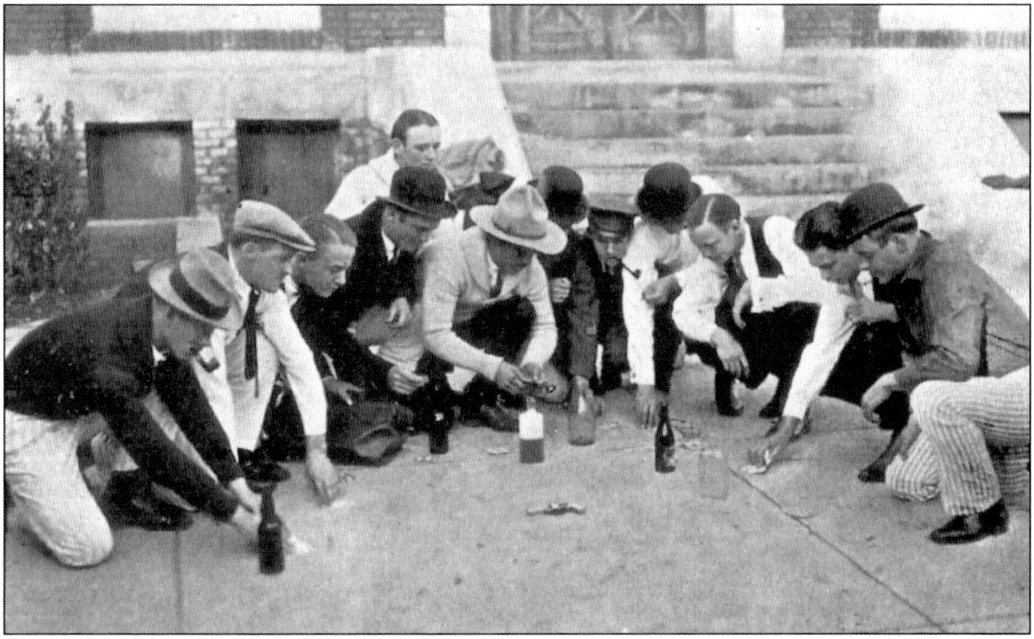

**Kard Krazy Klan, 1924.** In the early days, the college boasted some unusual clubs. Members of this club, whose motto was "Keep Konstantly Krooked," included Kap'n Banks, Karl Karson, Kruel Karson, Krook Kornwall, Kool Klinton, Krank McLendon, Knockout Knowles, Kute Berry, Kwit Lowry, Kant McLendon, Kanteen Weatherby, and Kid Poe. (Courtesy of 1924 *PaC SaC*.)

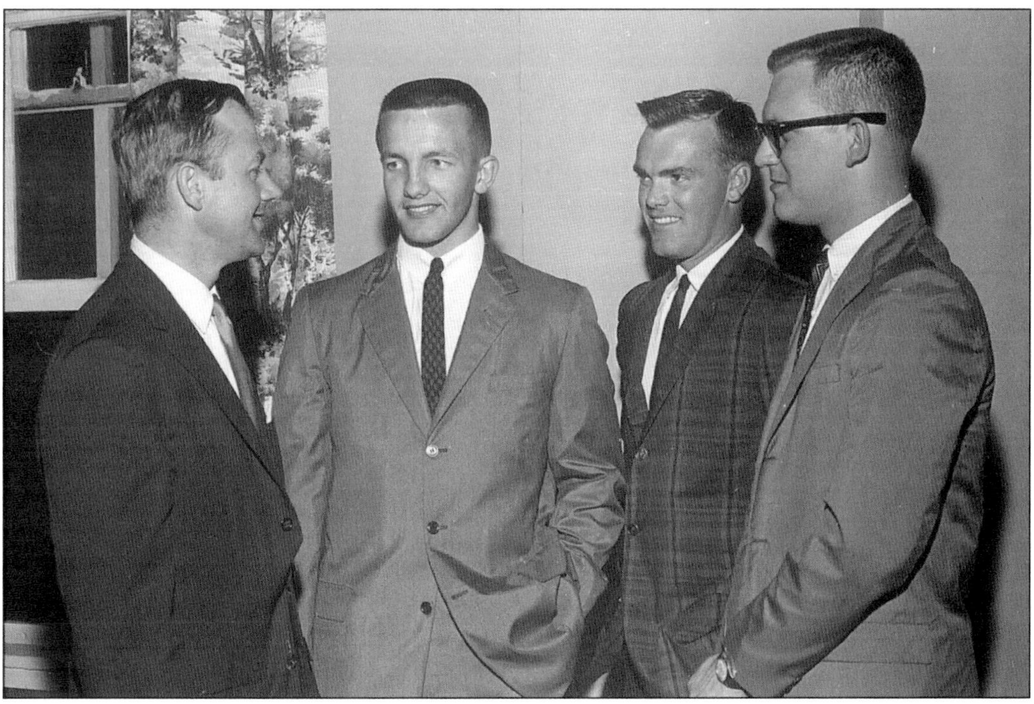

**Blue Key, 1961.** Blue Key, a national leadership fraternity, was organized on campus in 1932. Here South Carolina Lt. Gov. Burnet R. Maybank poses with Paul Ard, Herb Hammett, and Evin Varner. (Courtesy of Presbyterian College Archives.)

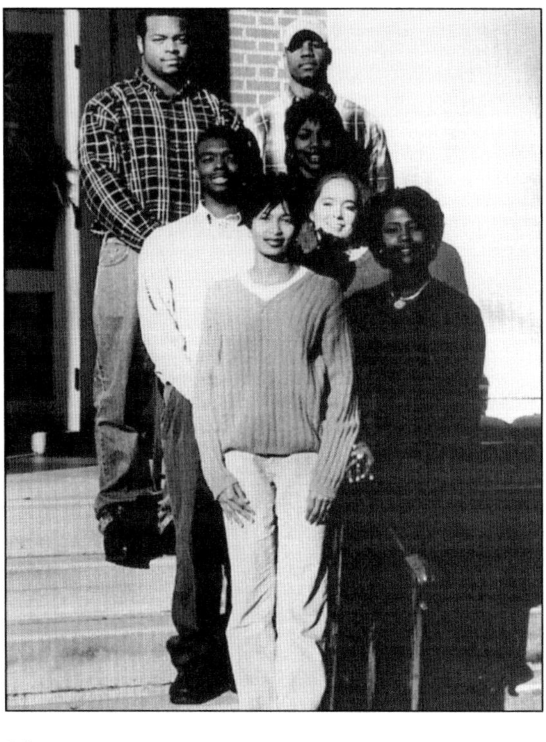

**Blue Key Symposium.** For a number of years, Blue Key sponsored an annual symposium on current events. (Courtesy of Presbyterian College Archives.)

**Multicultural Student Union, 2000.** Founded in 1987 as the Minority Student Union, MSU strives to create an awareness of minority concerns among members of the student body. Among the many activities sponsored by MSU are the African American Overnight project, and programs for Black History Month. (Courtesy of Presbyterian College Public Relations Office.)

# *Five*

# Student Life

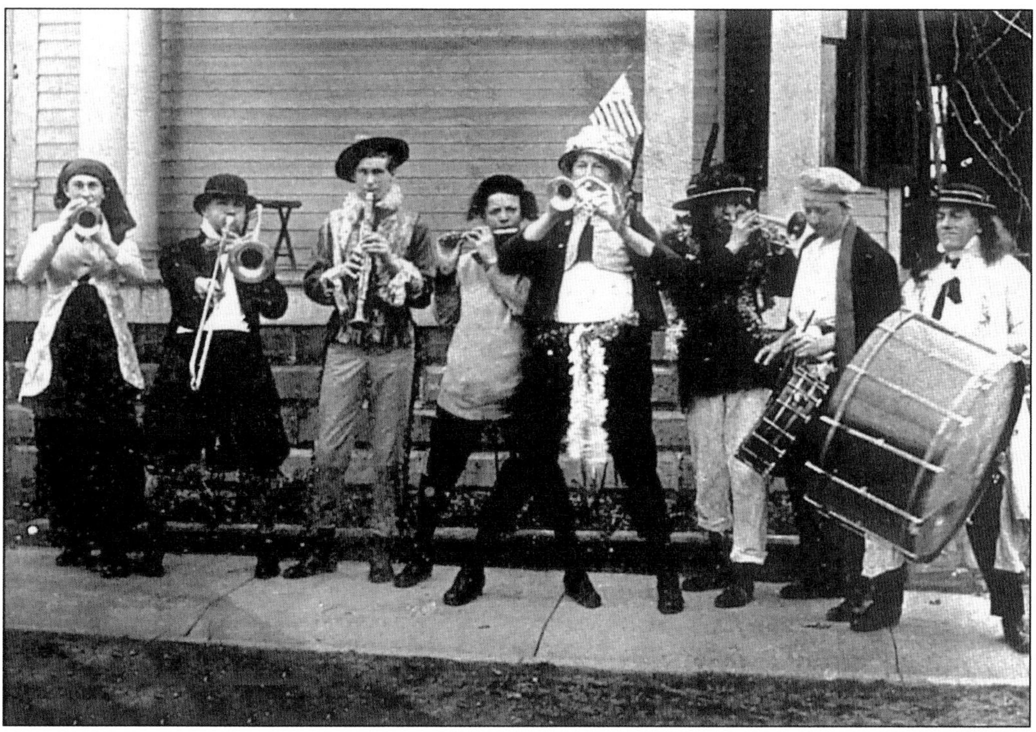

**The Jolly Serenaders, 1914.** The members of this group included H.D. Smith, supreme cornetist; W.P. Jacobs Jr., trombone slidist; H. Brimm, manipulator of the piccolo; H.A.D. Neely, red cornetist; H.K. Neely, clarinetist; J.A. Neely, black cornetist; J.C. Byrd, trap drums; and Hugh McLucas, beater of the bass drum. (Courtesy of 1914 *PaC SaC*.)

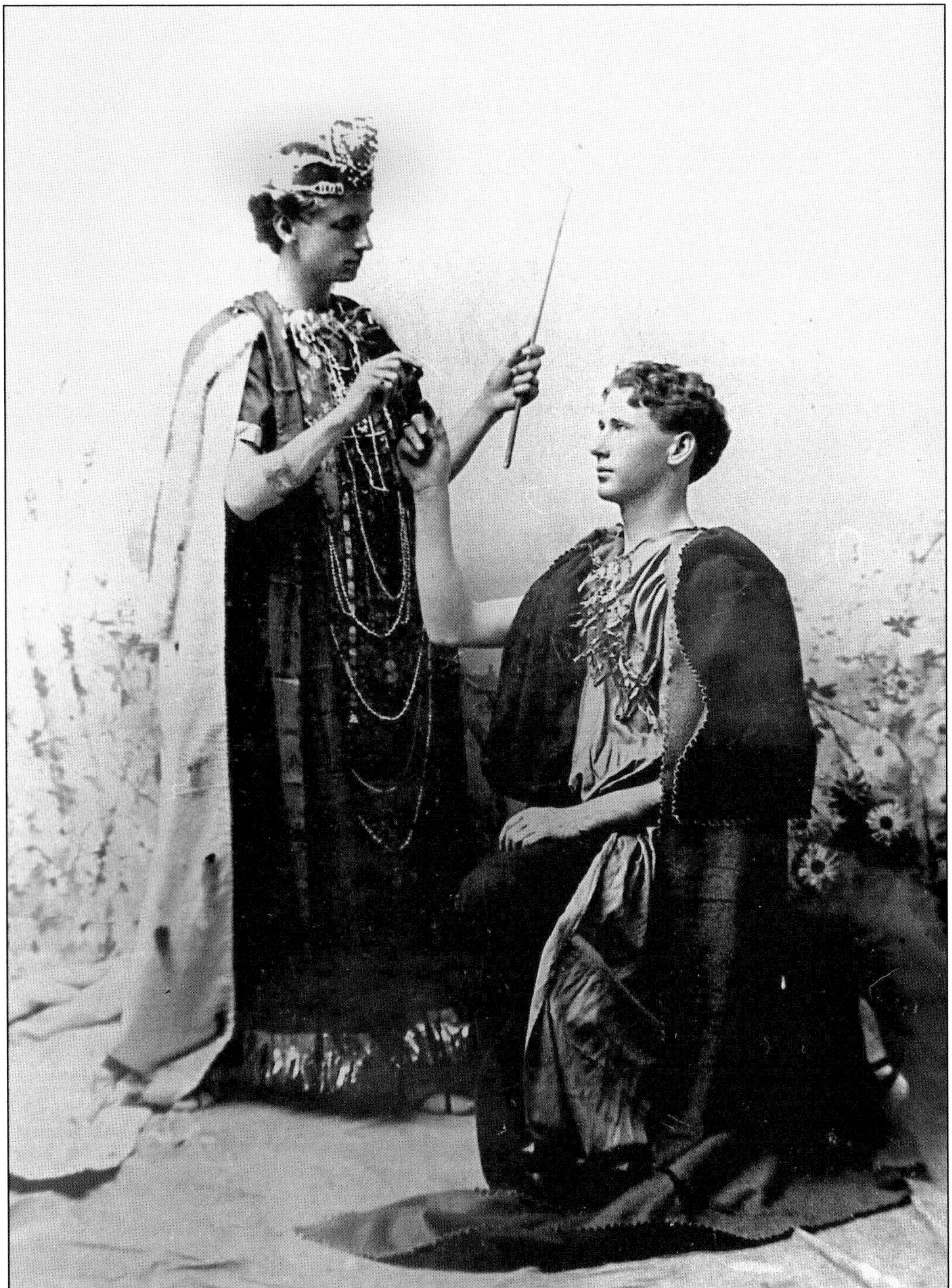

**Early Performance.** There has been a drama club on the PC campus since the late 1920s, and theatrical productions have always been popular. Here, Thornwell and Dillard Jacobs, sons of PC's founder, participate in a dramatic production around 1890. (Courtesy of Presbyterian College Archives.)

**Black Magic Theater.** During the 1960s, the old chemistry lab in Jacobs Hall was re-done in all black to create a theater-in-the-round. Many memorable performances were held there. It was replaced by a theater in Douglas House, and eventually by the Harper Center. (Courtesy of Presbyterian College Archives.)

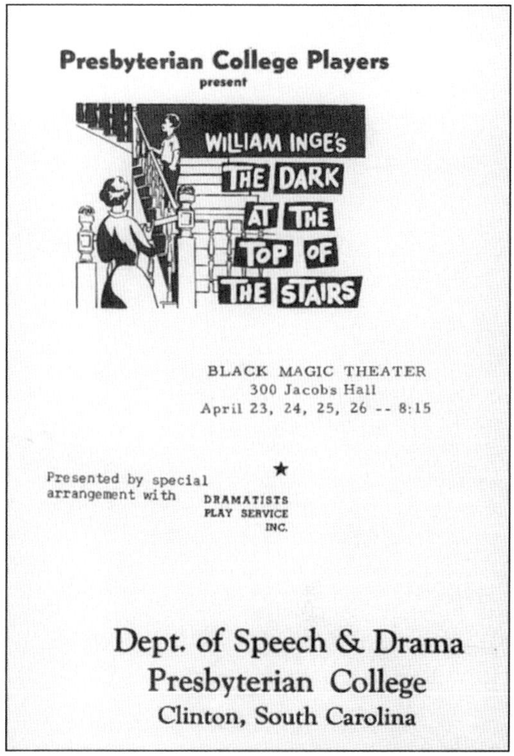

Presbyterian College Players
present

WILLIAM INGE'S
THE DARK AT THE TOP OF THE STAIRS

BLACK MAGIC THEATER
300 Jacobs Hall
April 23, 24, 25, 26 -- 8:15

Presented by special arrangement with DRAMATISTS PLAY SERVICE INC.

Dept. of Speech & Drama
Presbyterian College
Clinton, South Carolina

***The Oaks of Mamre*, 1966.** The PC Players, under the direction of Dr. James Skinner, presented three plays during 1966–1967, including *The Oaks of Mamre*. (Courtesy of Presbyterian College Archives.)

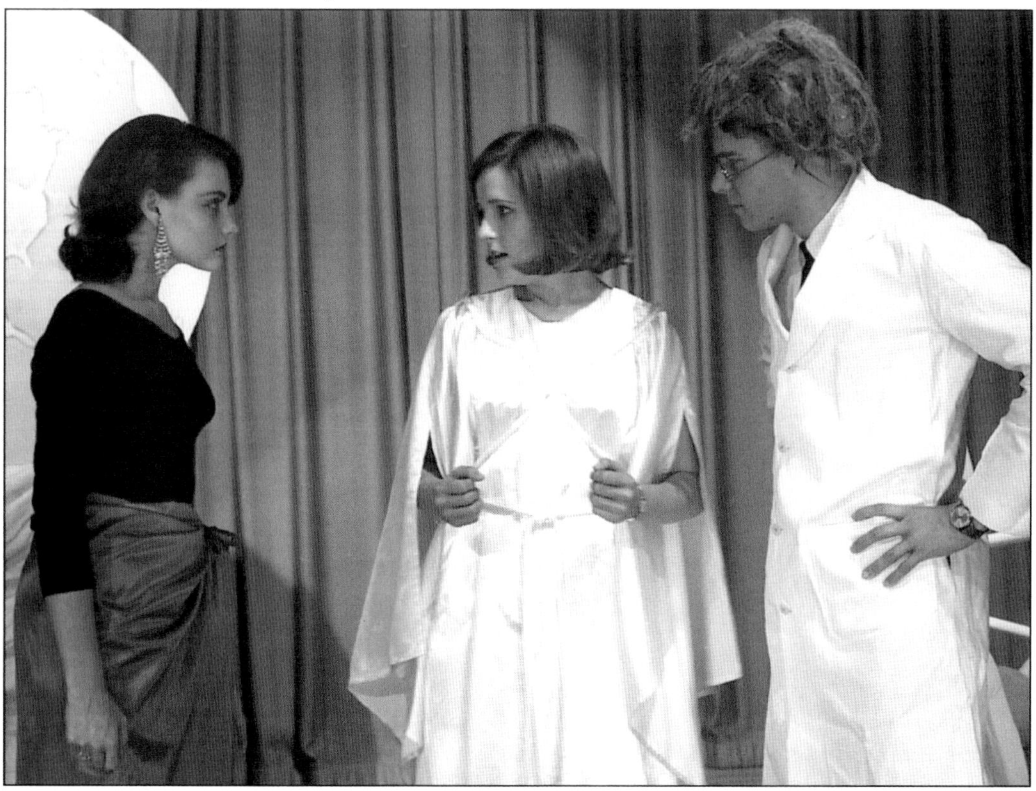

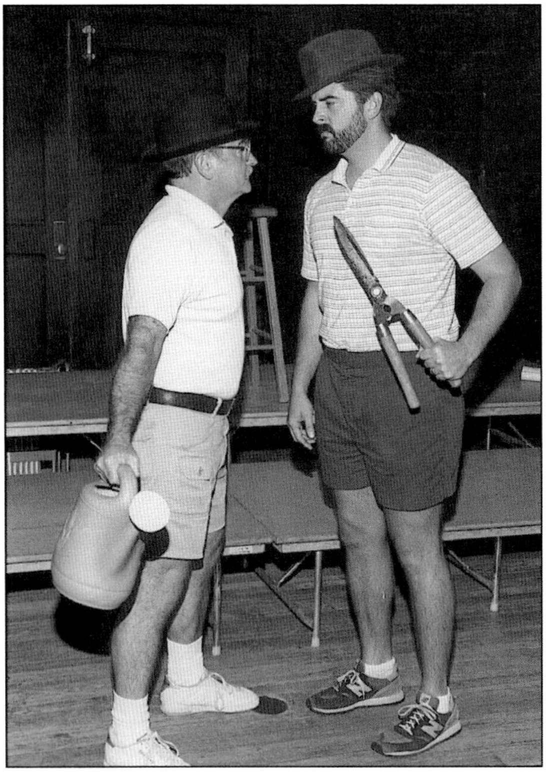

***The Fantastiks*, 1986.** A perennial favorite was *The Fantastiks*, seen here featuring Tom Stallworth (left) and Randy Randall. (Courtesy of Presbyterian College Archives.)

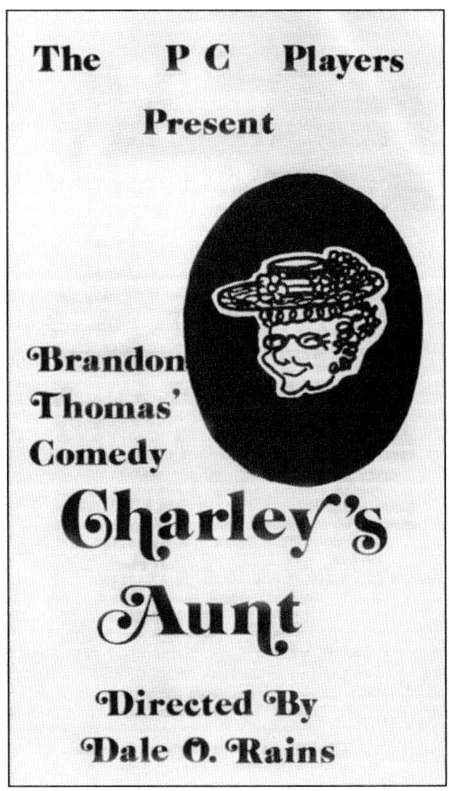


**Theater program.** *Charley's Aunt* was one of many plays directed by Dale Rains before his retirement in 2001. (Courtesy of Presbyterian College Archives.)

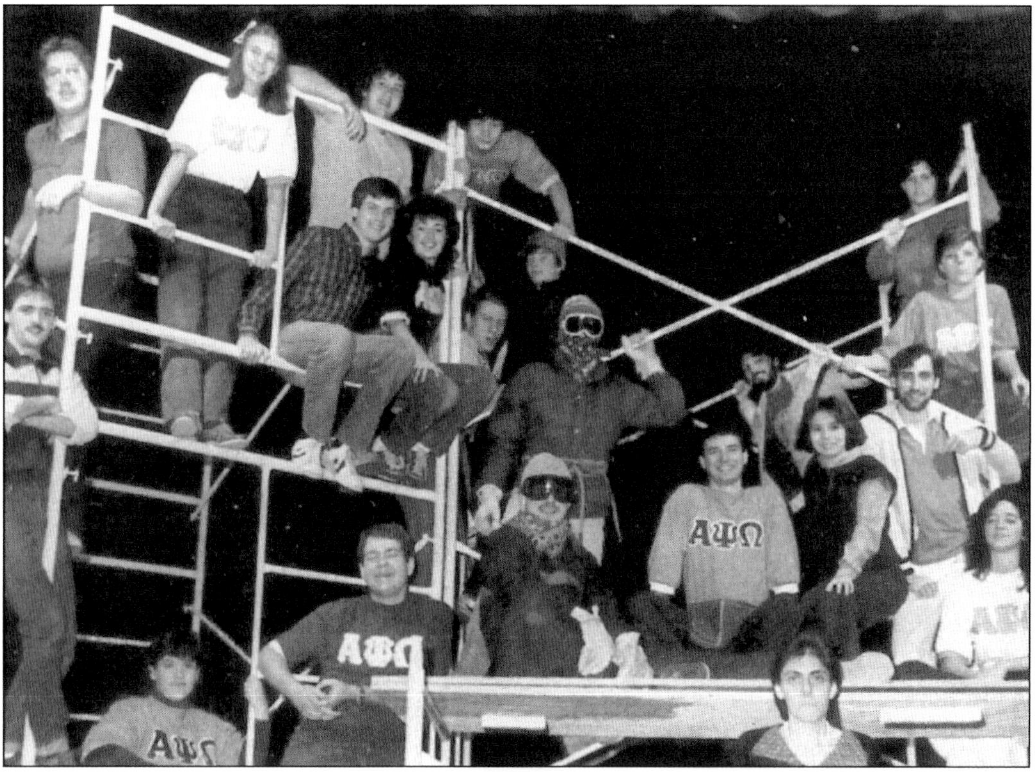

**PC Players, 1985.** Included in this photograph are Kevin Little, Paul Abernathy, Jenny Walstor, John Ladd, Todd White, Missy Gaston, Robert Gettys, Chris Bates, Michael Streeter, Bill Cunningham, Joe Alexander, Pam Walker, Donna Jarvis, Kathy Holliday, Mary Rogers, Danny Roberts, Kari Needham, and Jackie Gingrich. (Courtesy of Presbyterian College Public Relations Office.)

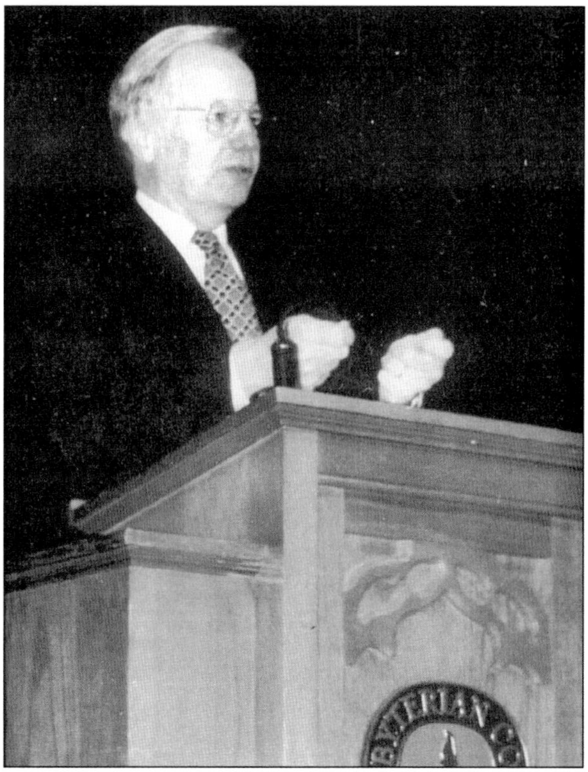

**Russell Program.** The Russell Program, founded in 1986, focuses on issues involving the media and mass communication. Over the years it has brought many notables to campus, including Bill Moyers. (Courtesy of Presbyterian College Public Relations Office.)

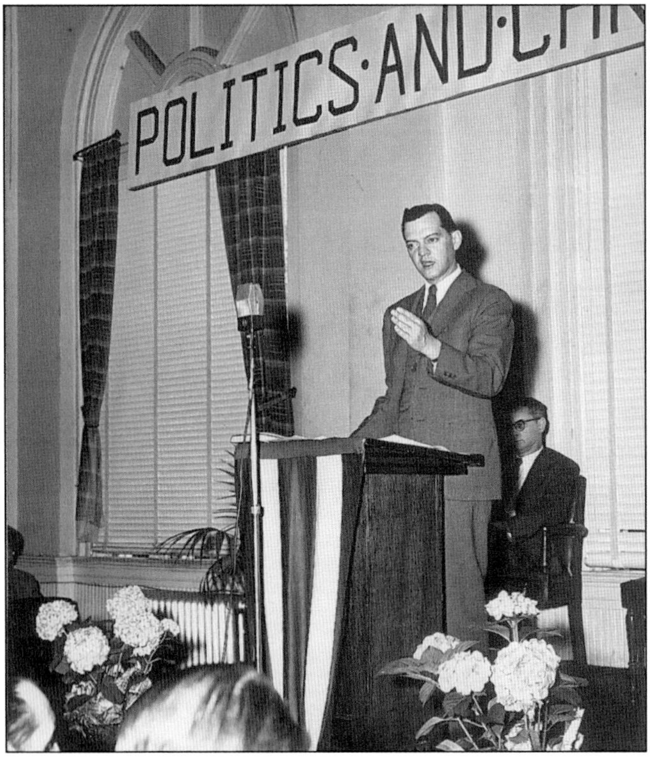

**POLITICAL EMPHASIS WEEK, 1950.** This yearly event, sponsored by the International Relations Club, featured nationally known speakers. The purpose of the club was to stimulate interest in world affairs and promote better international understanding. (Courtesy of Presbyterian College Archives.)

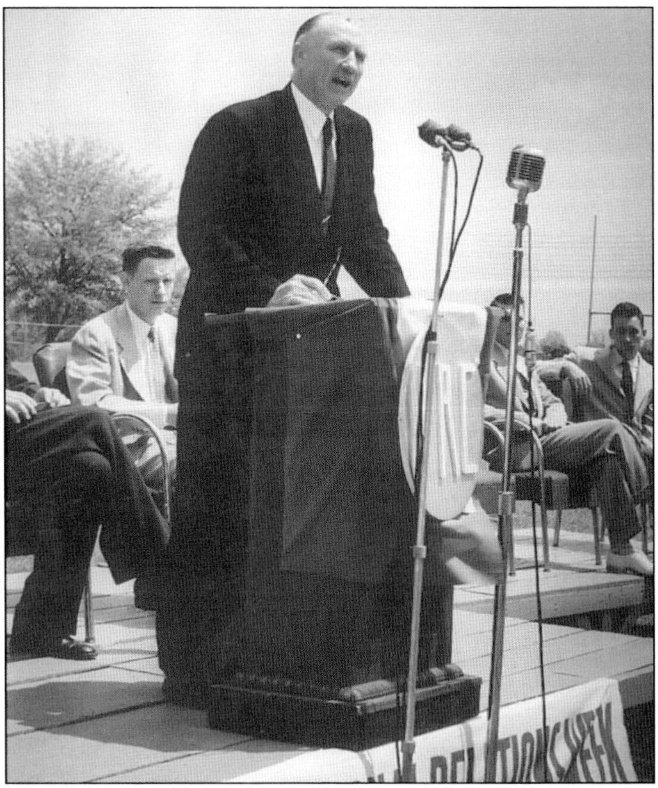

**INTERNATIONAL RELATIONS WEEK.** Strom Thurmond, current president pro tempore of the U.S. Senate and former governor of South Carolina, was the speaker for International Relations Week in 1955. (Courtesy of Presbyterian College Archives.)

**EARLY COMMENCEMENT PROGRAM.** Early commencement exercises were often combined with meetings of the Board of Trustees and featured debaters' and disclaimers' contests and an alumni oration. (Courtesy of Presbyterian College Archives.)

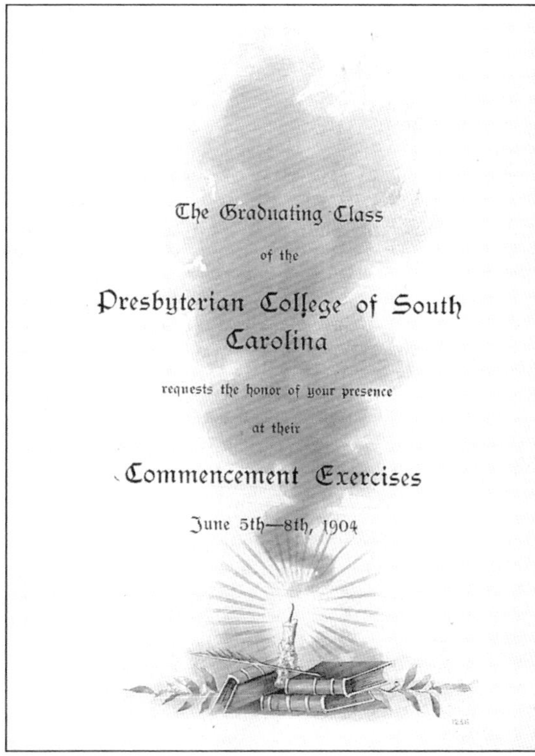

The Graduating Class

of the

Presbyterian College of South Carolina

requests the honor of your presence

at their

Commencement Exercises

June 5th—8th, 1904

**COMMENCEMENT, 1940s.** For many years, commencement was held in an outdoor chapel on the college campus. (Courtesy of Presbyterian College Archives.)

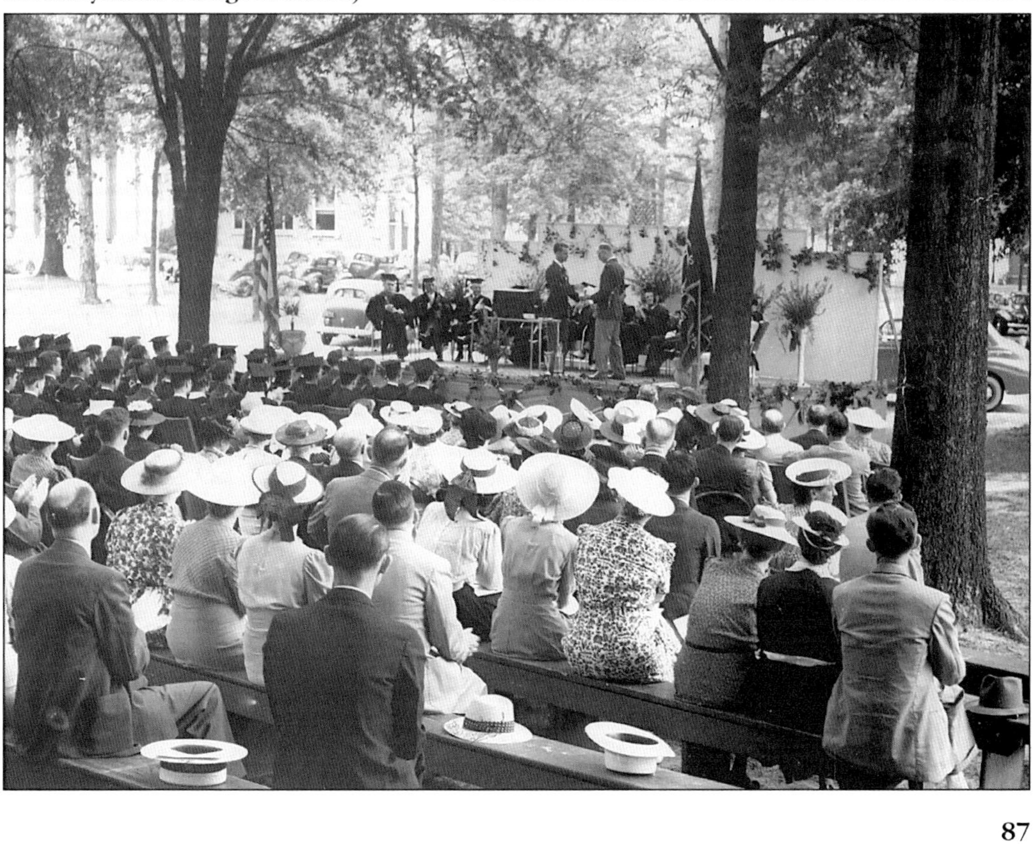

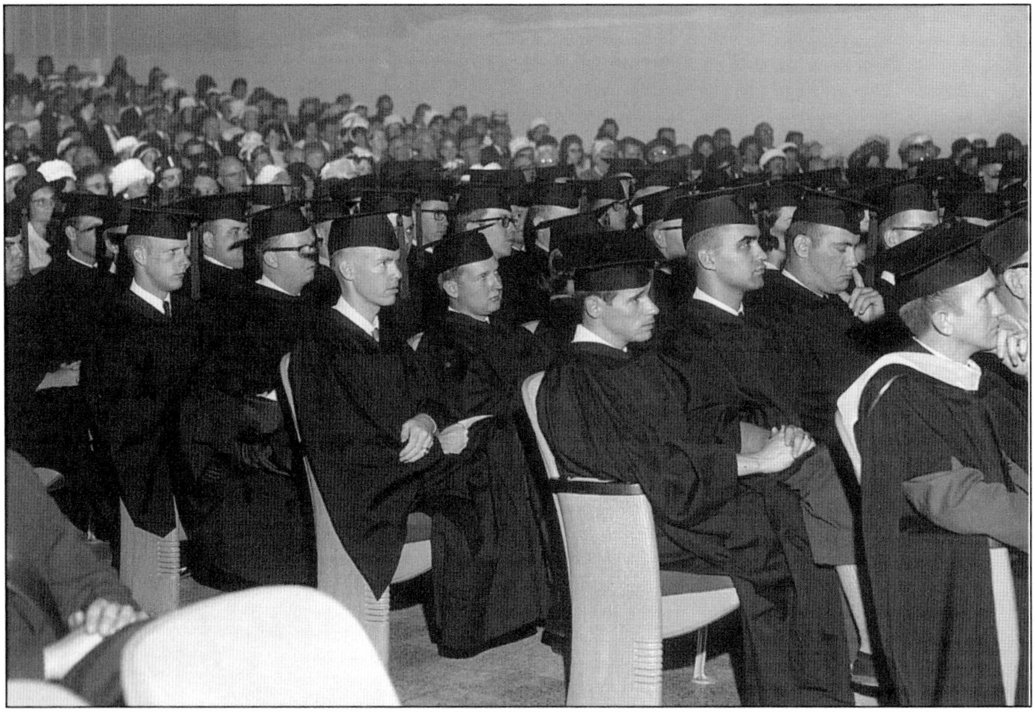

COMMENCEMENT, **1964**. Between 1961 and 1992, ceremonies were held indoors. This is a photograph of a 1964 ceremony that was held in Belk Auditorium. (Courtesy of Presbyterian College Archives.)

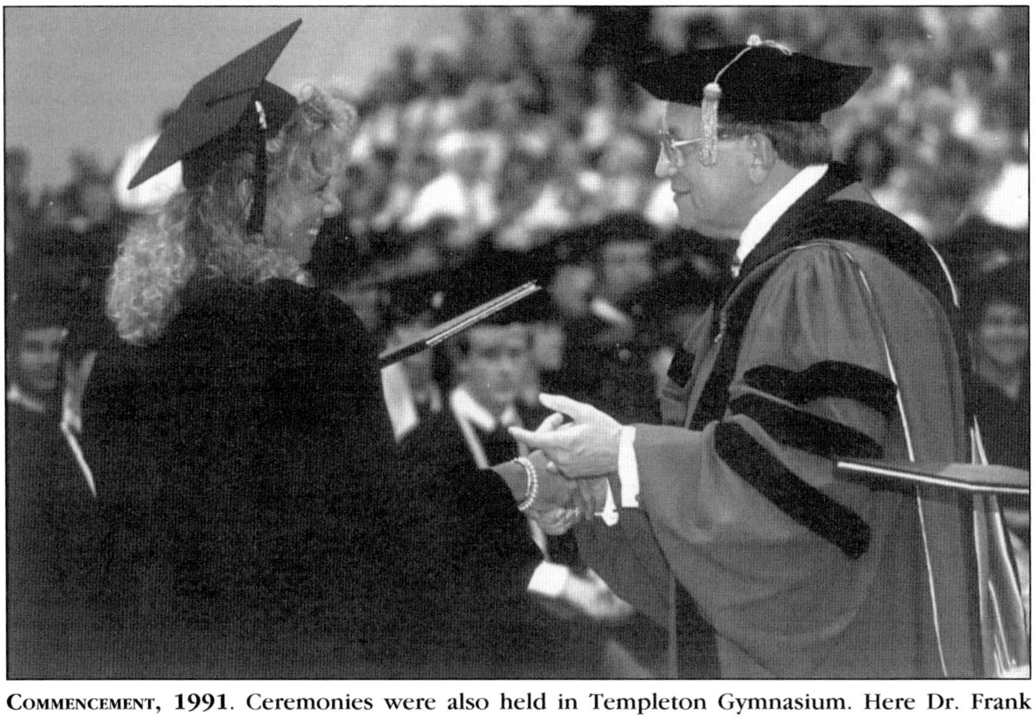

COMMENCEMENT, **1991**. Ceremonies were also held in Templeton Gymnasium. Here Dr. Frank Harrington presents a diploma to a 1991 graduate. (Courtesy of Presbyterian College Archives.)

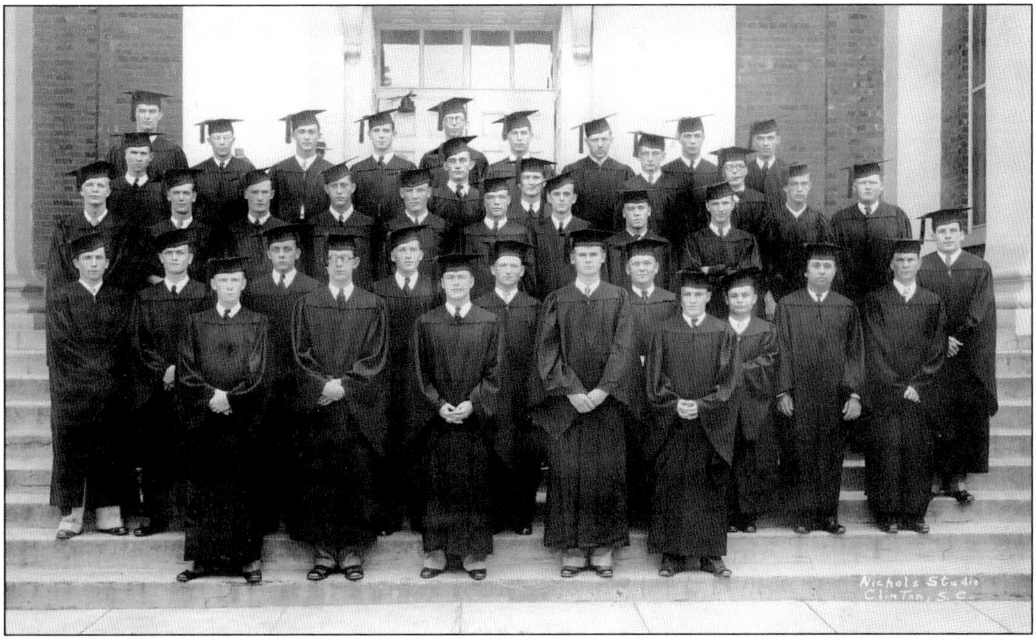


**CLASS OF 1931.** This all-male class graduated in 1931. Among notable campus figures that year were "Most Popular Professor" Capt. R.E. Wysor; "Most Cheerful Student" J.I. Copeland; and R.M. Lynn, who was voted "Best Sport," "Most Promising," "Best All-Round Athlete," and "Best All-Round Man." (Courtesy of Presbyterian College Archives.)

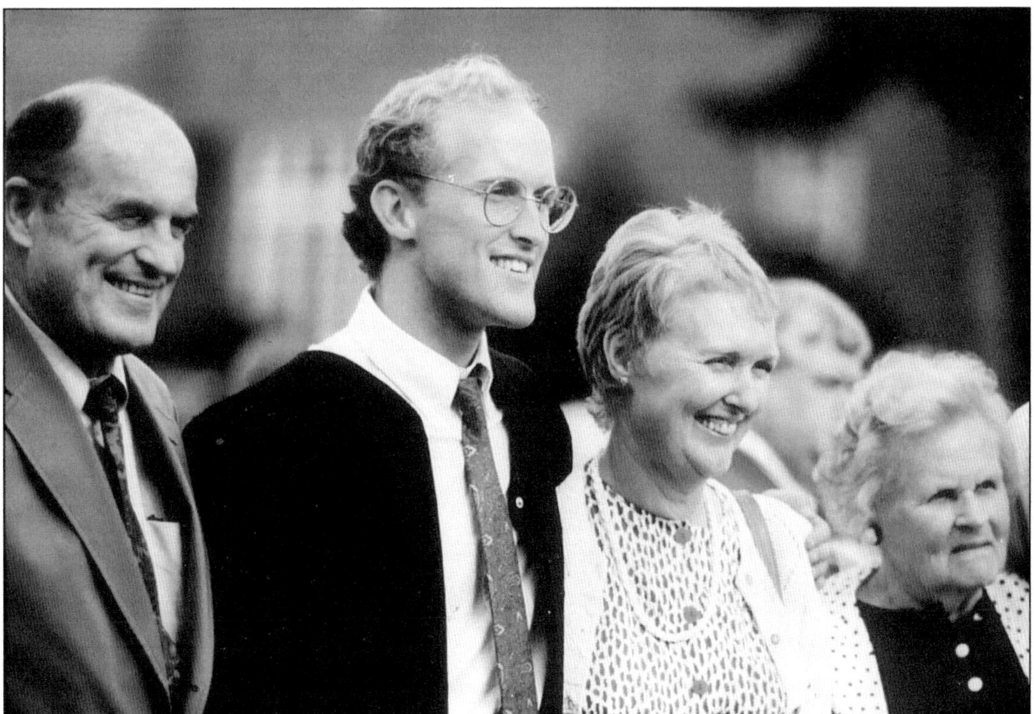

**A HAPPY GRADUATE.** Here a happy PC graduate poses with his family in 1990. (Courtesy of Presbyterian College Archives.)

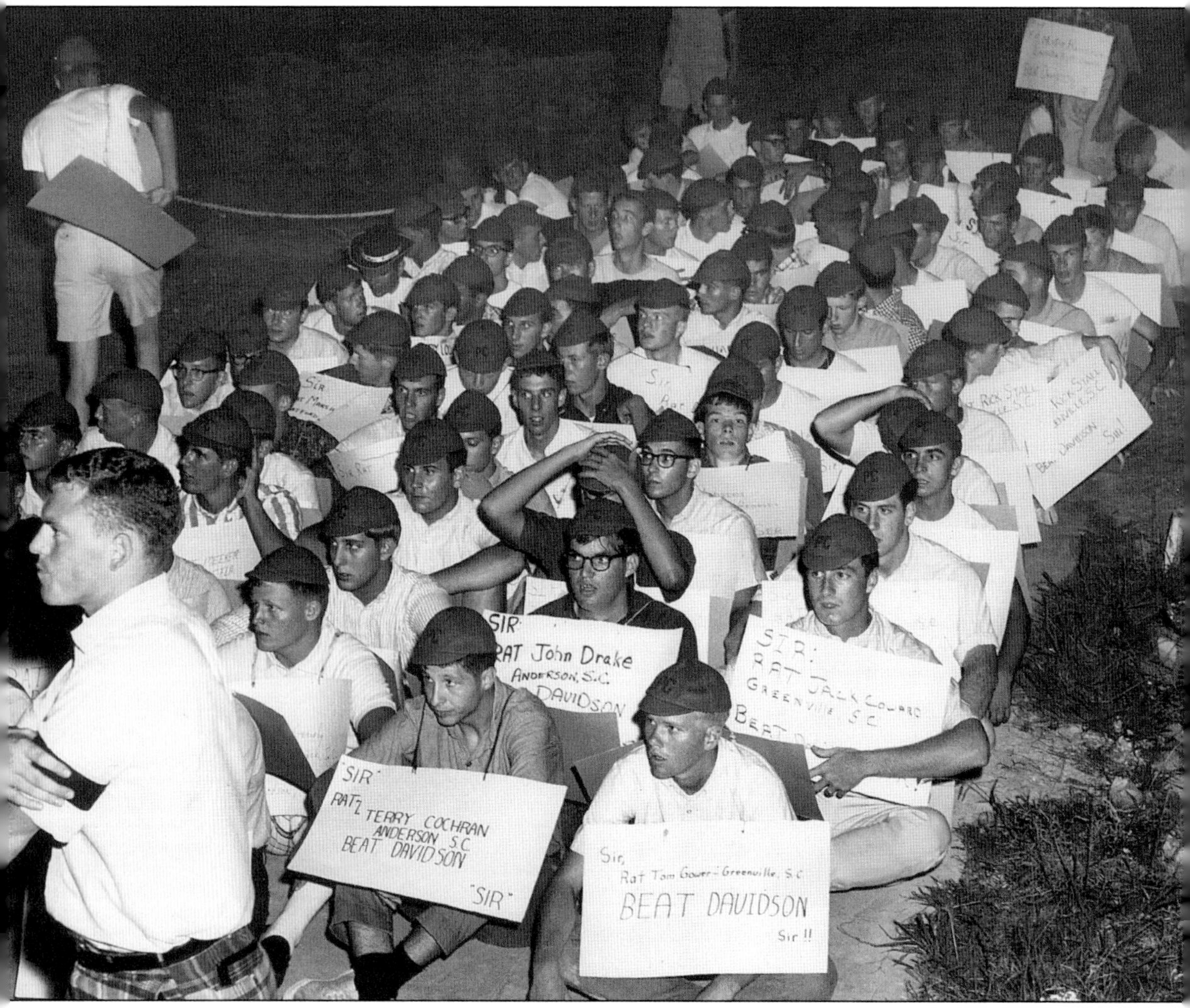


**Freshman "Rat Season," 1965.** From the early part of the century, freshmen were subjected to a mild form of hazing called "ratting." Here, students line up in their "rat hats" holding signs. (Courtesy of Presbyterian College Archives.)

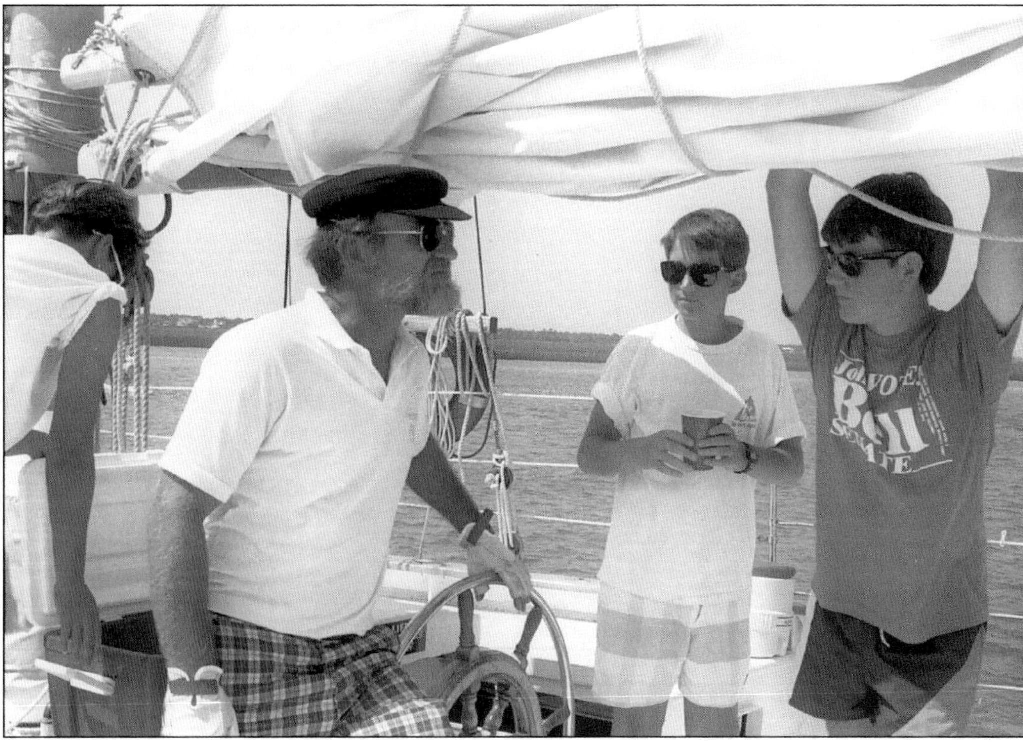

**Freshman Sailing Trip, 1990.** Eventually, other activities were added to the orientation schedule. One of the more popular was the summer sailing trip, established in 1989. Here Everett Catts and Max Vallotta are pictured with "Captain Bob." (Courtesy of Presbyterian College Archives.)

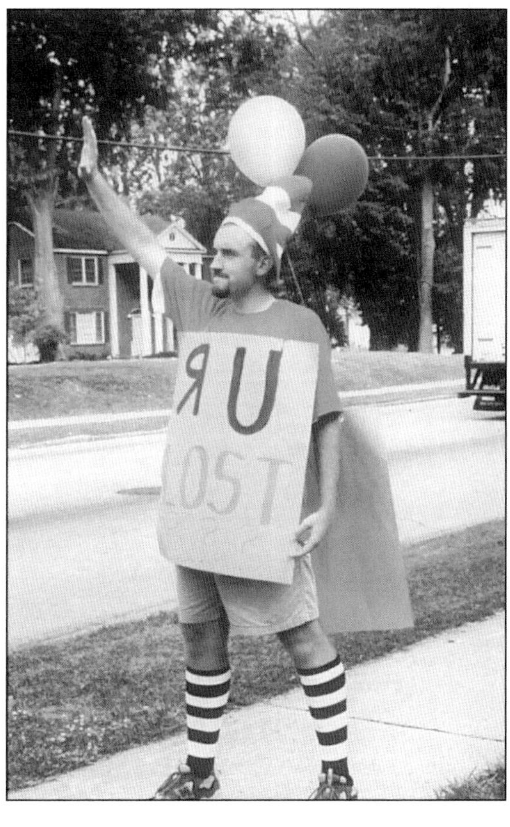

**Freshman Orientation, 2000.** In recent years, orientation leaders have developed imaginative ways to welcome arriving freshmen and their parents. (Courtesy of Presbyterian College Public Relations Office.)

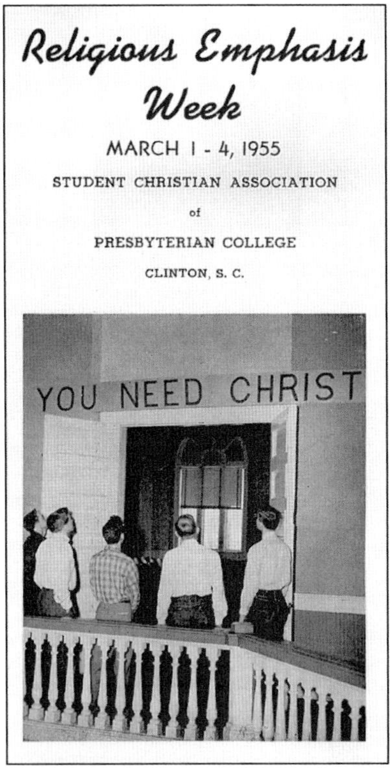


**RELIGIOUS EMPHASIS WEEK.** Religious Emphasis Week was held annually for many years. Designed to examine the Christian way of life, programs featured outstanding Christian laymen and ministers. Winter Conference eventually replaced the weeklong event in 1971. (Courtesy of Presbyterian College Archives.)

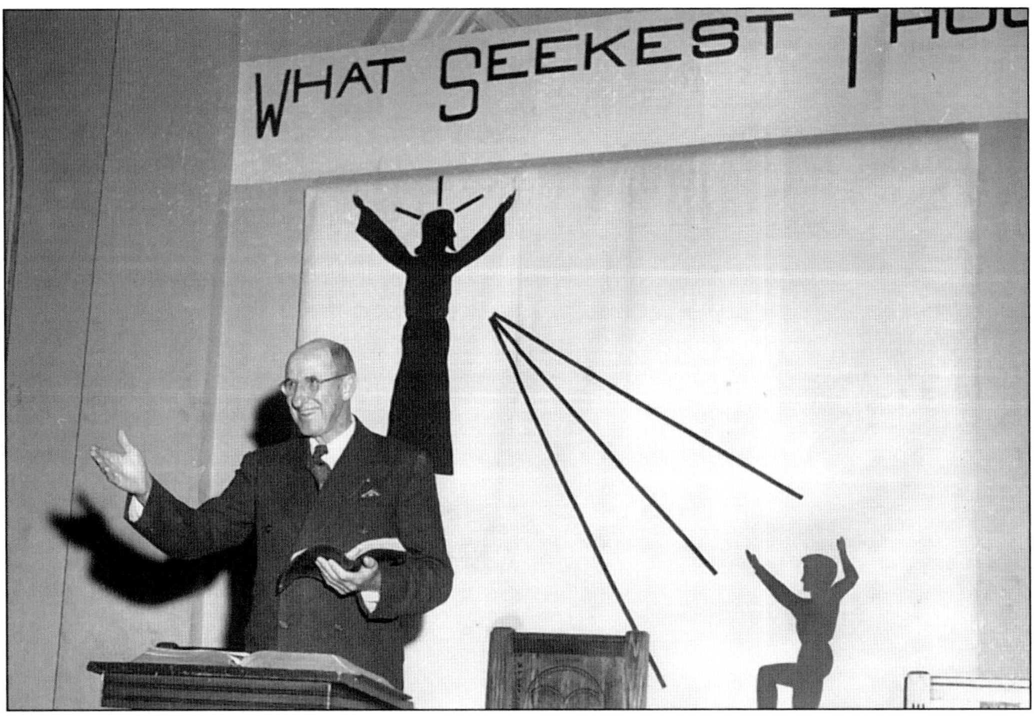


**FORMER PRES. JOHN MCSWEEN.** Former Pres. John McSween speaks at Religious Emphasis Week in 1956. (Courtesy of Presbyterian College Archives.)

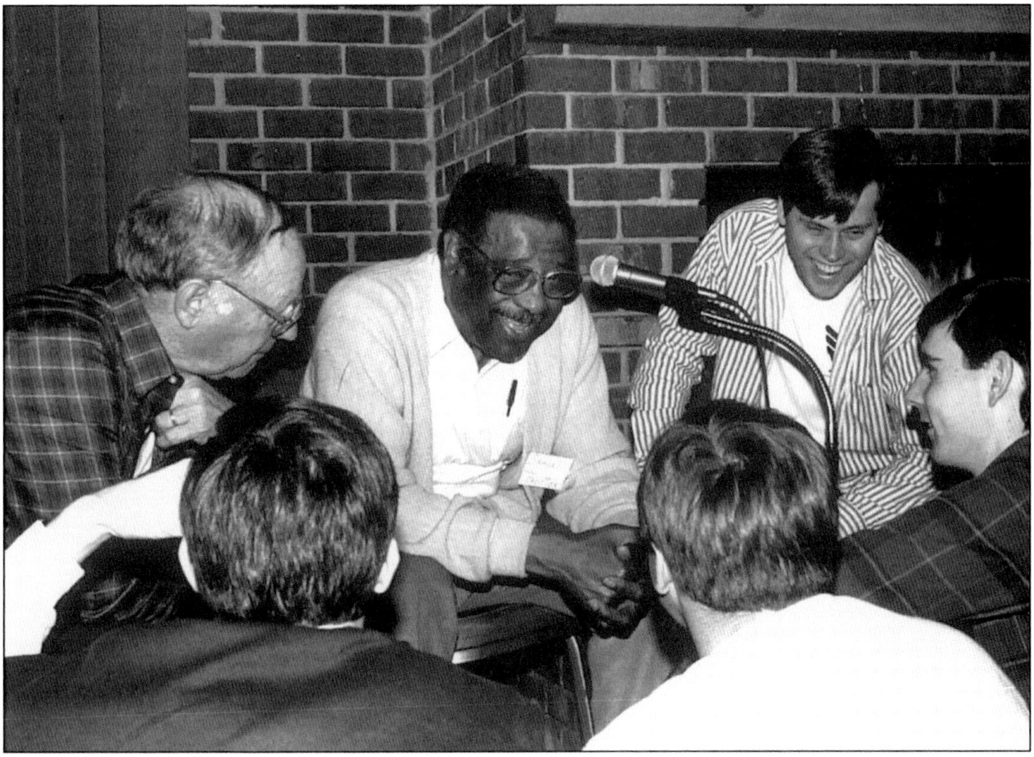

**Samuel Proctor.** Samuel Proctor leads Winter Conference at Camp Bethelwood in 1990. This popular weekend retreat for staff and students features well-known speakers, recreation, and fellowship. (Courtesy of Presbyterian College Archives.)

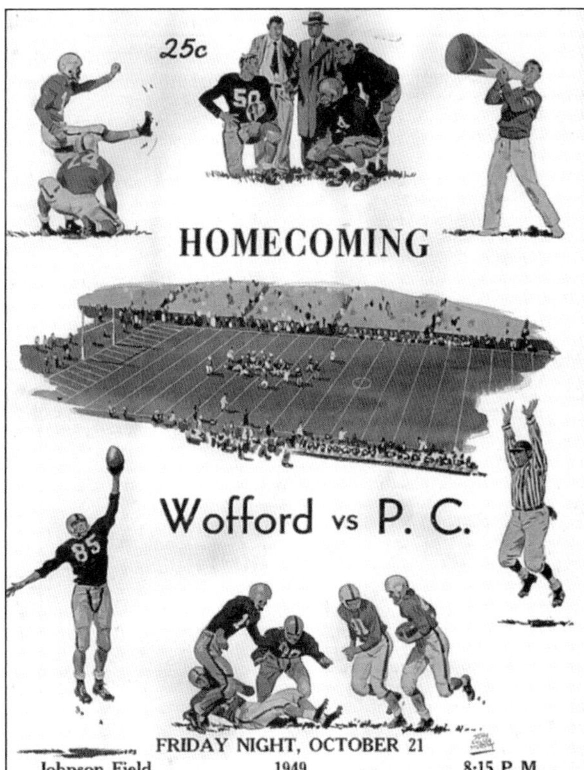


**Homecoming.** Homecoming was held at PC as early as 1929. (Courtesy of Presbyterian College Archives.)

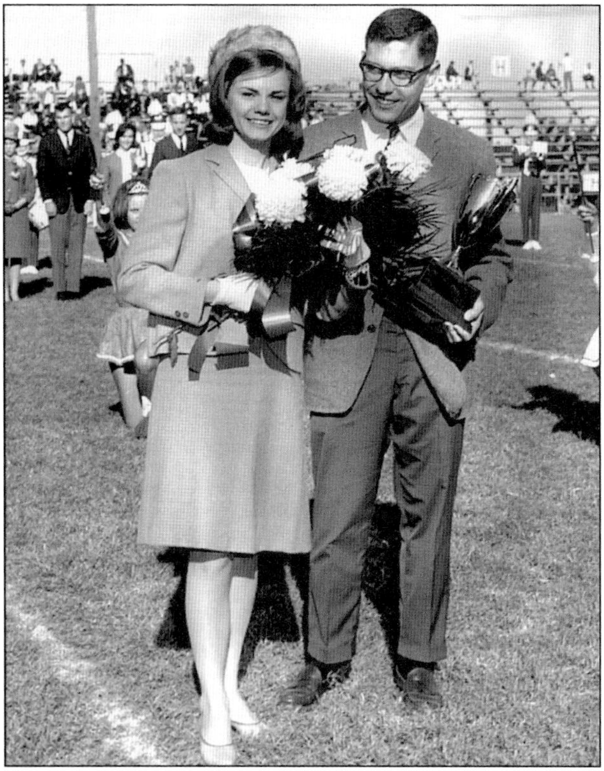

**Homecoming, 1964.** Even before the college became fully coeducational in 1965, homecoming queens were crowned. Here, Larue Gording of Limestone College is crowned in 1964. (Courtesy of Presbyterian College Archives.)

**Queen Amelia.** Gov. Robert McNair, Henry Lovett, and Pres. Marc Weersing crown homecoming queen Amelia Nichols in 1965. (Courtesy of Presbyterian College Archives.)

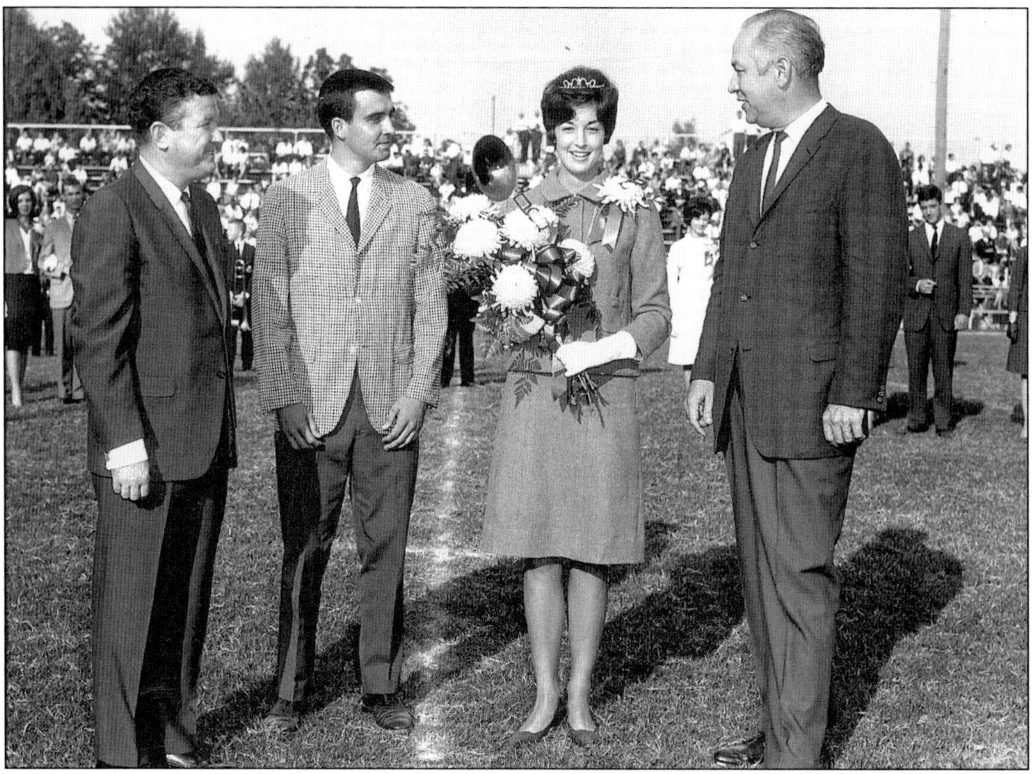

**HOMECOMING DISPLAY, 1954.** For many years, fraternities built elaborate displays before the homecoming game. (Courtesy of Presbyterian College Archives.)

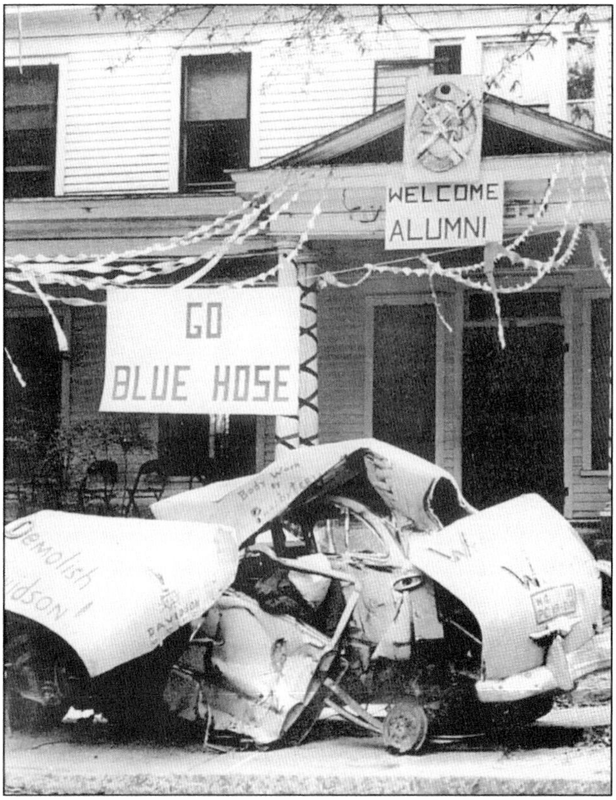


**HOMECOMING QUEEN AND ESCORT.** Vanessa McAlister and her escort Tyler Hudson circle the stadium at the homecoming football game, *c.* 1994. (Courtesy of Presbyterian College Archives.)

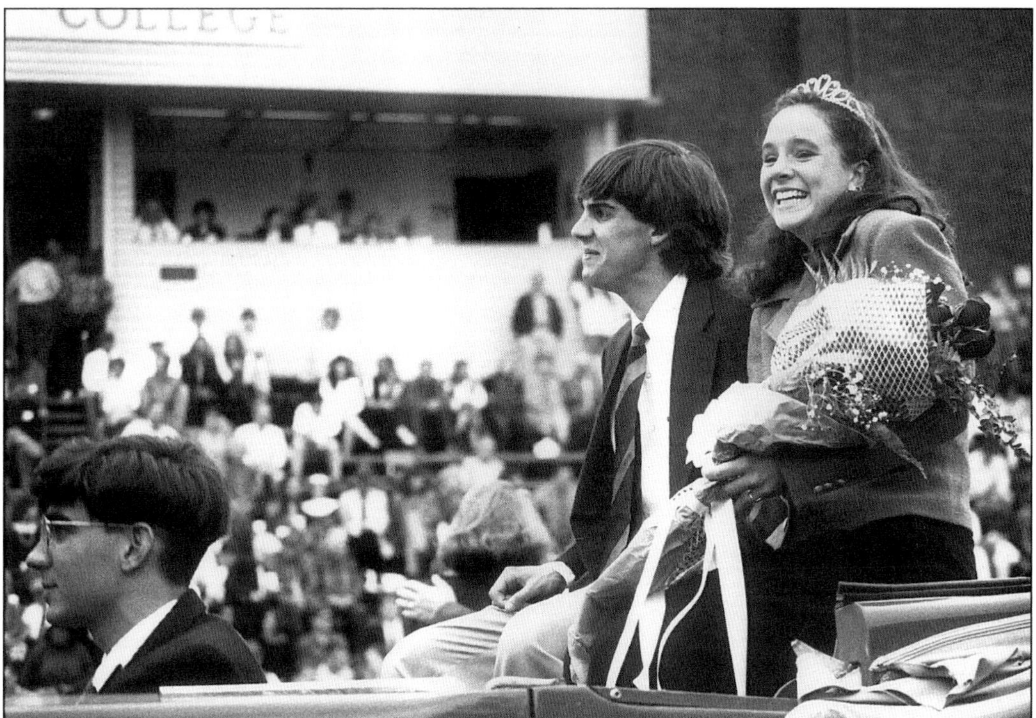

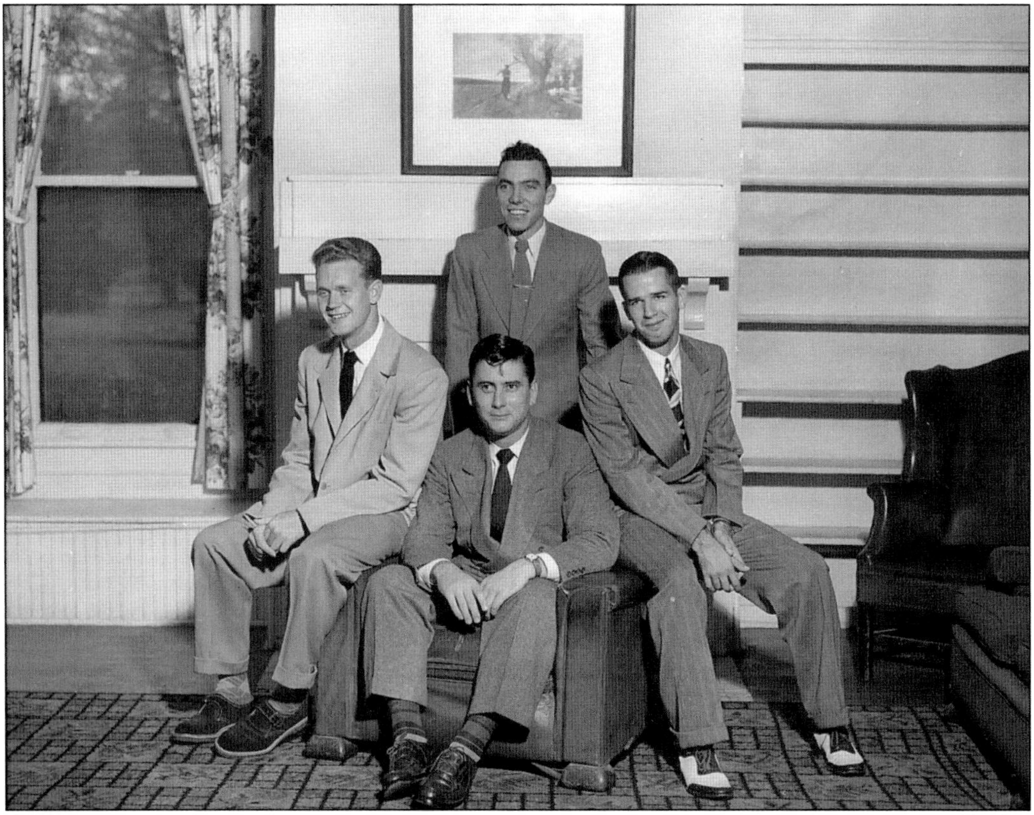

**JUNIOR CLASS OFFICERS, 1948–1949.** Pictured are Claude Howe, William Haithcock, H.L. Giles, and Ferdinand Jacobs. (Courtesy of Presbyterian College Archives.)

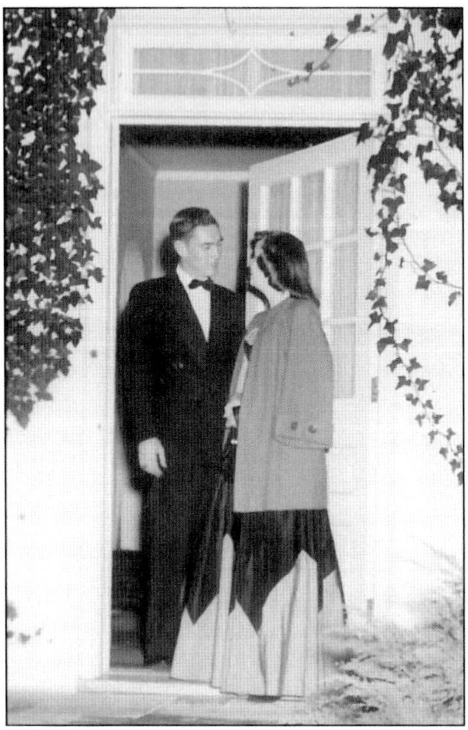

**"OPERATION FORMAL," 1948.** Ben Ivey picks up his date Kent Wysor in 1948. They later married, and he returned to PC to serve as professor of military science and dean of students. (Courtesy of Presbyterian College Archives.)

**Who's Who, 1957.** Elected to Who's Who in American Colleges and Universities in 1957 were, from left to right, T. Reeves, R. Veal, M. Tobias, C. Dukes, J. Hancock, and J. Finley (kneeling). (Courtesy of Presbyterian College Archives.)

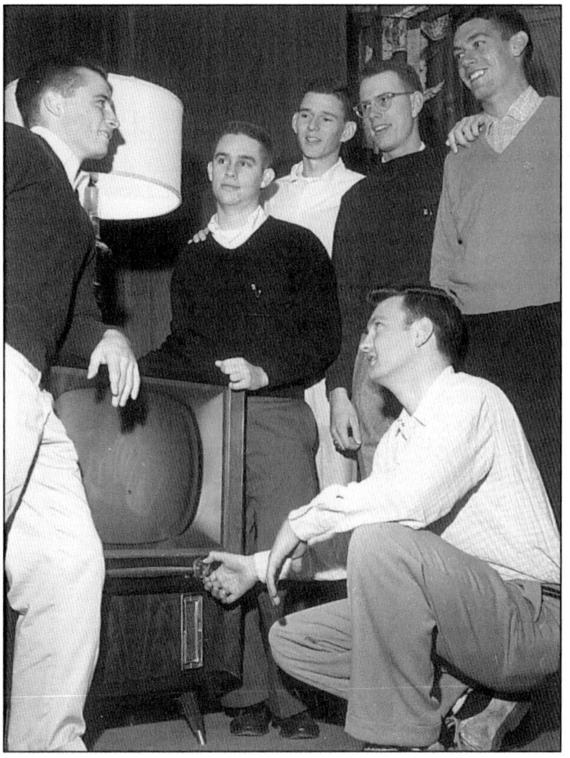

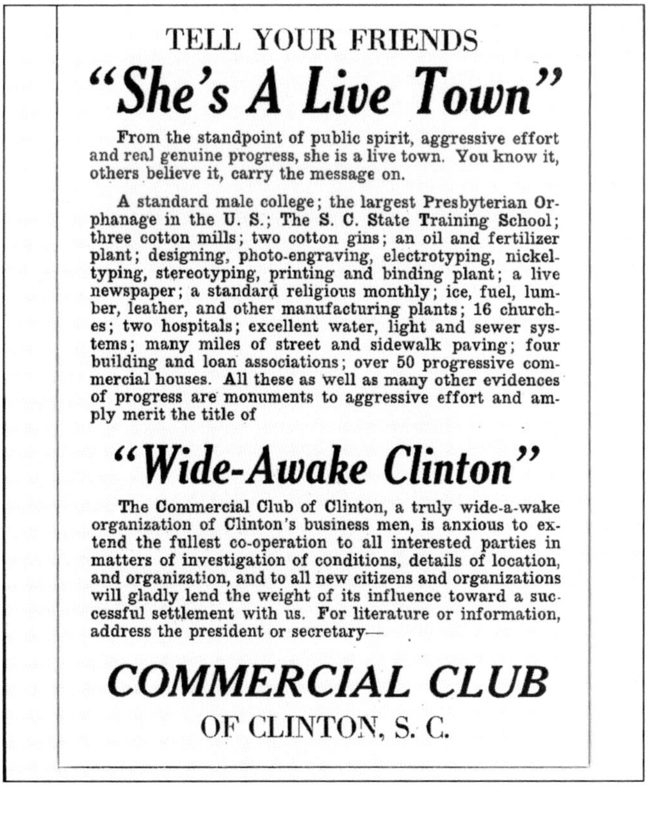

TELL YOUR FRIENDS

"She's A Live Town"

From the standpoint of public spirit, aggressive effort and real genuine progress, she is a live town. You know it, others believe it, carry the message on.

A standard male college; the largest Presbyterian Orphanage in the U. S.; The S. C. State Training School; three cotton mills; two cotton gins; an oil and fertilizer plant; designing, photo-engraving, electrotyping, nickeltyping, stereotyping, printing and binding plant; a live newspaper; a standard religious monthly; ice, fuel, lumber, leather, and other manufacturing plants; 16 churches; two hospitals; excellent water, light and sewer systems; many miles of street and sidewalk paving; four building and loan associations; over 50 progressive commercial houses. All these as well as many other evidences of progress are monuments to aggressive effort and amply merit the title of

"Wide-Awake Clinton"

The Commercial Club of Clinton, a truly wide-a-wake organization of Clinton's business men, is anxious to extend the fullest co-operation to all interested parties in matters of investigation of conditions, details of location, and organization, and to all new citizens and organizations will gladly lend the weight of its influence toward a successful settlement with us. For literature or information, address the president or secretary—

COMMERCIAL CLUB

OF CLINTON, S. C.

**Clinton, 1923.** Undoubtedly, many students over the years have disagreed with this assessment of Clinton. (Courtesy of 1923 *PaC SaC*.)

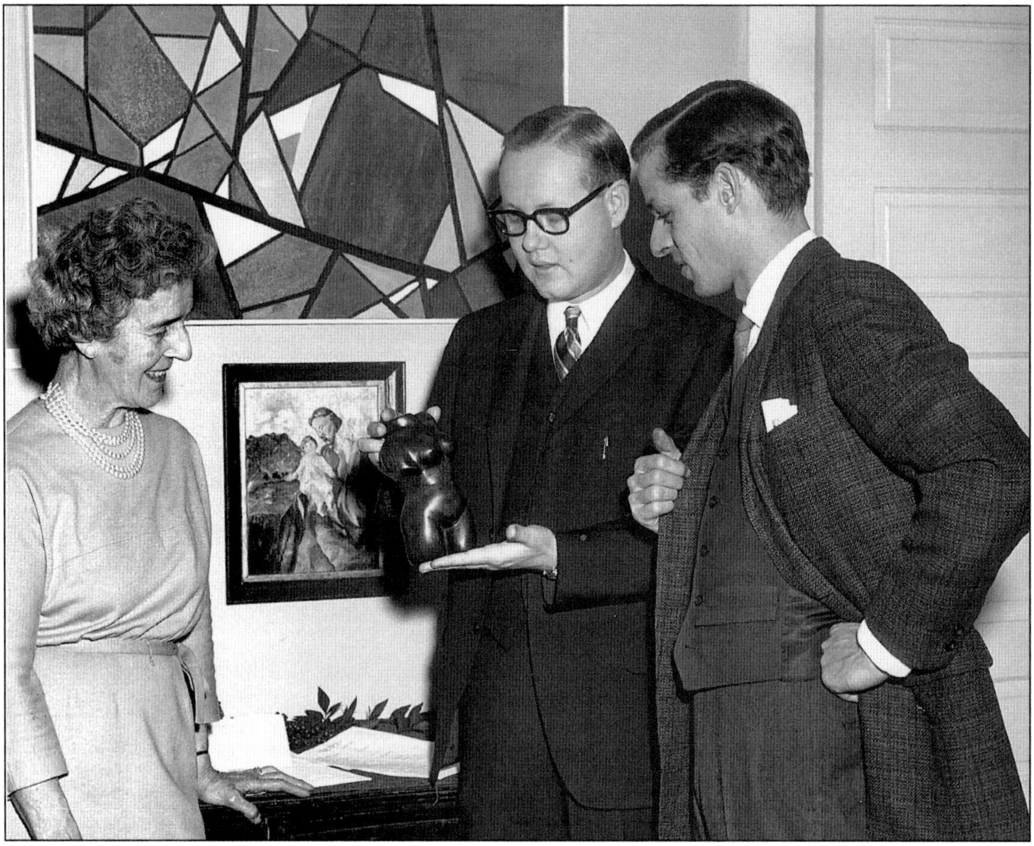

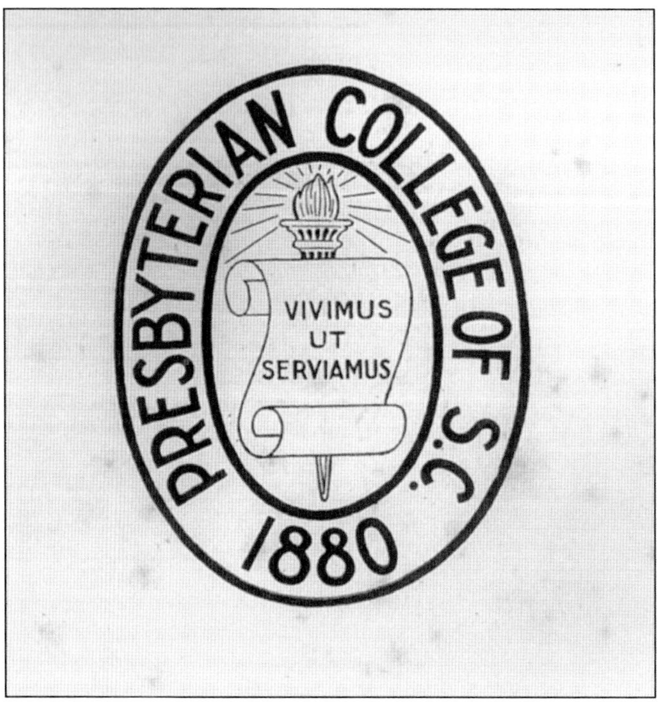


**Fine Arts.** Mrs. Edouard Patte, Prof. Carl J. Freeman, and Prof. Tony Brown examine a piece of sculpture at at the Second Annual Fine Arts Exhibit held in 1964. (Courtesy of Presbyterian College Archives.)

**Living to Serve.** This is the 1916 version of the college's seal. The motto now reads "Dum Vivimus Servimus," and expresses a central tenet of the PC education: the preparation of students for lives of service. (Courtesy of 1916 *PaC SaC*.)

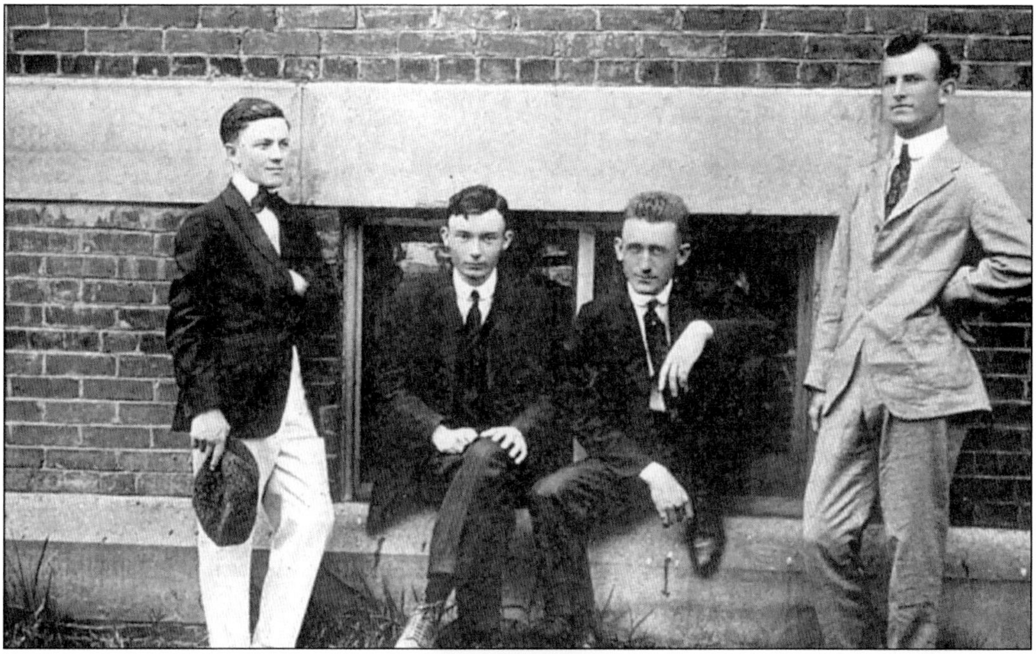

**Student Volunteer Band, 1917.** Members of this early precursor to Student Volunteer Services included W.B. Anderson, P.P. Boggs, S.W. Dendy, and J.W. Moore. (Courtesy of 1916 *PaC SaC*.)

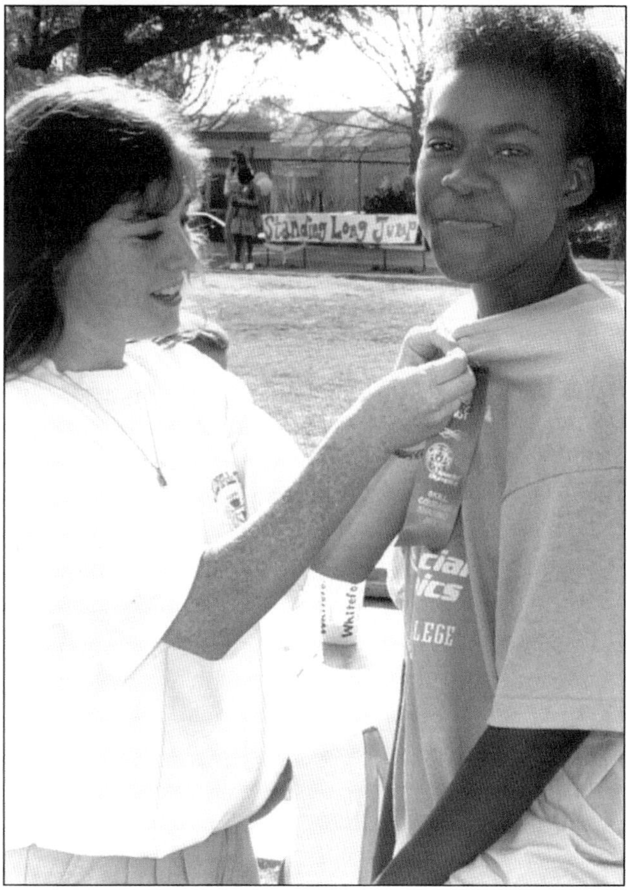


**Special Olympics.** Student Volunteer Services was organized in 1967 with the establishment of a joint program with Todd Memorial Church in Laurens. Since 1974, SVS has sponsored the Special Olympics at the college. Here a winner receives her ribbon in 1992. (Courtesy of Presbyterian College Archives.)

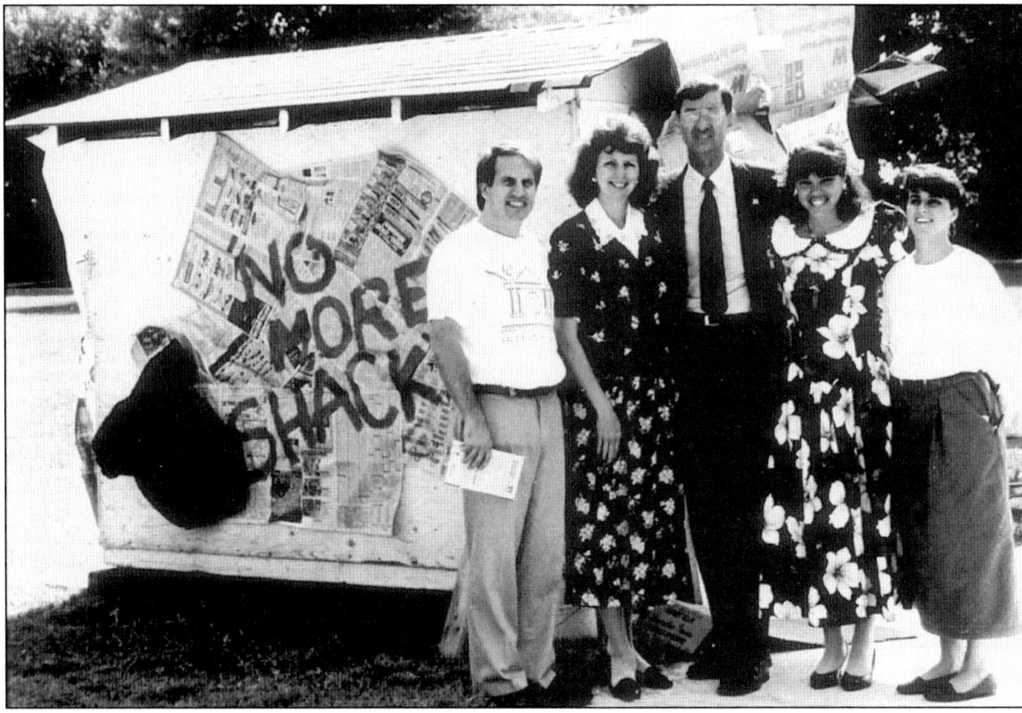


**HABITAT FOR HUMANITY.** Greg Henley (chaplain), Rhonda Peck, and Mary Ellen Vernon are seen with Habitat founders Millard and Linda Fuller in this 1990 photograph. (Courtesy of Presbyterian College Public Relations Office.)

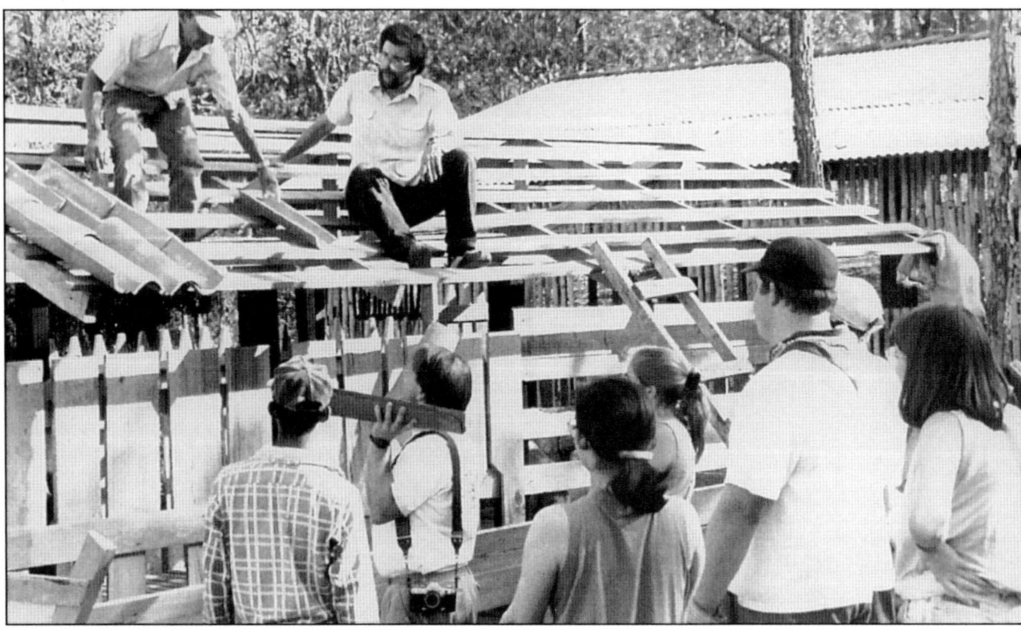

**SPRING BREAK SERVICE PROJECT, HONDURAS.** Here a group of PC students works on a construction project in cooperation with the Christian Commission for Development in 1992. Seated on the roof is Prof. Charles McKelvey. In the foreground with the camera is Chaplain Greg Henley. (Courtesy of Presbyterian College Public Relations Office.)

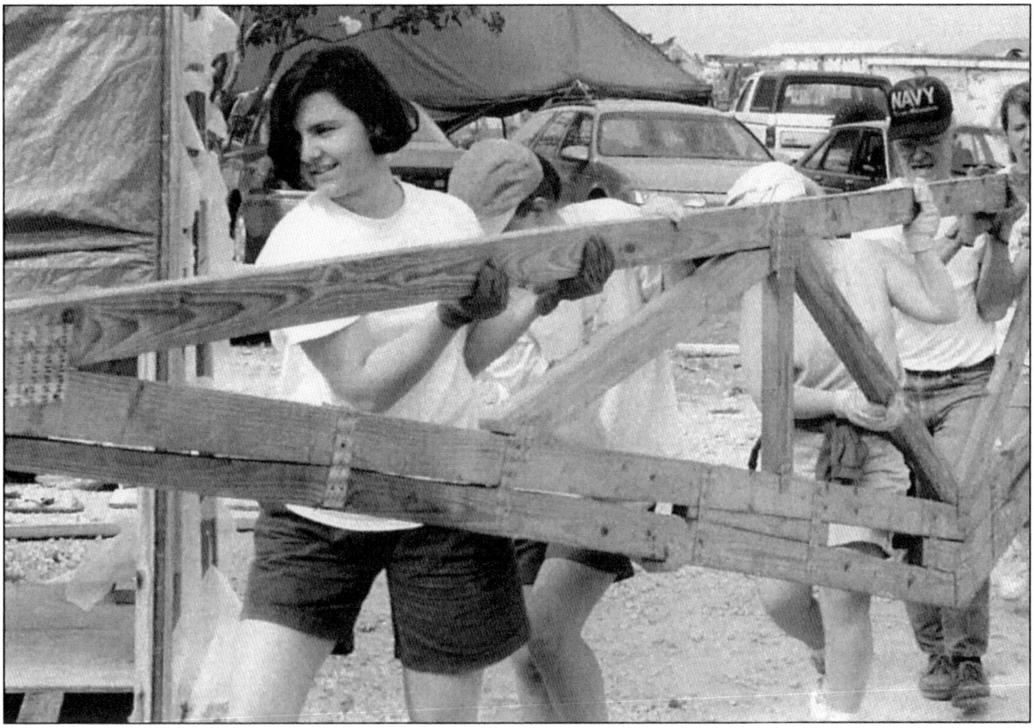


**Hurricane Andrew Relief, 1993.** Students traveled to Florida to help residents recover from Hurricane Andrew in 1993. (Courtesy of Presbyterian College Public Relations Office.)

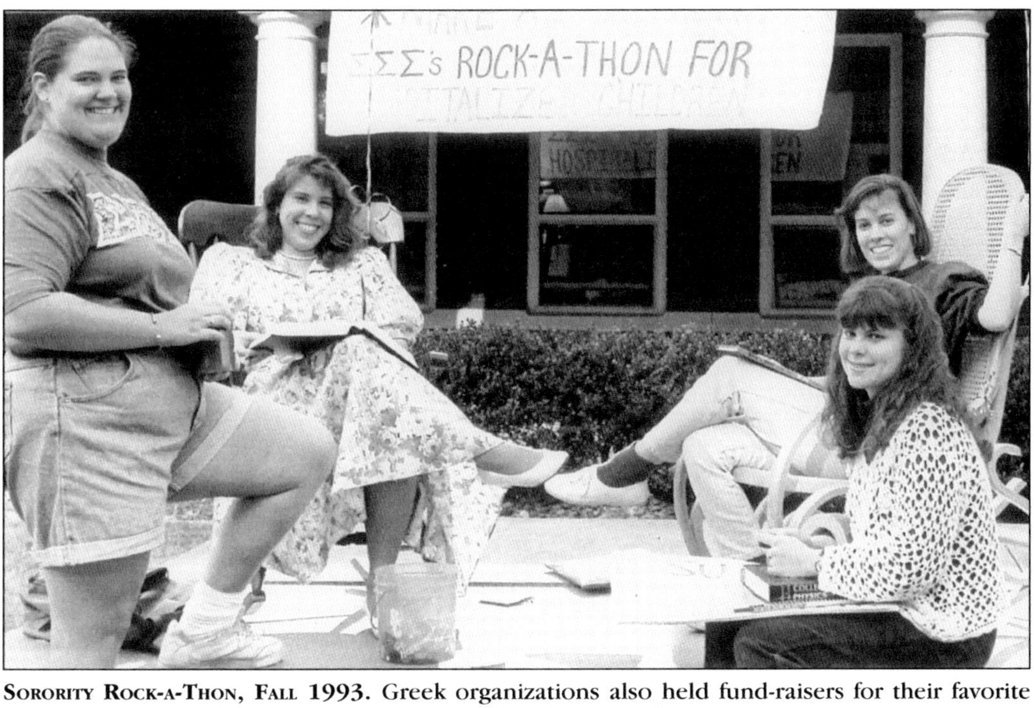


**Sorority Rock-a-Thon, Fall 1993.** Greek organizations also held fund-raisers for their favorite causes. (Courtesy of Presbyterian College Public Relations Office.)

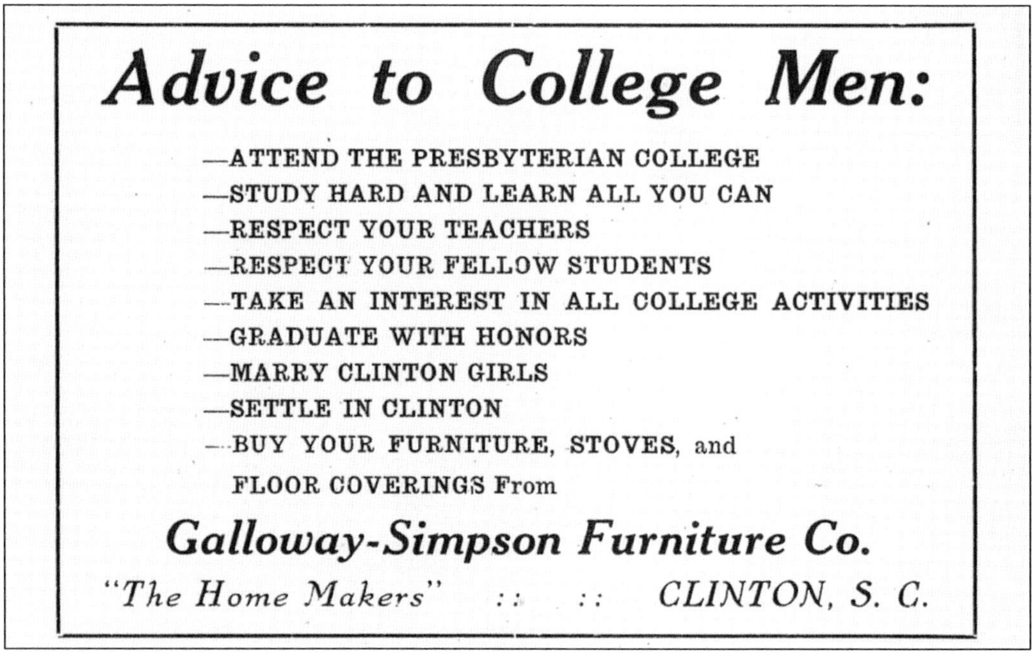


**ADVICE TO COLLEGE MEN, 1923.** Many students followed this advice, including the admonition to "marry Clinton girls." (Courtesy of 1923 *PaC SaC*.)

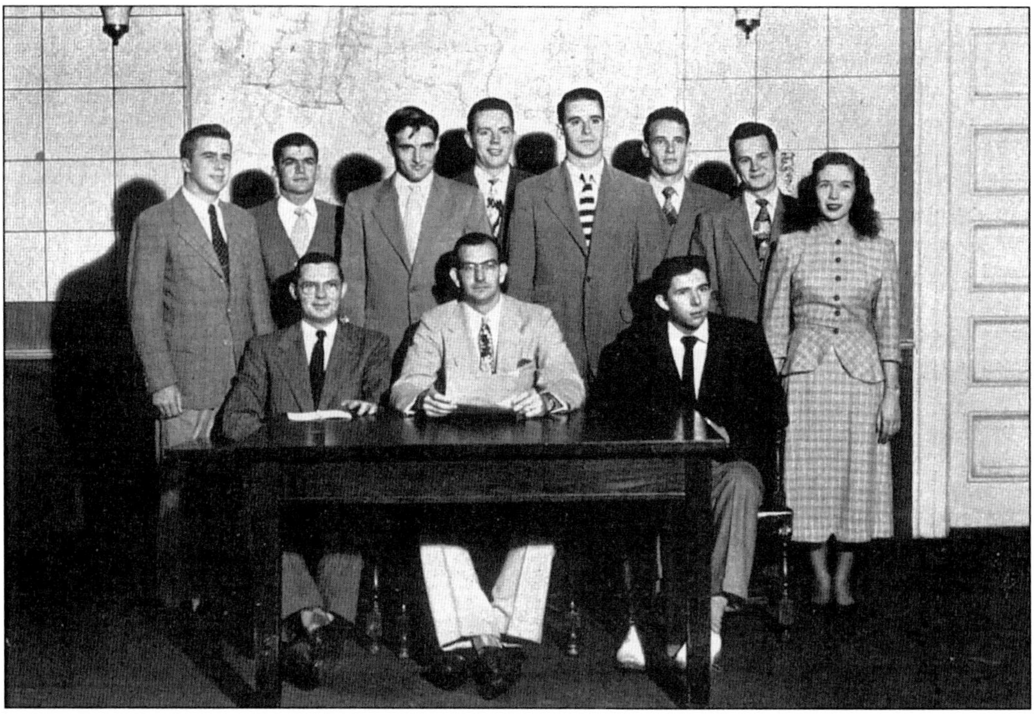

**STUDENT COUNCIL, 1948–1949.** For many years, a Student Council, made up of the officers of the student body and the class officers, governed students. From left to right are (seated) Hodge, Little, and Quick; (standing) Callahan, Copley, Watts, Tedards, Watt, Somerville, Johnston, and Hughes. (Courtesy of 1949 *PaC SaC*.)

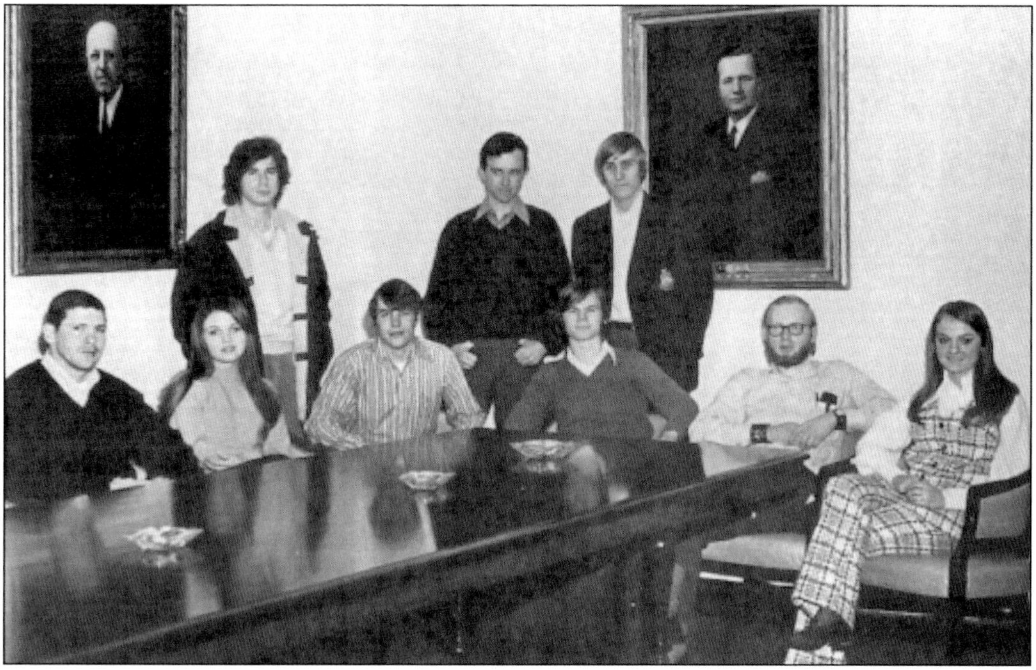

**Honor Council, 1970–1971.** PC has had a student honor code for almost a century. The Student Council, the Honor Council, and the Judiciary Council have administered it at different times. Shown from left to right are (seated) Elliott Poss, Cile Trippe, John Southern (chairman), Tim Chamberlain, Ted Tate, and Elaine Parker; (standing) Ed Dawson, Bill Brearley, and Rick Wilson. (Courtesy of 1971 *PaC SaC*.)

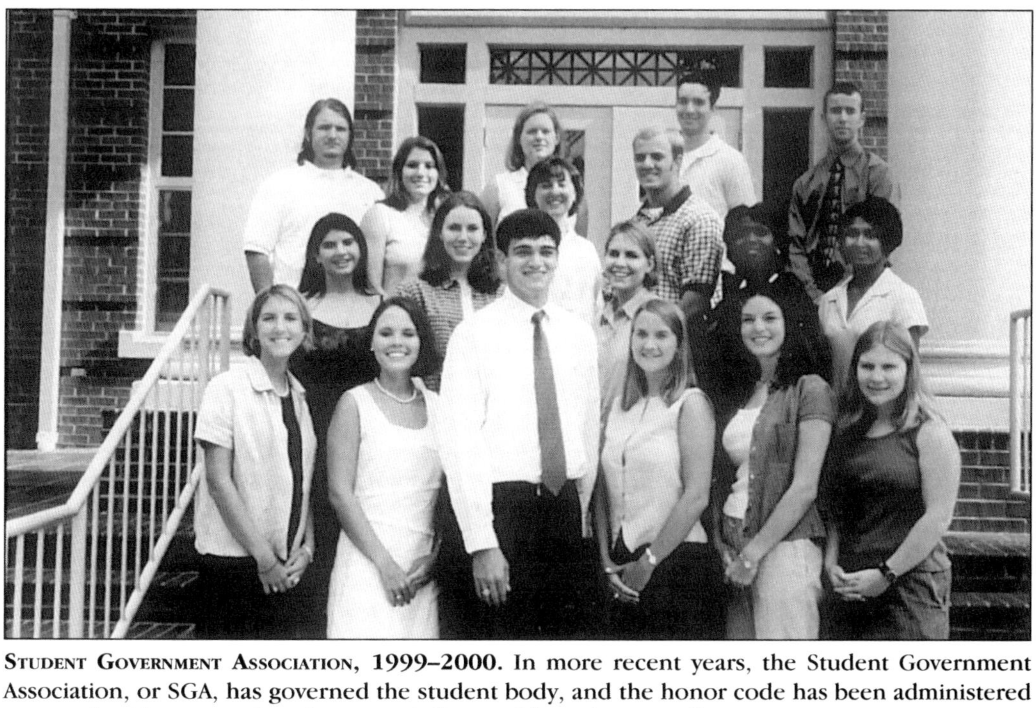

**Student Government Association, 1999–2000.** In more recent years, the Student Government Association, or SGA, has governed the student body, and the honor code has been administered separately. (Courtesy of Presbyterian College Public Relations Office.)

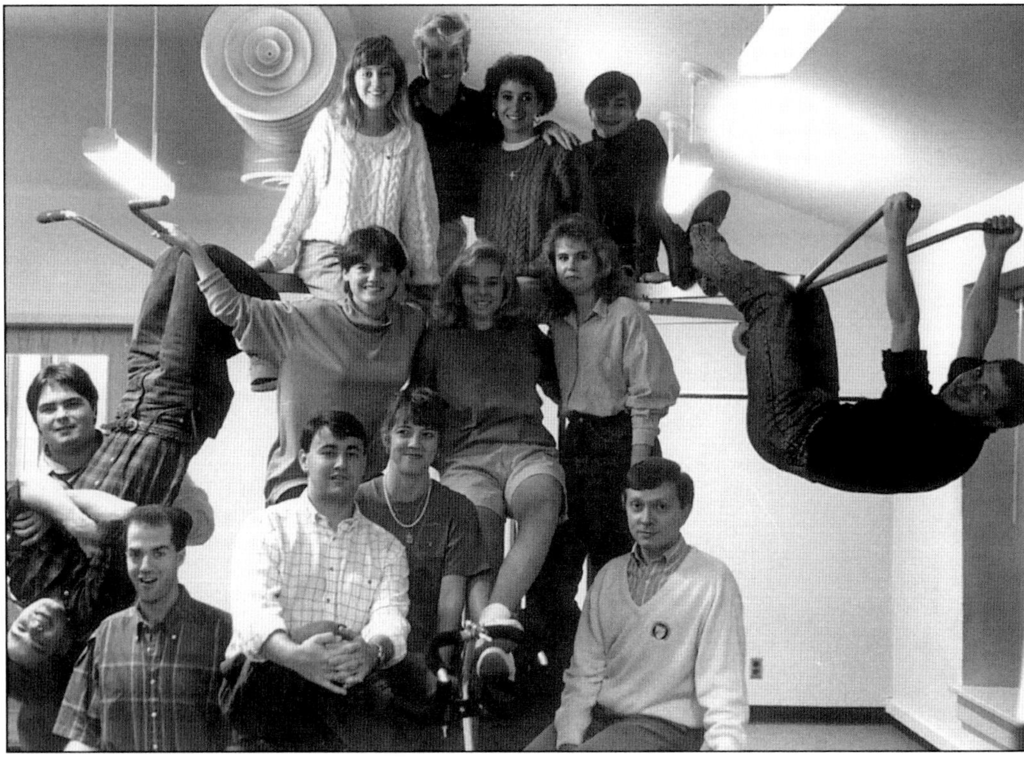

**Student Union Board, 1989.** Currently, the Student Union Board organizes many campus events. Members of the 1989 SUB are shown here with Dr. Dean Thompson (lower right). (Courtesy of Presbyterian College Archives.)

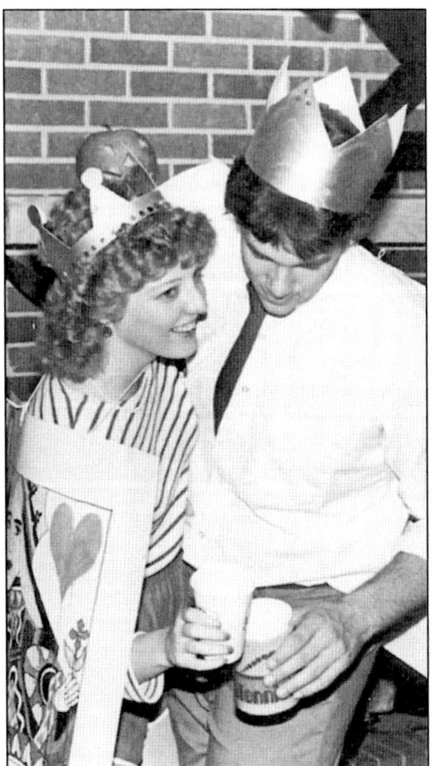

**Halloween Fun, 1983.** Halloween costume parties have long been a feature of campus life. (Courtesy of 1984 *PaC SaC*.)

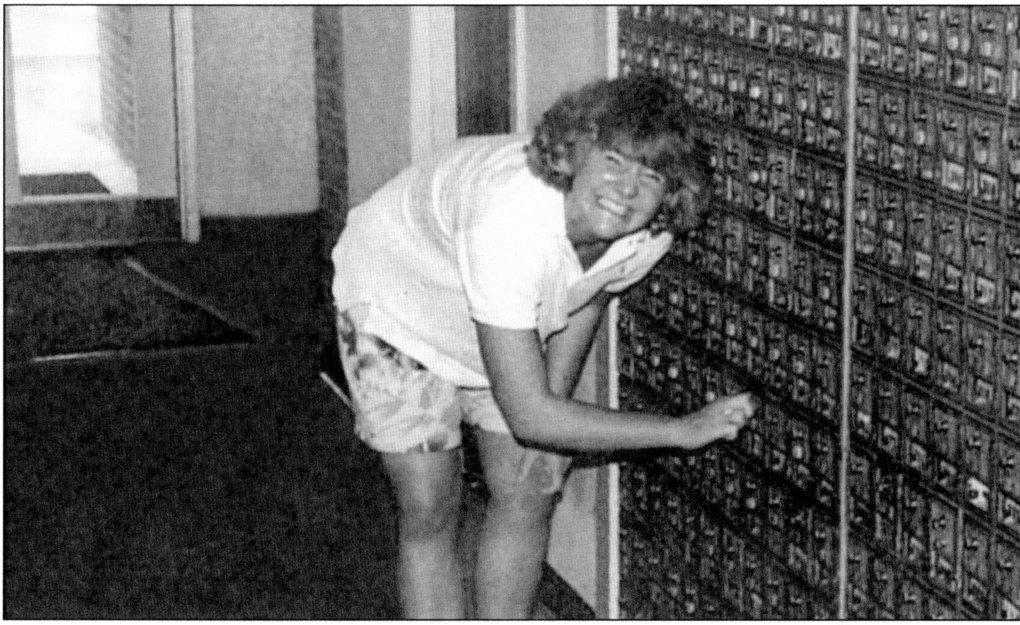

**Ever Hopeful.** Shannon Beery checks her mailbox in this 1987 photograph. (Courtesy of 1987 *PaC SaC.*)

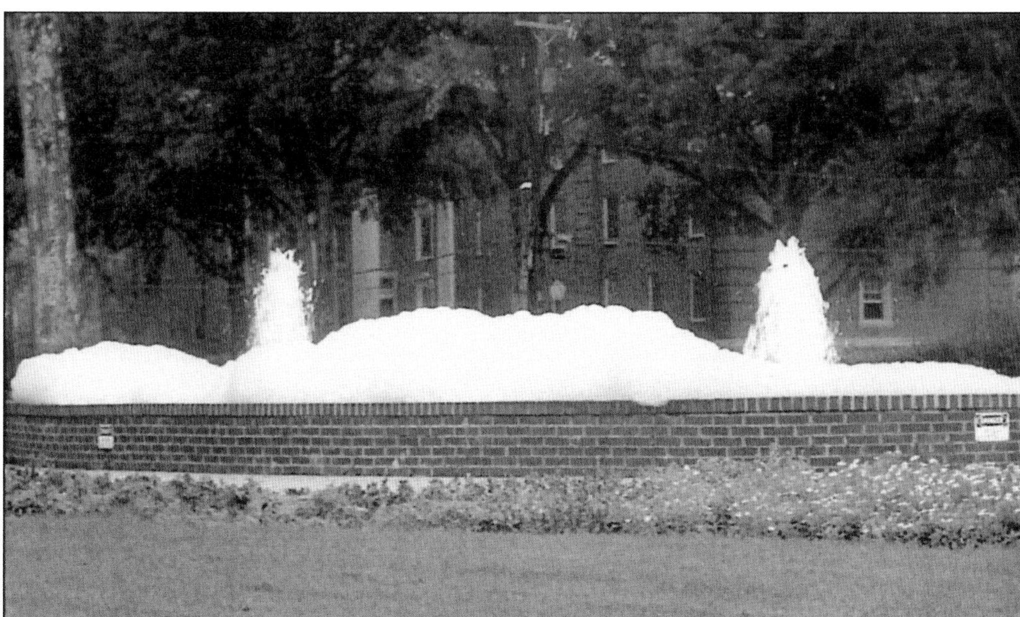

**A Familiar Sight.** What good is a fountain, if you can't put soap in it? (Courtesy of 1987 *PaC SaC.*)

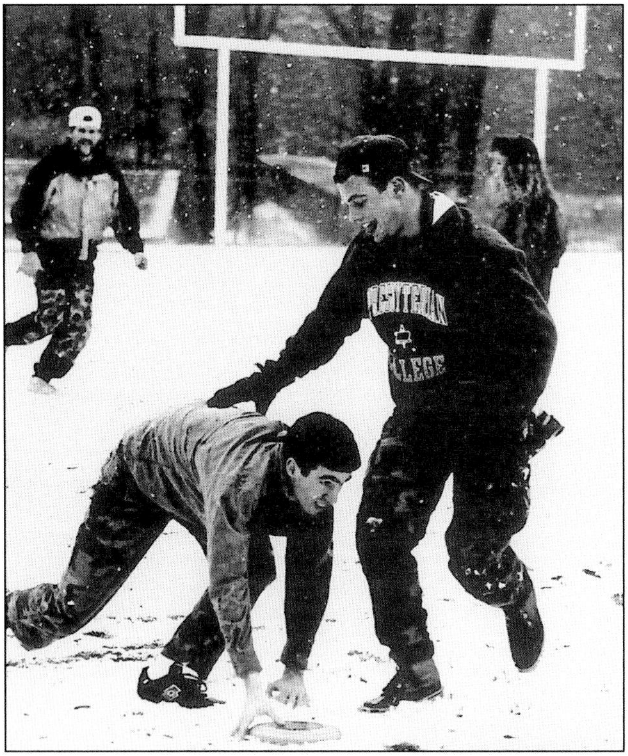

**Fun in the Snow.** While it doesn't snow often in Clinton, students have learned to take full advantage of it when it does. The 1970s even featured a "snow riot." (Courtesy of Presbyterian College Public Relations Office.)

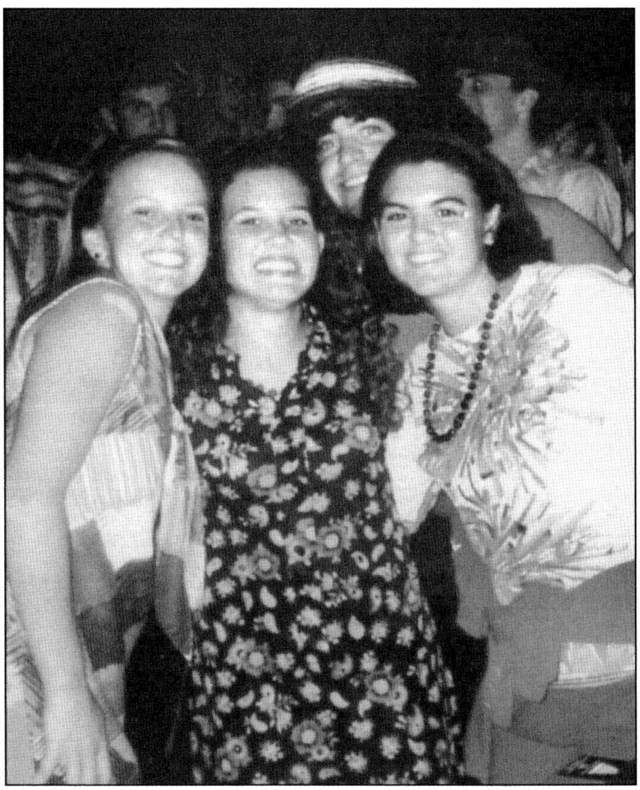

**Disco!** Tiffany Worrell, Summer Hendley, Tom Swift, and Jessica Glenn are pictured at right while at a 1998 disco party. (Courtesy of 1998 *PaC SaC*.)

# *Six*

# Athletics

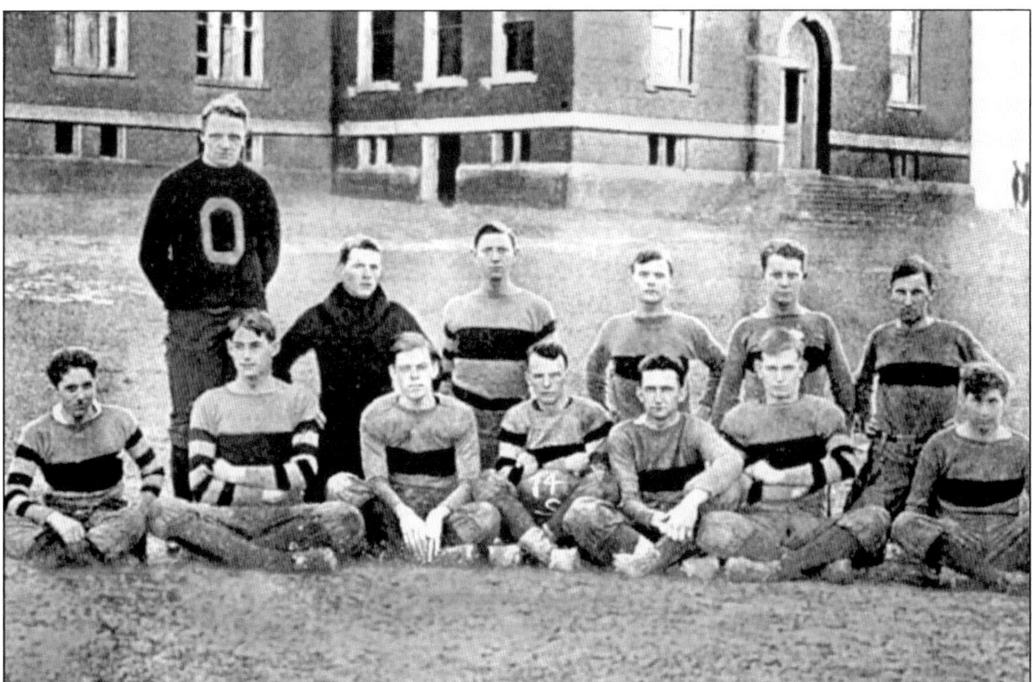

**Scrub Football Team, 1915.** Members of the "scrubs" in 1915 were M.S. Woodson, G.R. Cousar, E.P. McIlwain, O.E. White, J.M. Thompson, D.M. McIntyre, W.G. Neville, J.T. Ballenger, H.K. Neely, H.J. Williams, and B.C. Barksdale.(Courtesy of 1915 *PaC SaC*.)

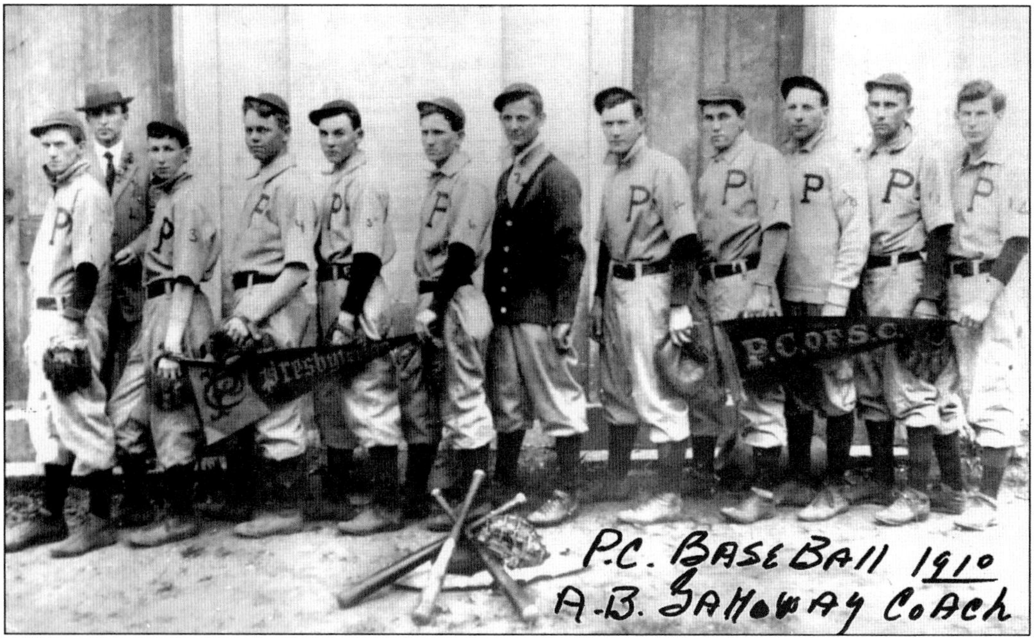


**BASEBALL TEAM, 1910–1911.** Baseball was the first intercollegiate sport to be played at PC, with the first team being organized around 1895 under coach (and professor) A.V. Martin. Team members from left to right are M.M. Sellars, Coach A.B. Galloway Sr., D. Fulton, E. Fullers, S.L. Leaman, J. Simpson, H. Winn, T. Simpson, P.D. Mayzck, ? Brown, J. McGregor, and S. Fulton. (Courtesy of Presbyterian College Archives.)

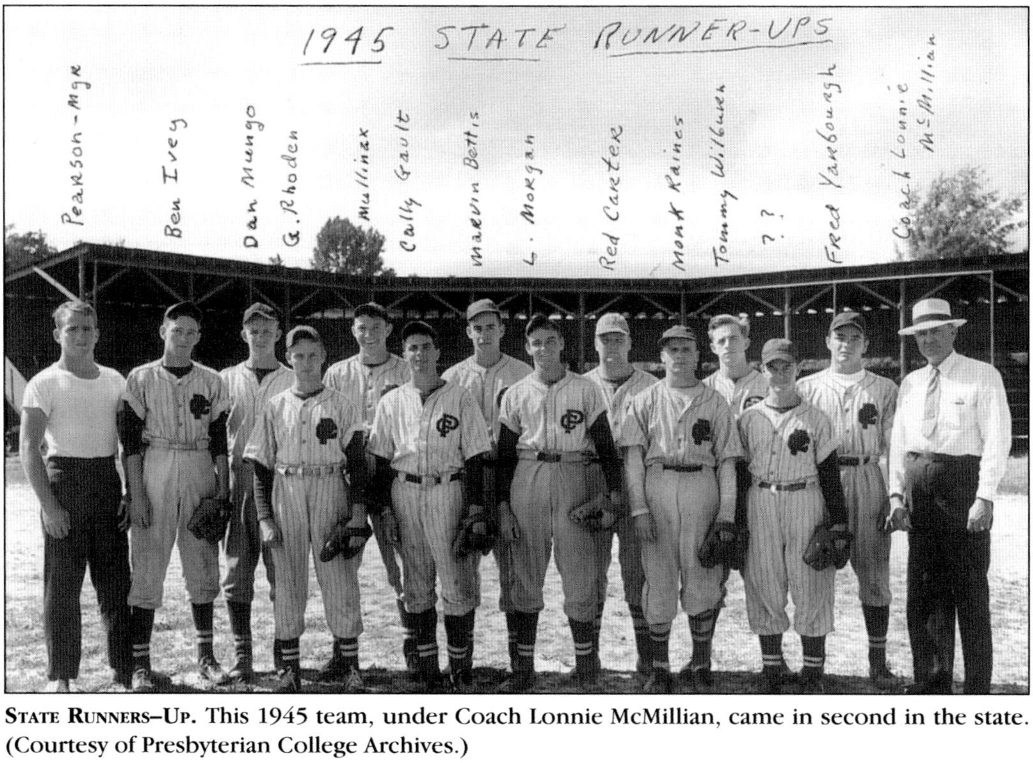


**STATE RUNNERS–UP.** This 1945 team, under Coach Lonnie McMillian, came in second in the state. (Courtesy of Presbyterian College Archives.)

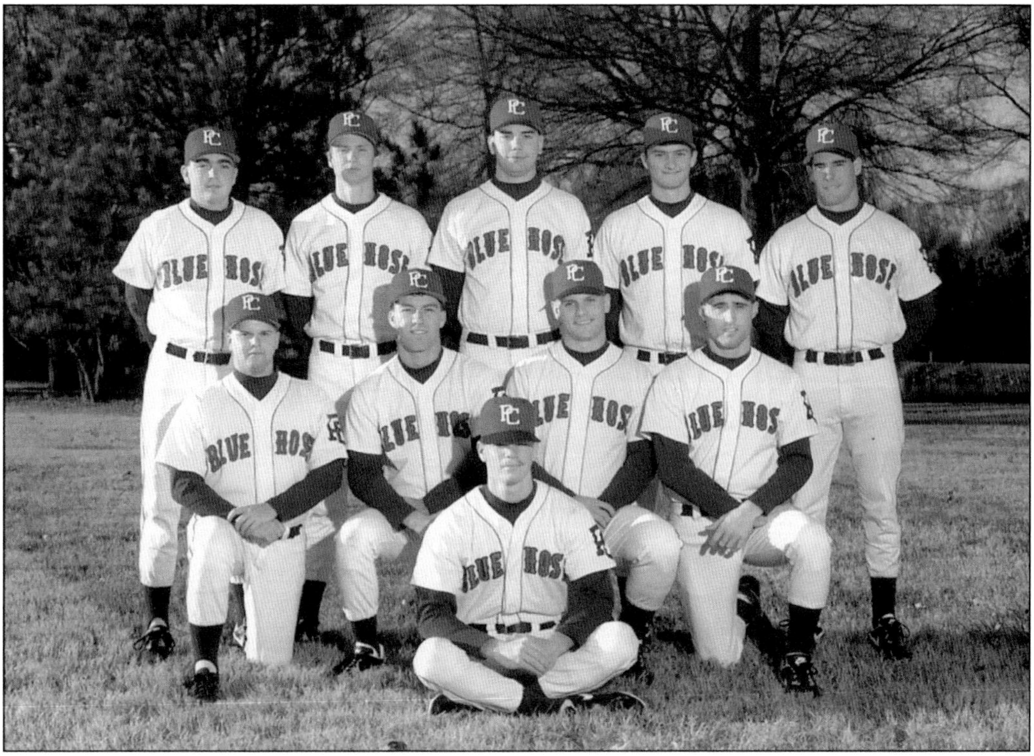


**A New Era.** Baseball was re-established at the college in 1988, after a 21-year absence. This is the first team of that new era. Pictured from left right are (top row) Alewine, Budinger, Canady, Kirkland, and Lanier; (kneeling) Huntsberger, Gilstrip, Fields, and Niles; (sitting) Jones. (Courtesy of Presbyterian College Archives.)

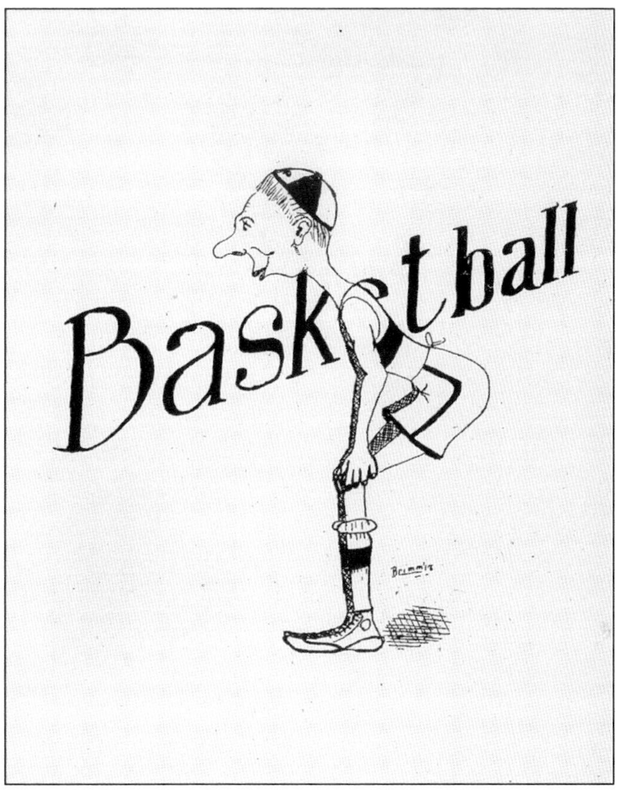


**Basketball.** Basketball was introduced as a sport in 1913. (Courtesy of 1917 *PaC SaC*.)

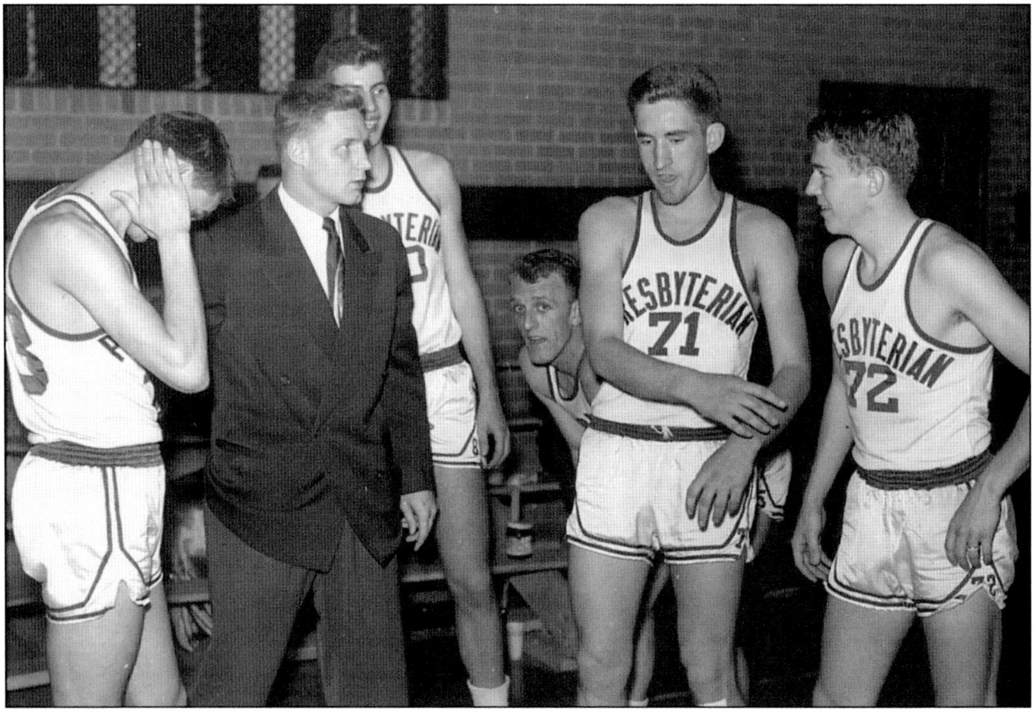

**Advice from the Coach.** Here coach Norm Sloan talks with players Clyde Beaumont (71) and Bill Toole (72). (Courtesy of Presbyterian College Archives.)

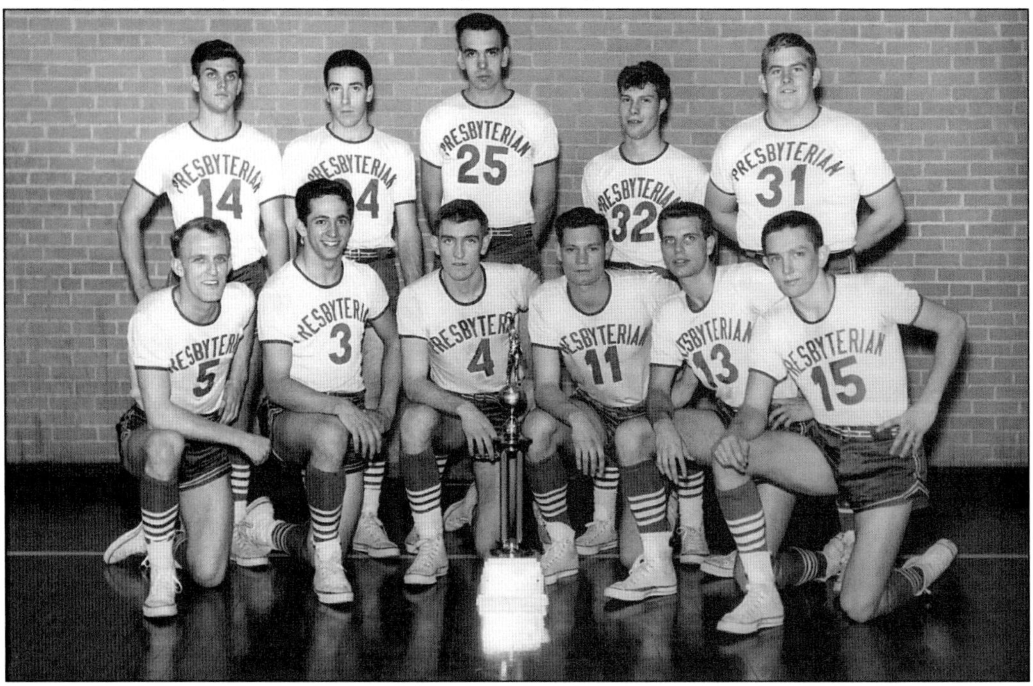

**State Champs.** The 1950–1951 basketball team won the state championship. From left to right are (kneeling) Nye, Hawkins, Groninger, K. Hill, Blewett, and Skinner; (standing) Jackson, Carter, Thompson, H. Hill, and Horn. (Courtesy of Presbyterian College Archives.)

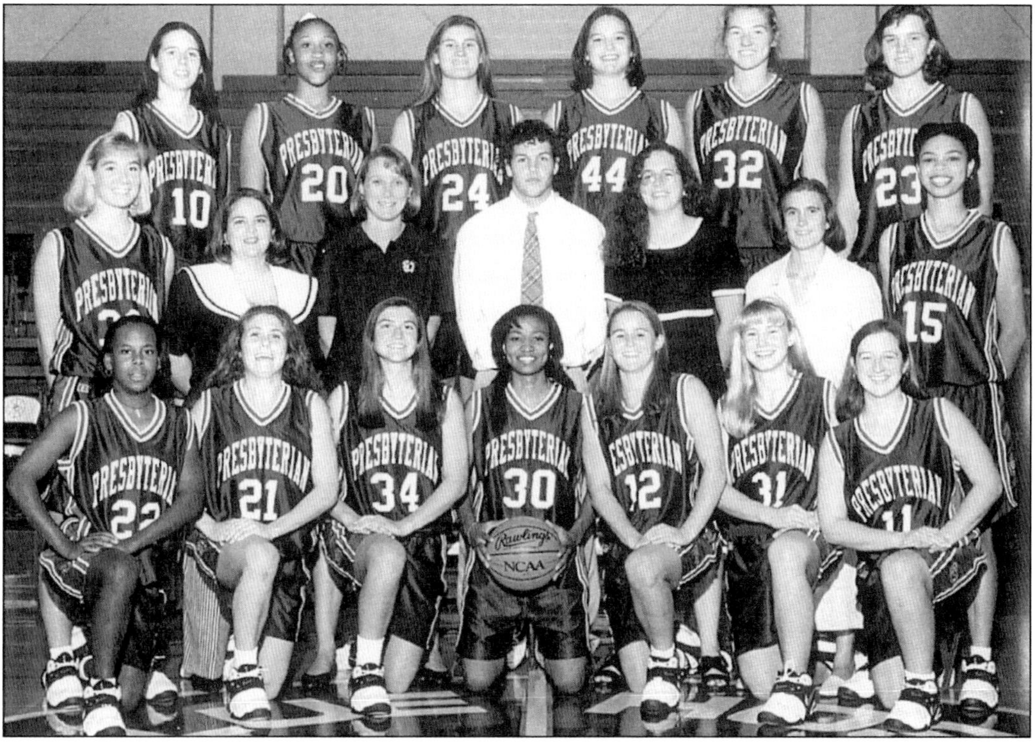

**WOMEN'S BASKETBALL TEAM, 1997–1998.** Although women's basketball existed briefly in the 1930s, intercollegiate women's basketball was started in 1977, the fourth sport available for female students. From left to right are (front row) C. McRae, J. Neumann, A. Monroe, A. Ridgell, D. Huffman, S. Smyrl, and H. Couch; (second row) T. Woody, D. Youngblood, Coach Couture, M. Mannely, Coach Mannely, Coach Timmons, and C. Choice; (third row) J. Ray, R. Sloan, D. Barman, J. Condon, T. Kelley, and L. Jones. (Courtesy of 1998 *PaC SaC*.)

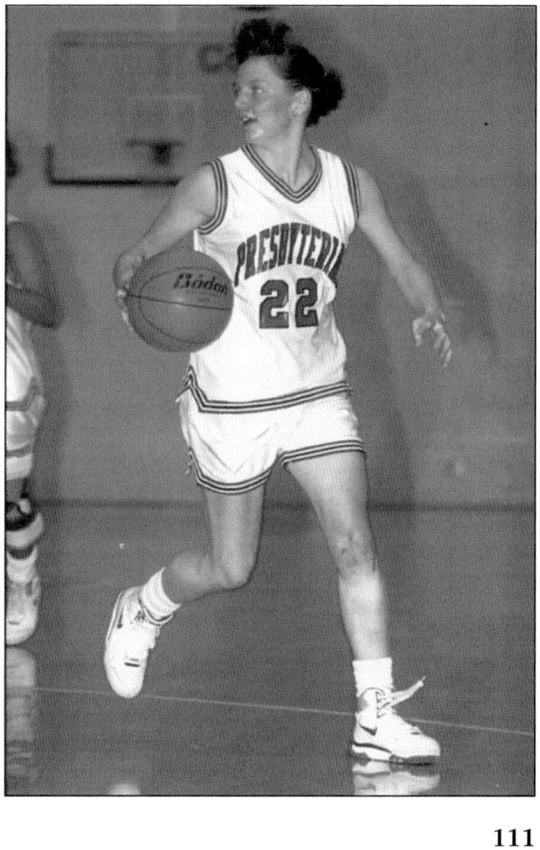

**ALLISON HUBBARD, *c.* 1992.** Senior Allison Hubbard drives down the floor. (Courtesy of Presbyterian College Archives.)

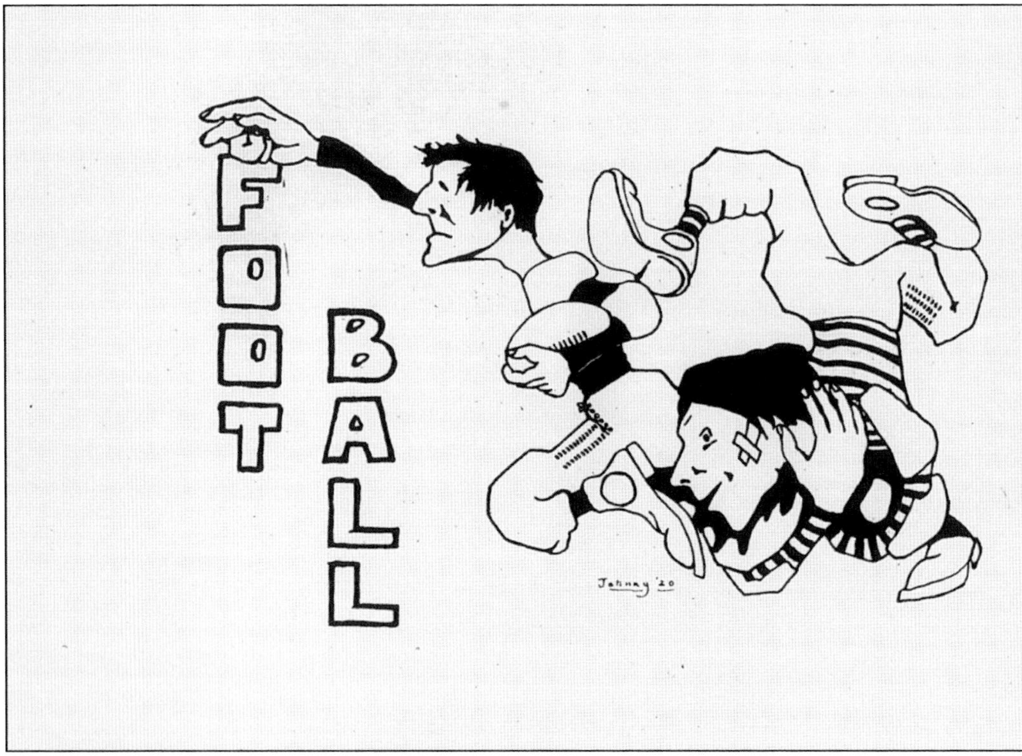


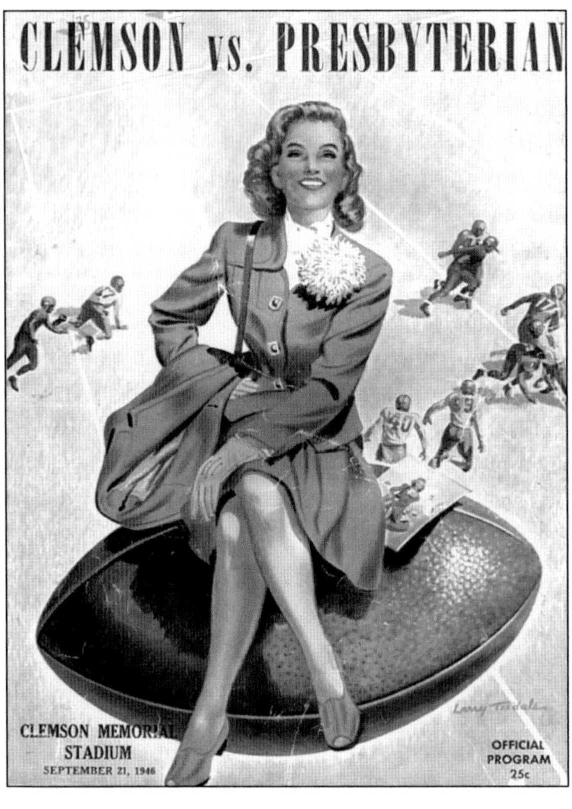


**FOOTBALL.** Football was introduced as an intercollegiate sport in 1915. The team has had a proud tradition over the years, and has boasted a number of well-known coaches and assistants, including Walter Johnson, Lonnie McMillian, Callie Gault and, for a brief period, Edward "Bo" Schembechler. (Courtesy of 1917 *PaC SaC*.)

**DAVID AND GOLIATH.** For a number of years, PC played Clemson in football, actually emerging with a 13-12 victory in 1943. (Courtesy of Presbyterian College Archives.)

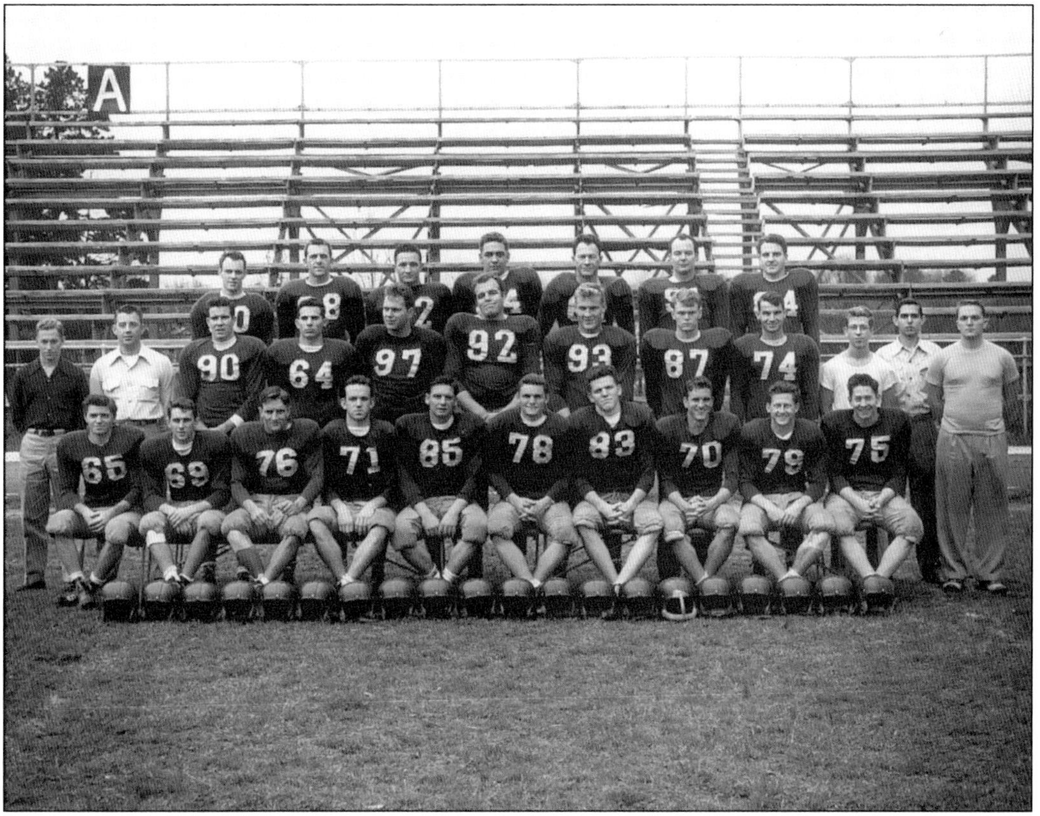

**FOOTBALL TEAM, 1949.** The roster for the 1949 team included J. Weingartner, R. Stutts, L. Hawkins, C. Howe, M. Lanter, F. Yarborough, W. Gooch, V. Dusenbury, L. Edwards, J. Dodd, H. Cate, B. Copeland, B. Atkinson, B. Ogletree, D. Lindsay, B. Neely, B. Watts, B. Jolly, G. Fleming, K. McCutcheon, G. Watt, R. Johnston, R. Tedards, H. Martin, S. Stevenson, B. Pierce, K. Jackson, J. Lindsay, J. McKissick, F. Honea, F. Barnum, H.C. Starnes, B. Weir, L. Surls, K. Horn, A. Beckum, and S. Baker. (Courtesy of Presbyterian College Archives.)

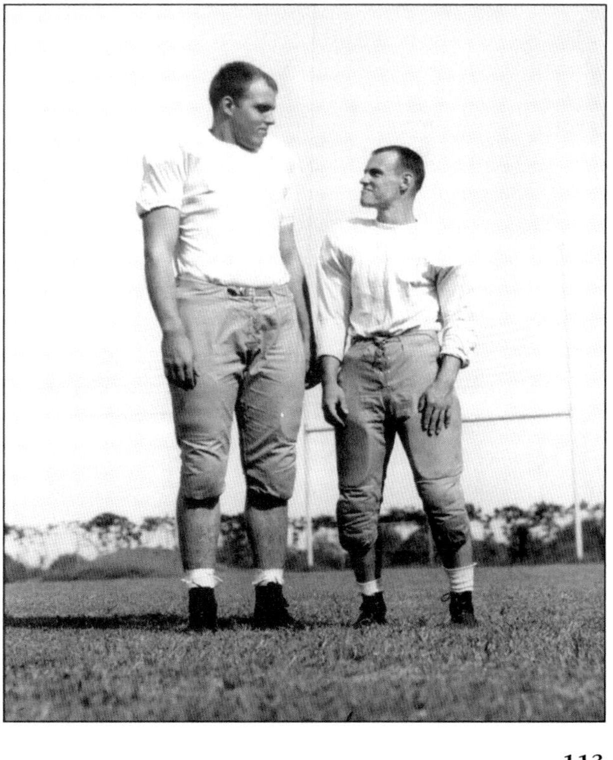

**THE ODD COUPLE, 1949.** William "Bozo" Weir and Jo Jo Weingarten presented quite a contrast in size. (Courtesy of Presbyterian College Archives.)

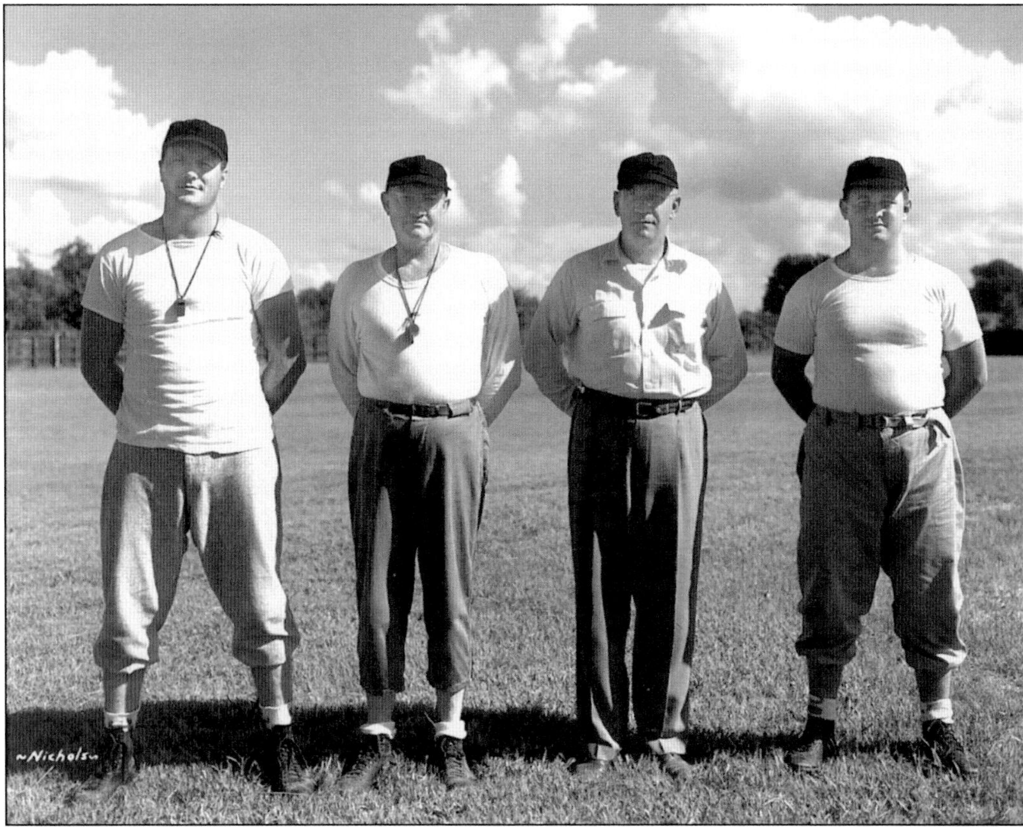


**Football Coaches.** Pictured in this 1950 photograph are, from left to right, Gene Lorendo, Lonnie McMillian (head coach), Walter A. Johnson (athletic director), and Sid Varney. Walter Johnson arrived at PC as coach and physical director in 1915, and Lonnie McMillian was a star on his first team. Between them, they eventually coached almost every sport at the college, and developed a well-respected athletic program. (Courtesy of Presbyterian College Archives.)

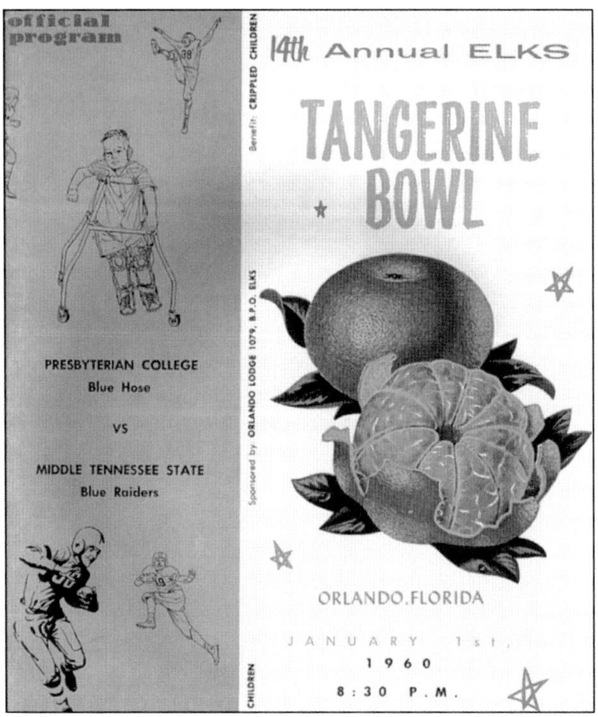


**Tangerine Bowl, 1960.** Presbyterian battled Middle Tennessee State in the Tangerine Bowl on New Year's Day in 1960. (Courtesy of Presbyterian College Archives.)

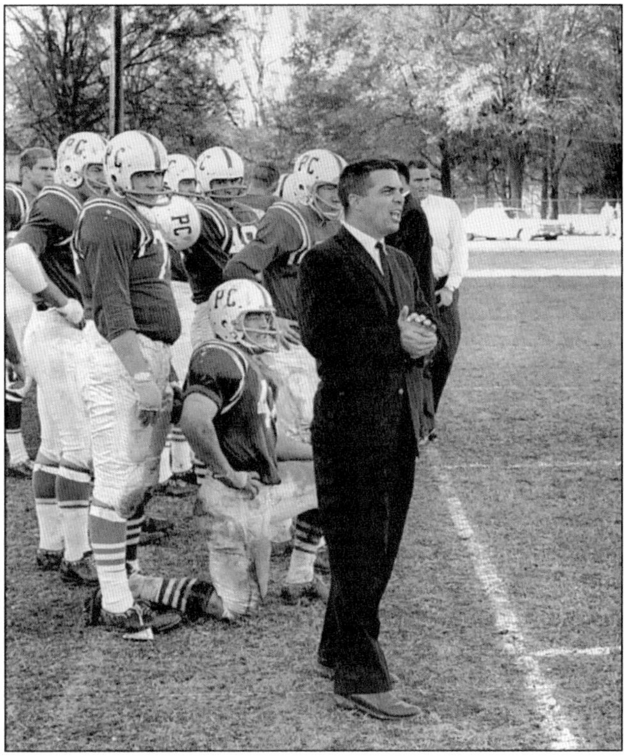


**Coach Gault.** Longtime coach and athletic director Cally Gault is seen on the sidelines in this 1964 photograph. (Courtesy of Presbyterian College Archives.)

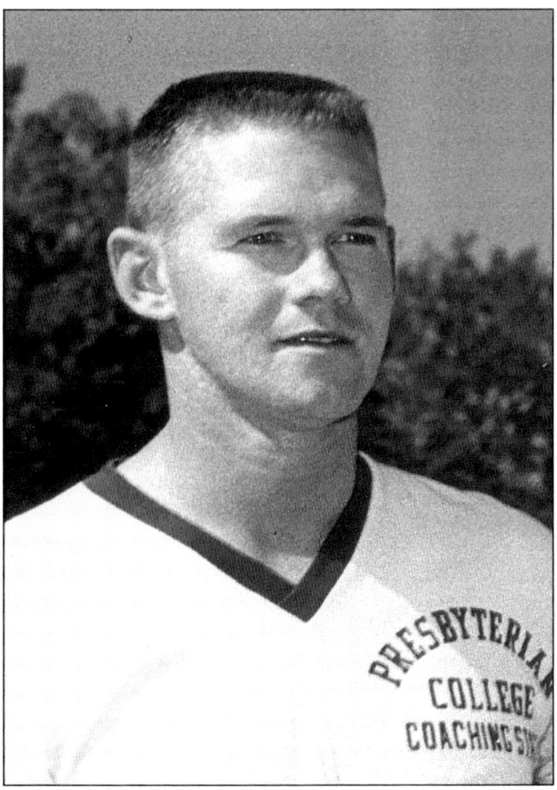


**Joe Nixon.** PC grad Joe Nixon joined the ranks of football coaches in 1965; he later went on to serve as dean of admissions and dean of students. (Courtesy of Presbyterian College Archives.)

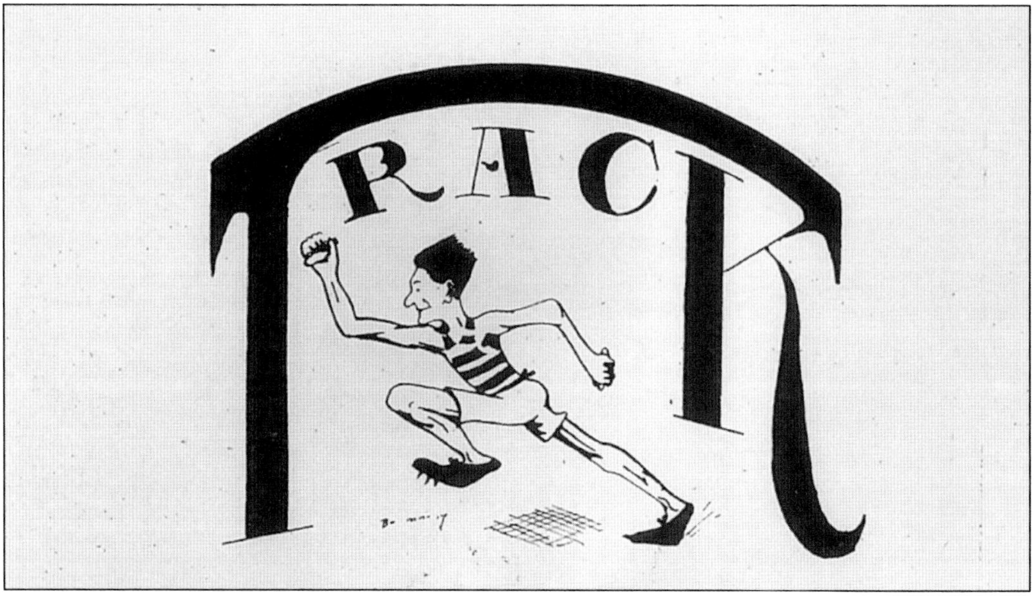


**Track.** Track was introduced as a sport at PC in 1913. (Courtesy of 1917 *PaC SaC*.)

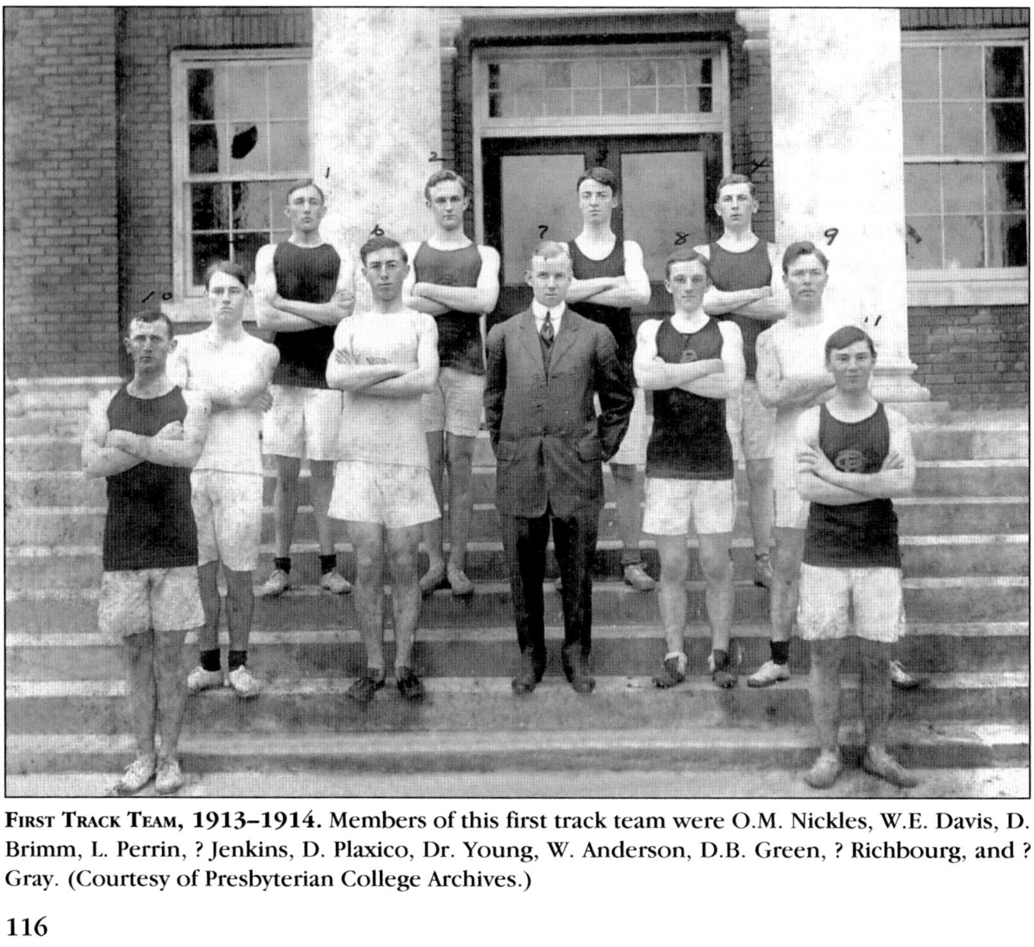

**First Track Team, 1913–1914.** Members of this first track team were O.M. Nickles, W.E. Davis, D. Brimm, L. Perrin, ? Jenkins, D. Plaxico, Dr. Young, W. Anderson, D.B. Green, ? Richbourg, and ? Gray. (Courtesy of Presbyterian College Archives.)

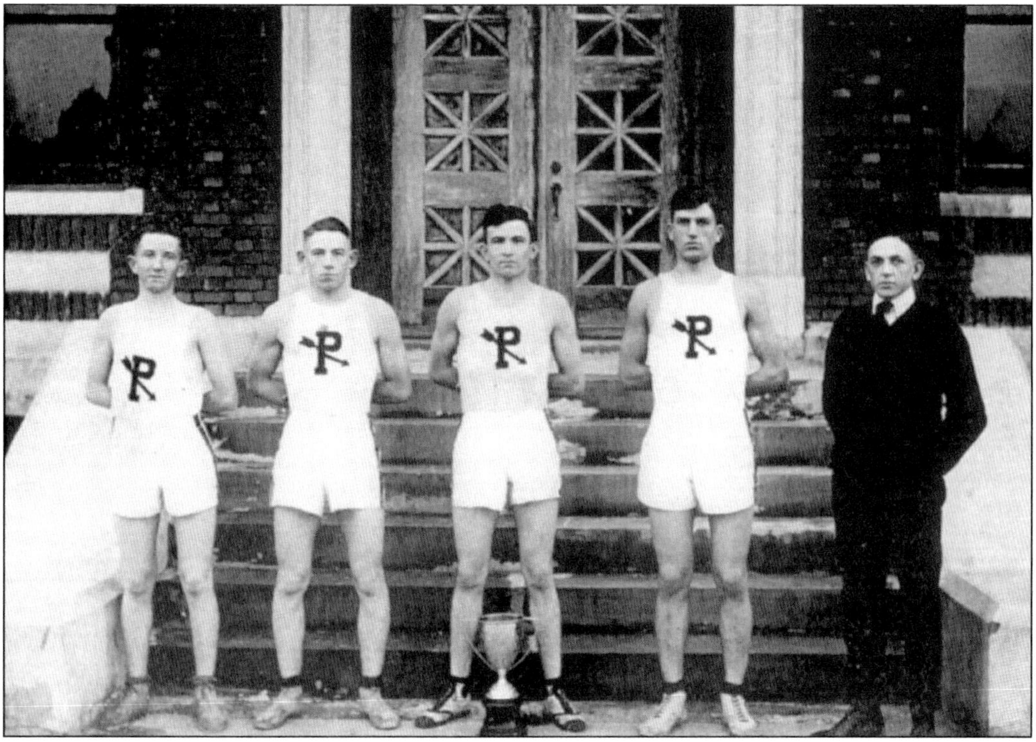

**Cross-Country Team, 1920.** Cross-country was introduced as a sport by 1915. Although the people in this photograph have not been identified, members of the team that year included Neely, Dick, Matheson, Dilling, Utility, and Park. (Courtesy of 1920 *PaC SaC*.)

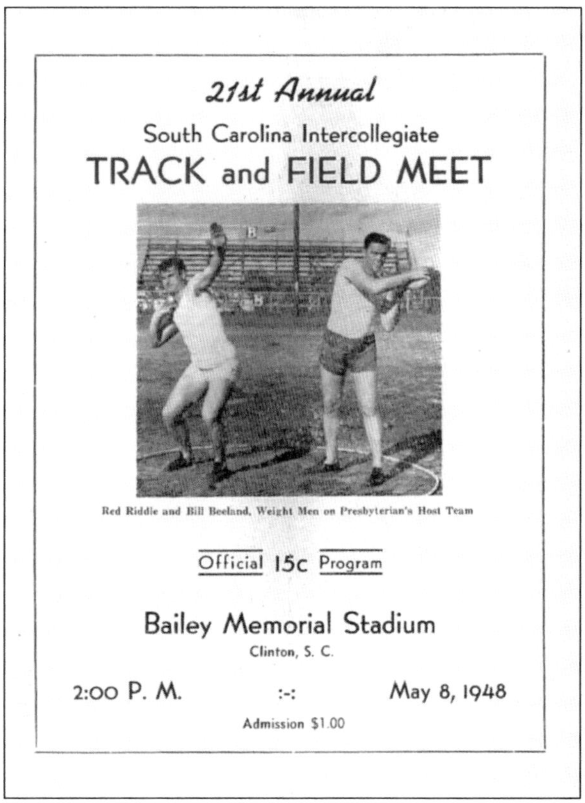


**State Track Meet Program.** Because of the college's excellent cinder track (which was built by students), the state intercollegiate track meet was held at PC for many years. This "Little Olympics" sometimes brought 2,500 spectators to Clinton. (Courtesy of Presbyterian College Archives.)

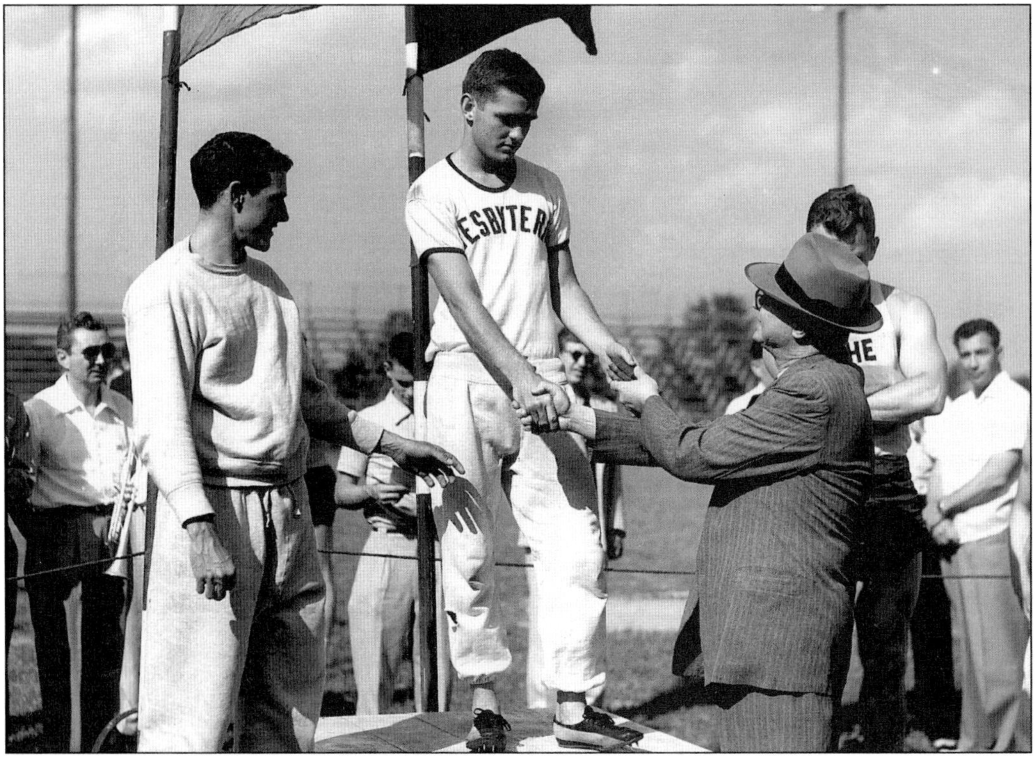

**State Track Meet, 1954.** The college's own Bobby Vass won a medal in the broad jump competition in 1954. (Courtesy of Presbyterian College Archives.)

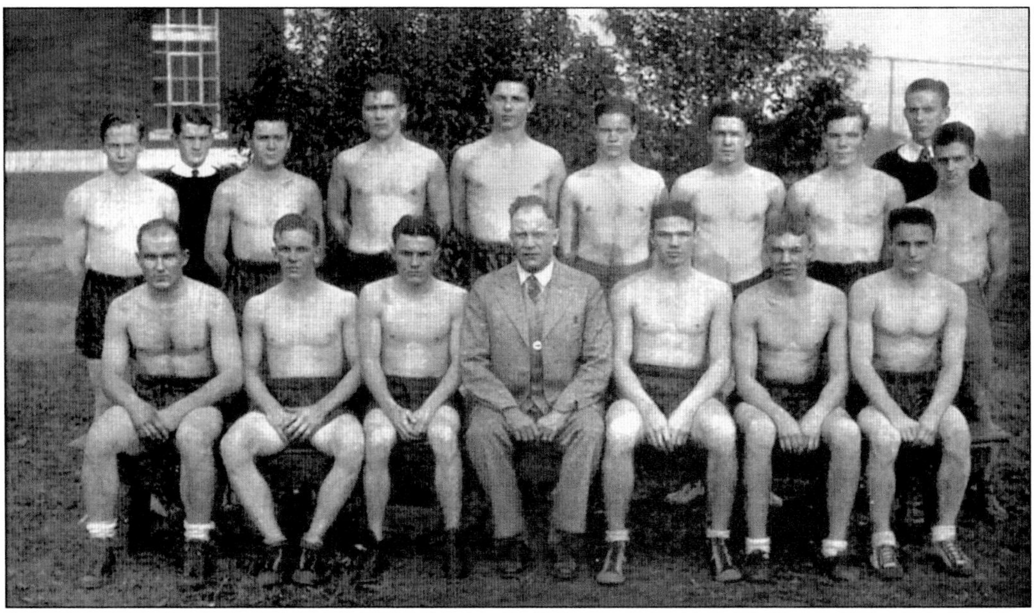

**Boxing.** Boxing was one of the short-lived sports at the college. Here the team poses with Coach Walter Johnson in 1931. Members included Truesdell, McQueen, Caskey, Cheatham, Parker, Graham, Horton, and Boyd. The manager was L.C. Jackson. (Courtesy of Presbyterian College Archives.)

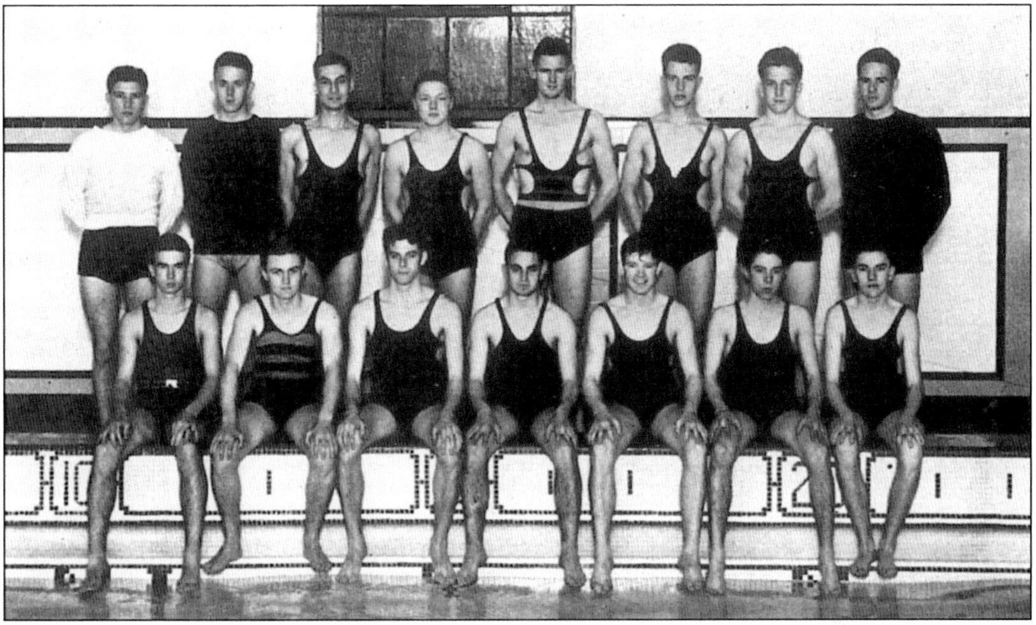

**Swimming.** The completion of the swimming pool addition to Springs Gymnasium in 1929 allowed for the formation of a team. While the members pictured in this 1933 photo are not specifically identified, the team included McFadden, Wilson, Danny, Parker, Hays, Valley, Walter, Adams, Carson, and Hannah. (Courtesy of Presbyterian College Archives.)

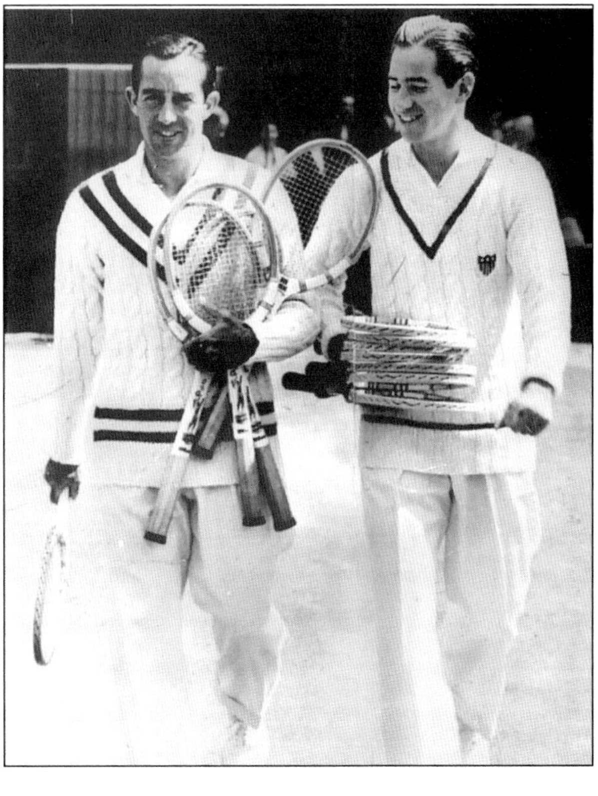

**Tennis.** Tennis was played at PC as early as 1913, and was a prominent part of college life during the 1930s, 1940s, and 1950s. In addition to intercollegiate matches, many clinics and exhibition games were held on the campus. Elwood Cooke (left) and Bobby Riggs were photographed at one such match. Riggs actually served for a time as a traveling public relations agent for the college. (Courtesy of Presbyterian College Archives.)

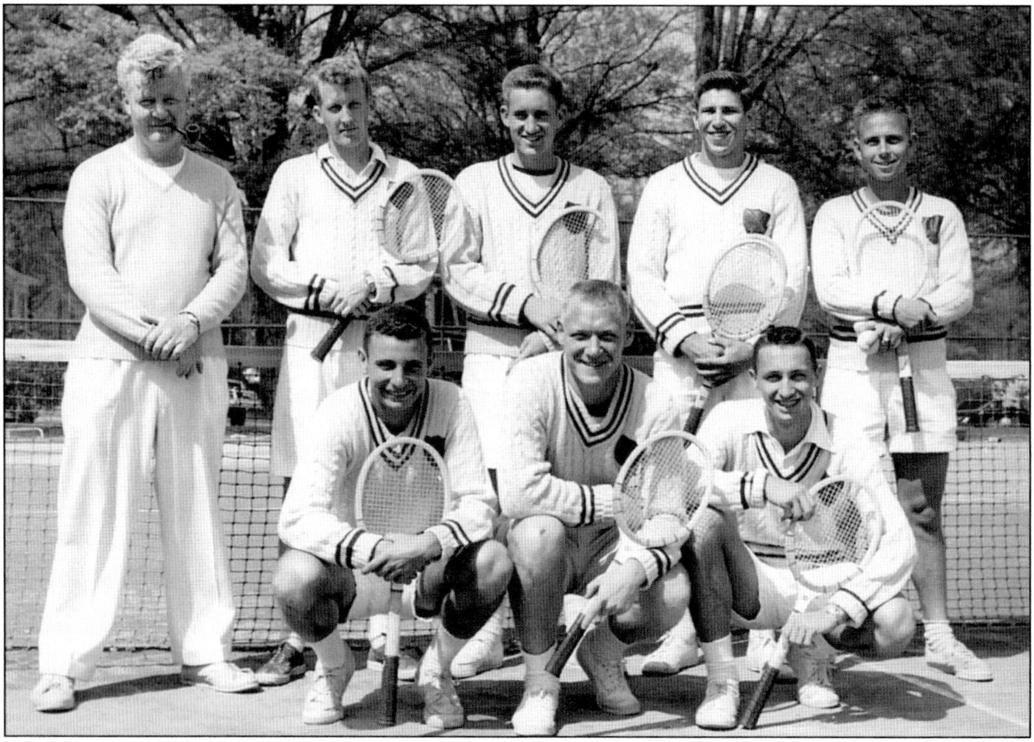

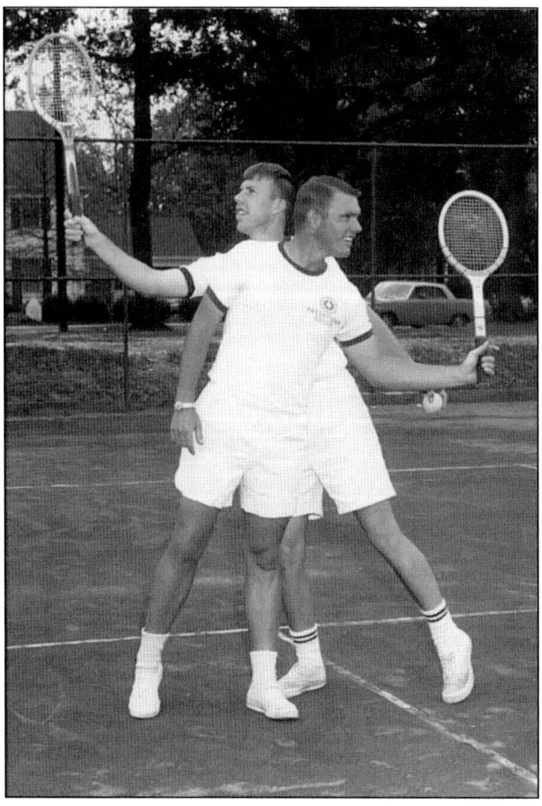

**Tennis Team, 1952–1953.** From left to right are (kneeling) Hunt, Morris, and Bradley; (standing) Coach Leighton, Toole, Beaumont, Thompson, and Bradley. In his 12 years as coach, Leighton's teams compiled a 155-57 record. (Courtesy of Presbyterian College Archives.)

**Howdy Letzrig and Larry Conley.** Here the #2 doubles team strikes a comic pose in 1965. (Courtesy of Presbyterian College Archives.)

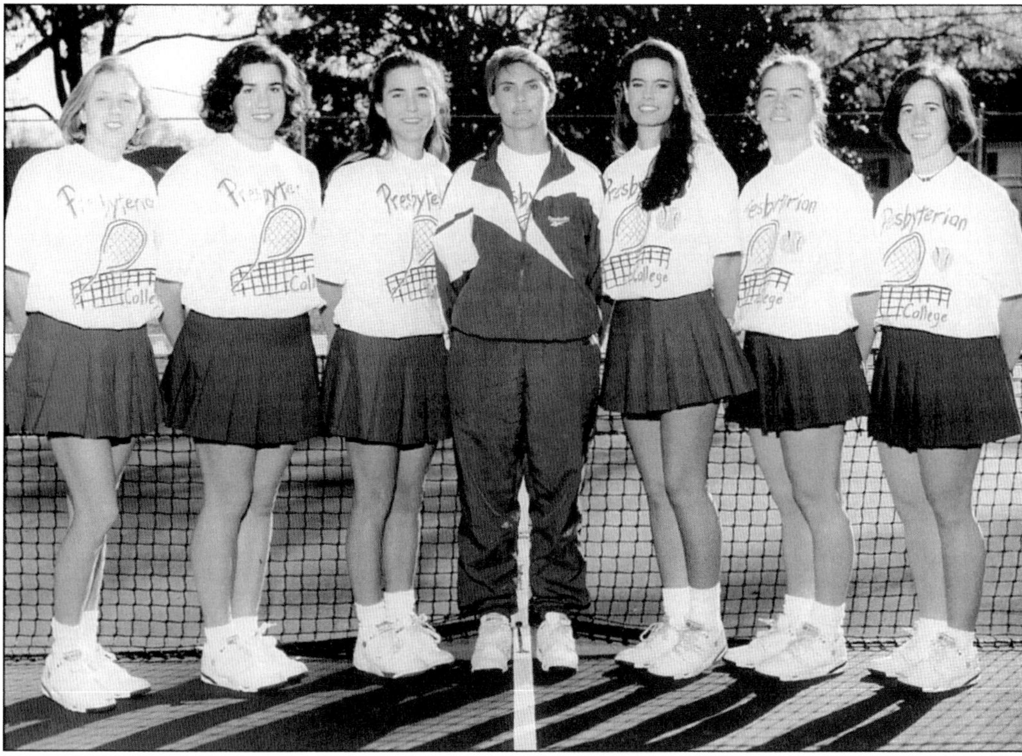

**Women's Tennis.** Women's tennis was first played at PC in 1972, and became a varsity sport two years later. The 1995 team was composed of (from left to right) Jennifer Brim, Dawn Dachelet, Dana Davis, Coach Donna Arnold, Stacie Buttorff, Chrissie Bolt, and Jessica Clark. (Courtesy of Presbyterian College Public Relations Office.)

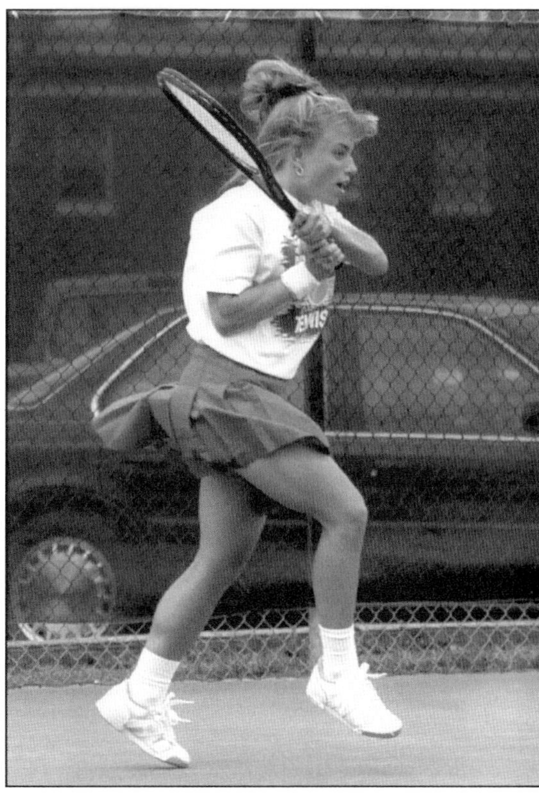

**Catherine Scott, All-Conference, 1992.** The women's team had a 15-6 record in 1992, winning the SAC and regional tournaments and qualifying for the national tournament. (Courtesy of Presbyterian College Archives.)

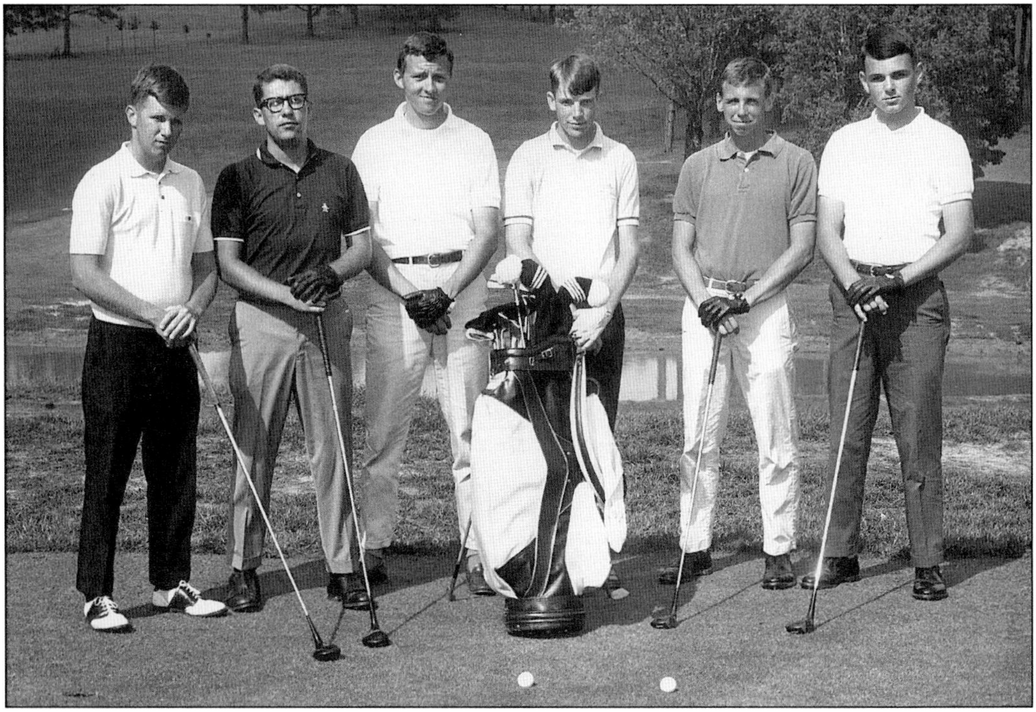

**GOLF TEAM, 1965.** Bruce Lawrence, Bunky Hanks, Larry Preston, Allen Parsons, Bill Kellam, and Joe Dunlap were members of PC's golf team in 1965. (Courtesy of Presbyterian College Archives.)

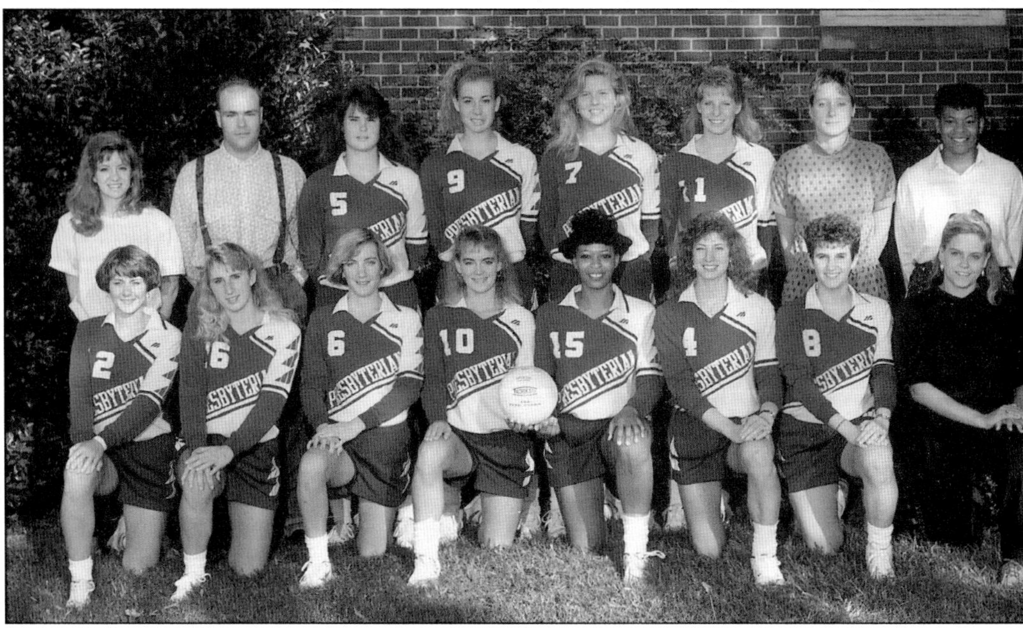

**VOLLEYBALL TEAM, 1990.** The first volleyball team appeared in 1976, under Coach Jane Hammet. In this 1990 volleyball photograph team members from left to right are (front row) S. Carter, K. Brown, S. Dodd, K. James, D. Williams, C. Wynn, J. Smith, and S. Fleming (manager); (back row) S. Stone (scorekeeper), T. Pysell (trainer), A. Jenkins, K. Lockwood, D. Wycoff, L. Kimbrell, B. Couture (coach), and T. Williams (assistant coach). (Courtesy of Presbyterian College Archives.)

**BROOKE FLEMING AND JENNIFER SMITH.** Volleyball players Brooke Fleming and Jennifer Smith set up to return a serve. (Courtesy of Presbyterian College Archives.)

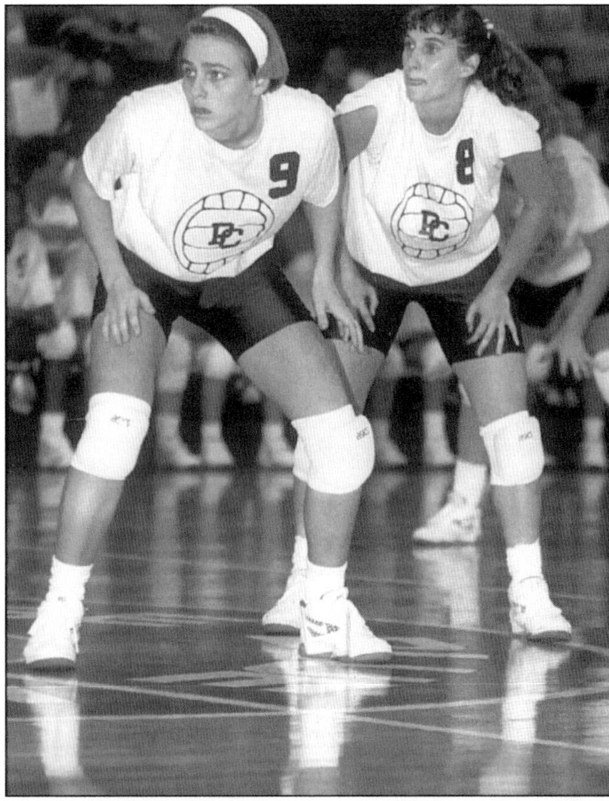

**SOCCER TEAM, 1995.** Men's soccer has been played at Presbyterian since 1977. (Courtesy of PC Athletic Department.)

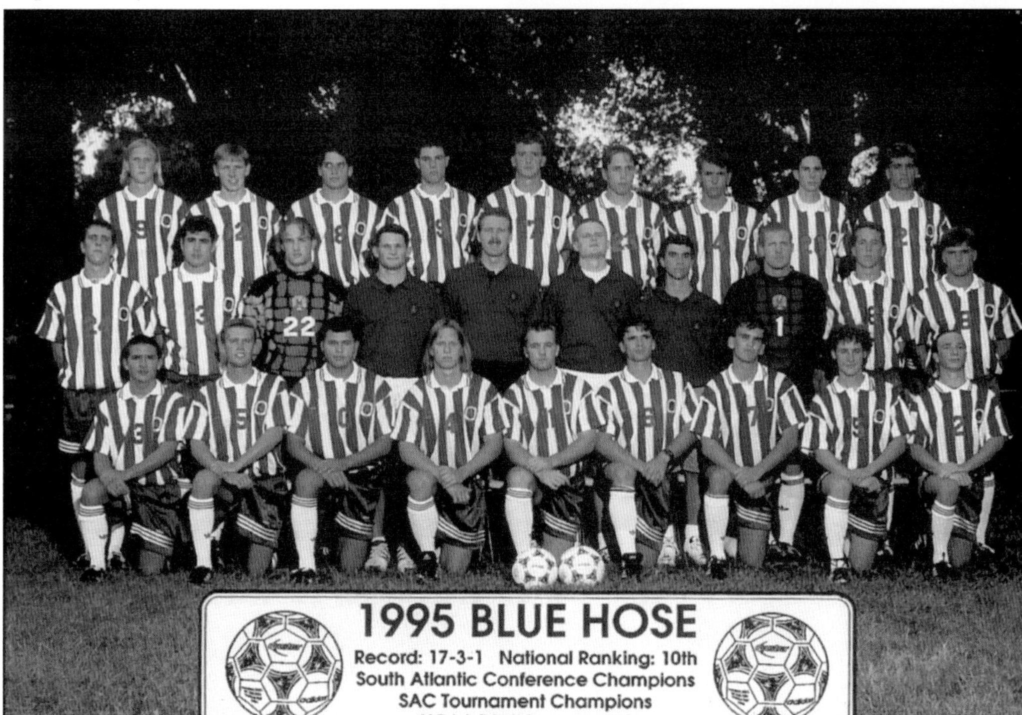

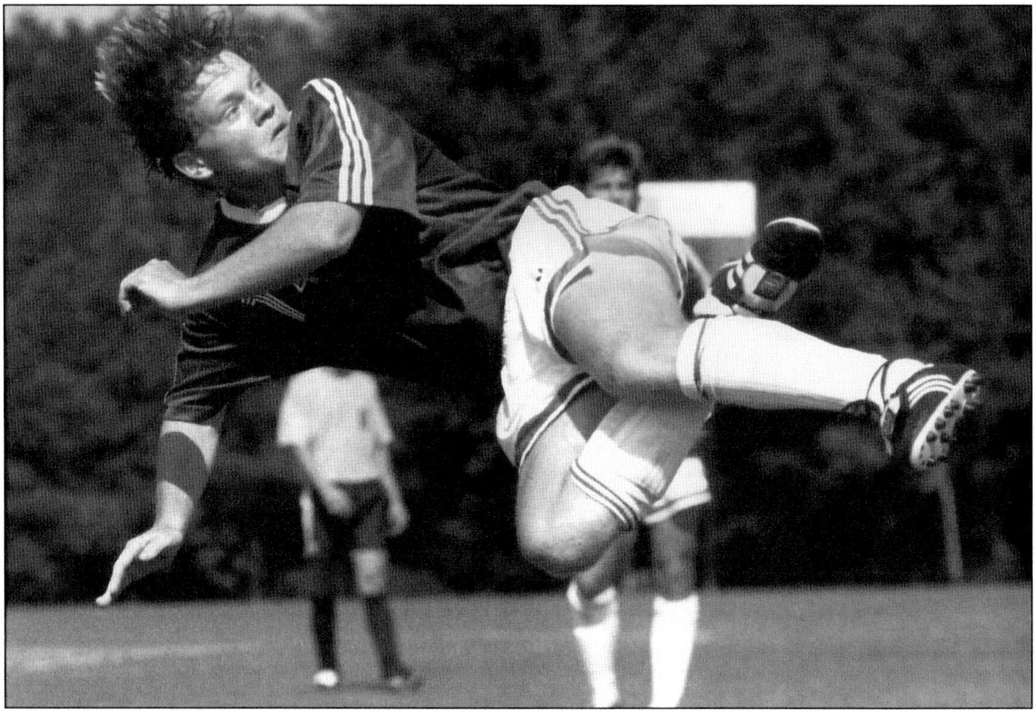

**Men's Soccer.** Here freshman Richard Wright makes an airborne play in 1991. (Courtesy of Presbyterian College Archives.)

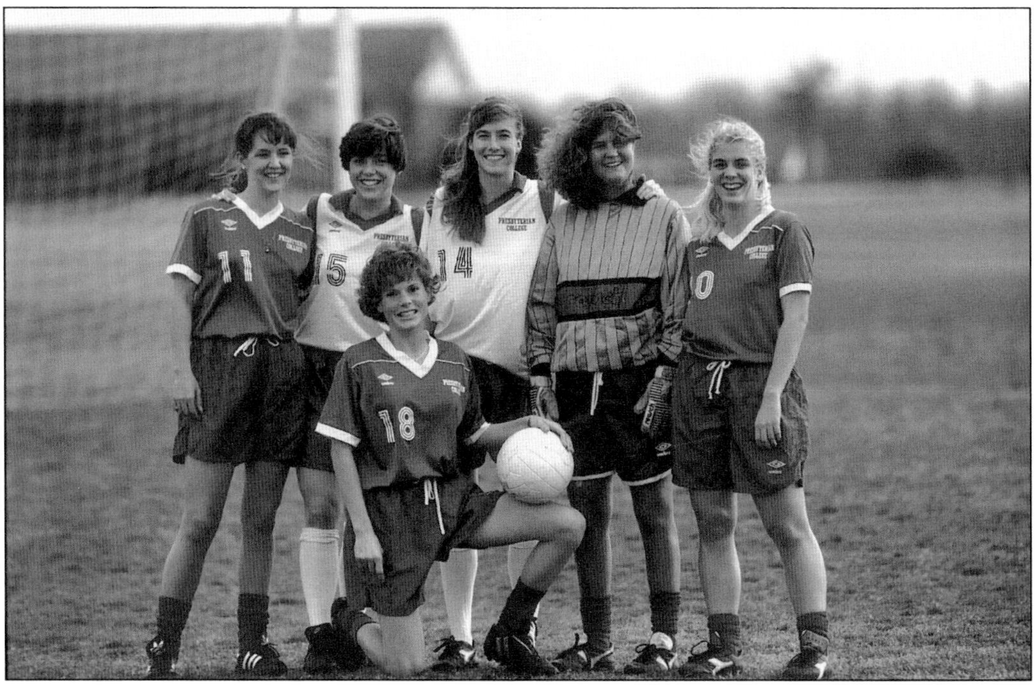

**Women's Soccer.** Lady Blue Hose soccer was begun in 1989. Among the players the following year were Amanda Bowers, Kathy Sawyer, Sandy Spear, Kristen Beleos, and Tricia McIlwain. (Courtesy of Presbyterian College Archives.)

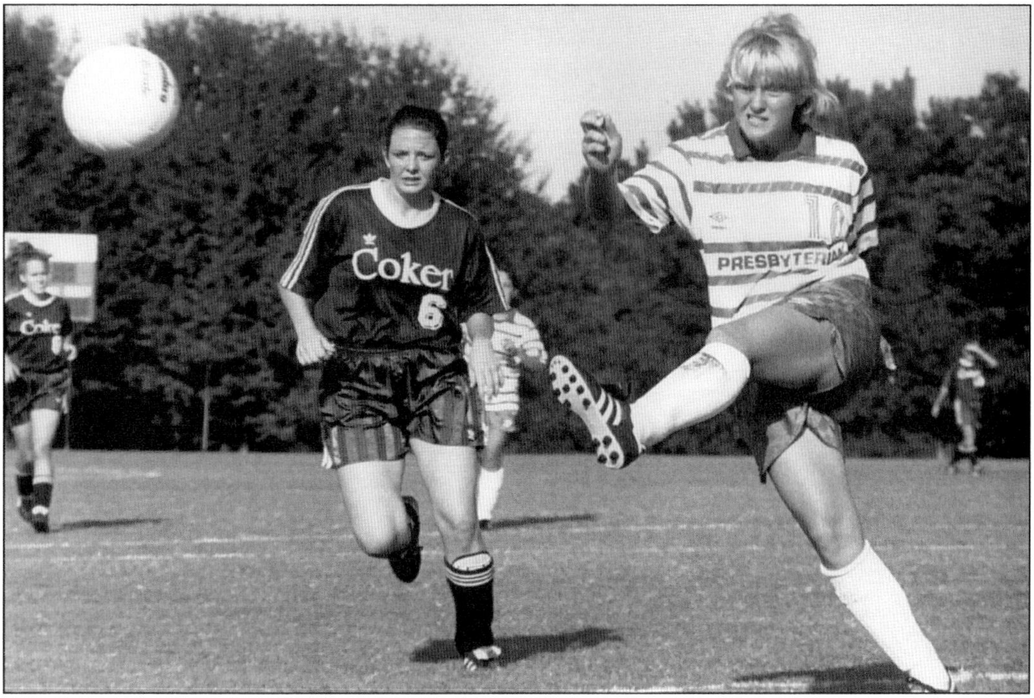


**Christi Flack Makes a Play Against Coker.** Women's soccer player Christi Flack makes a play against Coker College. (Courtesy of Presbyterian College Archives.)

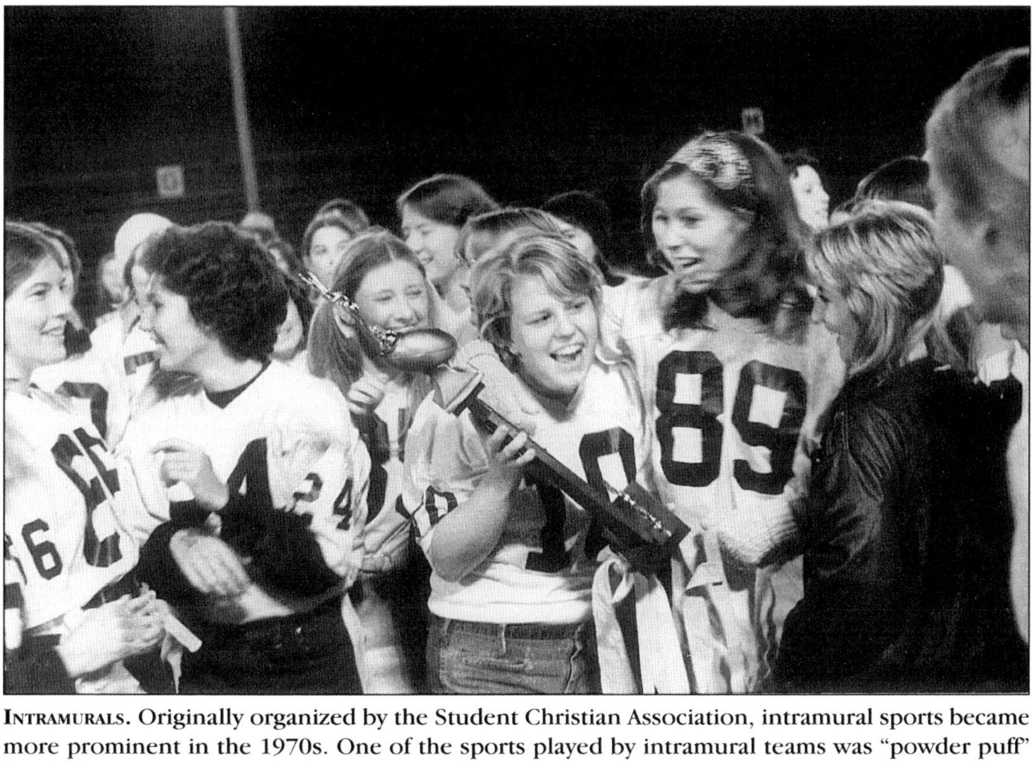

**Intramurals.** Originally organized by the Student Christian Association, intramural sports became more prominent in the 1970s. One of the sports played by intramural teams was "powder puff" football, shown here in 1974. (Courtesy of Presbyterian College Archives.)

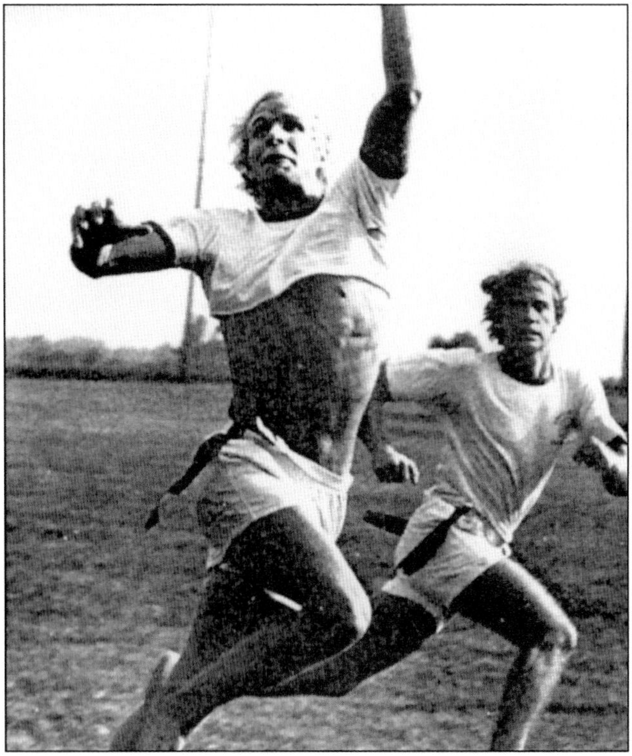

**Bill Thompson Avoids a Tackle.** Intramural football is a perennial favorite. Here Bill Thompson avoids a tackle by Billy Wade in 1974. (Courtesy of 1974 *PaC SaC*.)

**Cheerleaders.** Cheerleaders in 1965, from left to right, were Suzanna Jeans, Mavis Harrop, Mary Anne Arnette, and Bruce Hughes. (Courtesy of Presbyterian College Archives.)

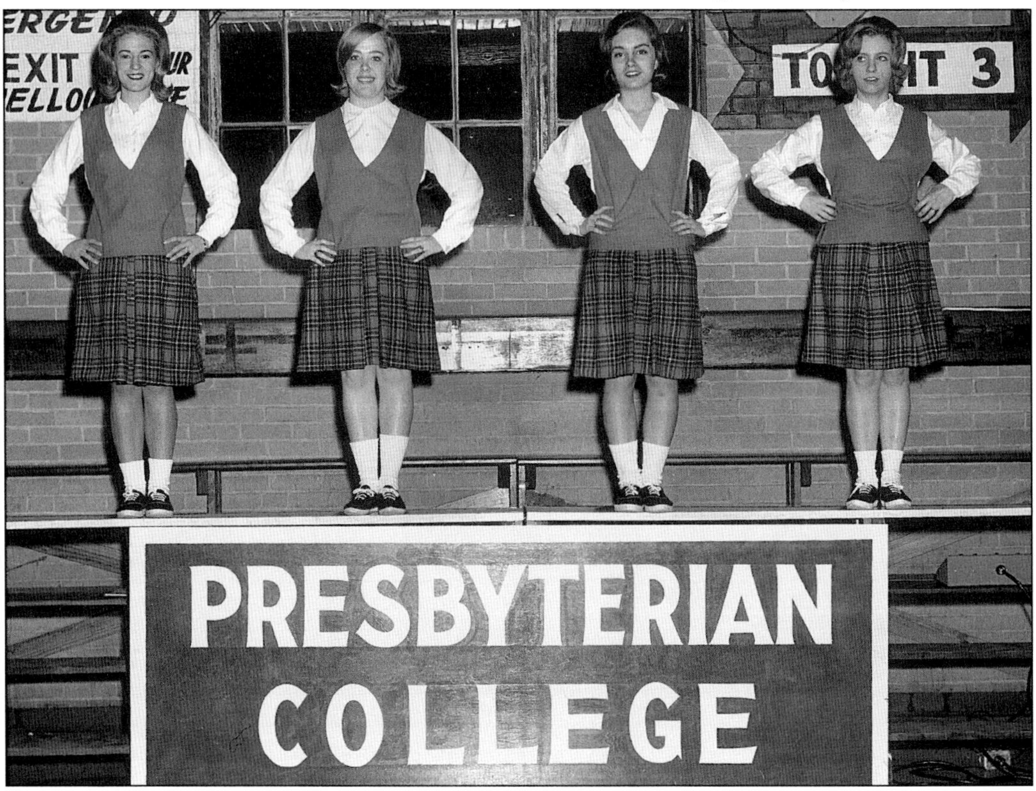

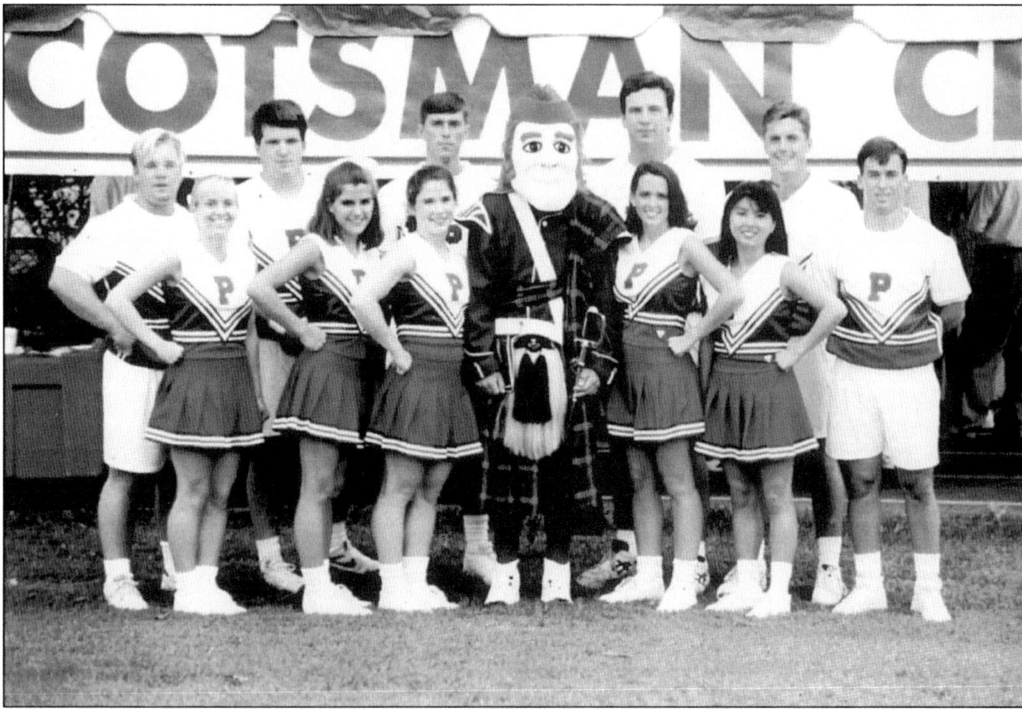


**Cheerleaders and Mascot, 1993.** From left to right are the following: (front row) Jenny Knox, Tabitha Stokes, Mary Beth Brumbelow, Harris Gaines, Laura Pate, and Jeanie Kim; (back row) Chris Woodall, Chris Adair, Ian Twombly, Brian McGill, Lance Dauby, and Keith Walker. (Courtesy of Presbyterian College Public Relations Office.)

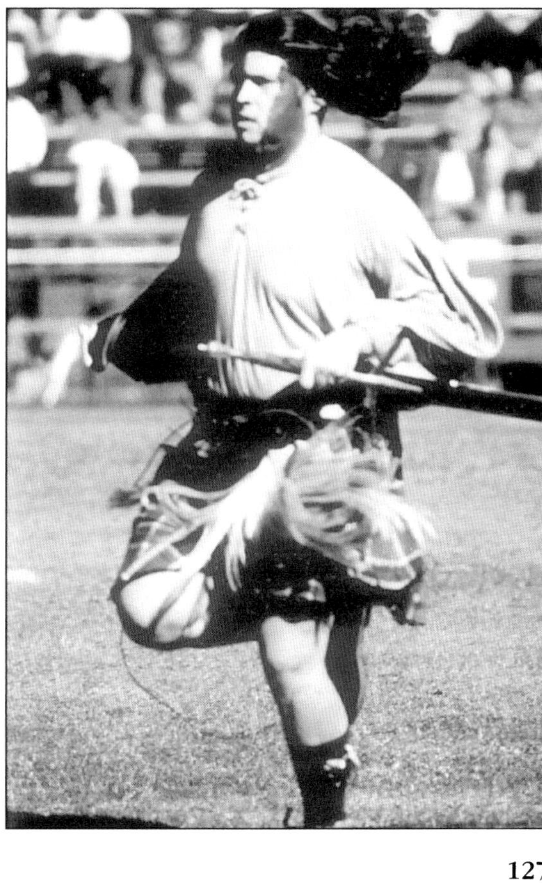

**Mascot, 2000.** The Scotsman mascot changed quite a bit over the years. Here is Michael York in the newest costume, which debuted in the fall of 2000. (Courtesy of Presbyterian College Public Relations Office.)

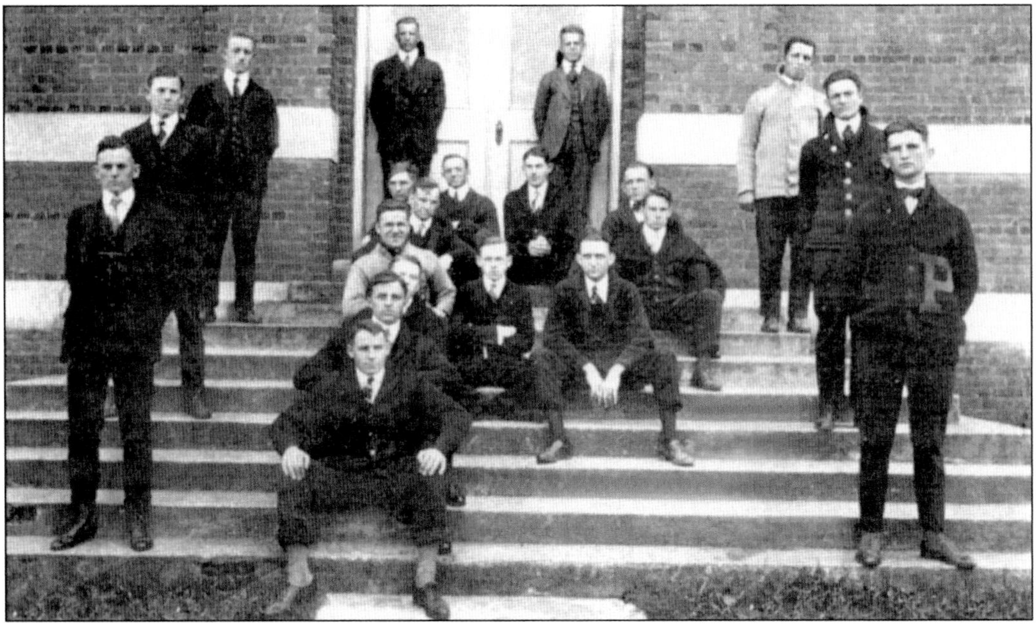

**Wearers of the "P," 1916.** An organization called "Wearers of the P" existed on the campus as early as 1913. Composed of men who had earned a varsity letter in any sport, the group was later renamed "Block P." (Courtesy of 1916 *PaC SaC*.)

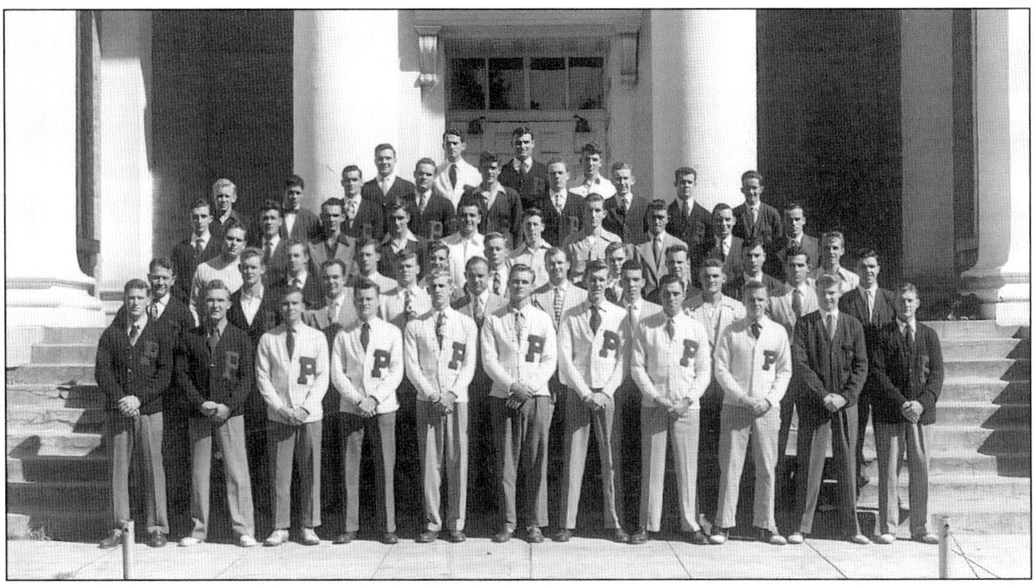

**Block P.** The members of the Block P club in 1949 included, from left to right, (front row) Bowles, Brake, Rollins, Wood, Vassy, Howie, Wilkinson, Berry, West, Moore, and McMillan; (second row) Stutts, Howe, Starnes, J. Lindsay, Spurrier, Davidson, Giles, Fleming, Lanter, and Logan; (third row) Baker, Cooper, McCutcheon, Harper, Maxwell, Young, Weingartner, Graham, and Cavaleri; (fourth row) Liles, Allred, Turner, Watts, Yarborough, Neville, Massey, Brown, Hodge, and Gooch; (fifth row) Currie, Cunningham, Hughes, Dusenbury, Draughon, Tedards, Roark, Norton, and McKinney; (sixth row) Puryear, Andrews, Riddle, and Kaiser. (Courtesy of Presbyterian College Archives.)